KNIGHTS
OF THE
SKULL

CONTENTS

BATTLE GROUP PEIPER
Originally appeared as a one shot issue from Tome Press, a division of Caliber Comics.

TANK KILLER
Originally appeared as a series in Caliber Comics' Negative Burn anthology.

WITCHES CALDRON
Originally appeared in a one shot issue from The Heritage Collection.

KNIGHTS
OF THE
SKULL

TALES OF THE WAFFEN SS BY
WAYNE VANSANT

The famous Panzer division that led the Ardennes Offensive, also known as the Battle of the Bulge. This tells the tale of the young commander as he spear-headed the offensive. Time was of the essence and he sacrificed tanks, his own men, and when it came time to take prisoners...he shot them instead. In what is now known as the Malmedy massacre, Peiper's reputation would forever be linked to his slaughter of prisoners rather than his battlefield prowess.

Battle Group Peiper

written and illustrated by

WAYNE VANSANT

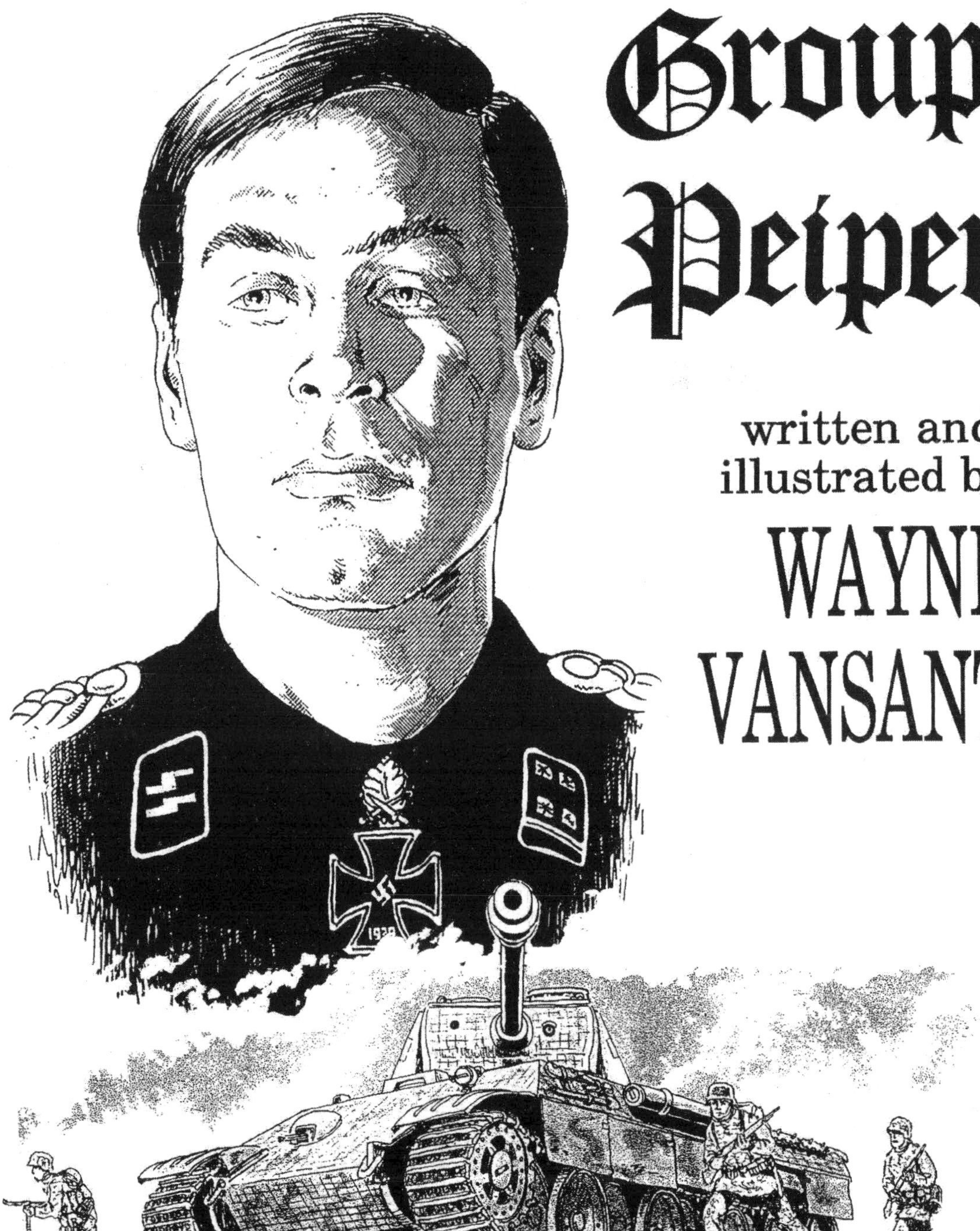

1939

Battle Group Peiper

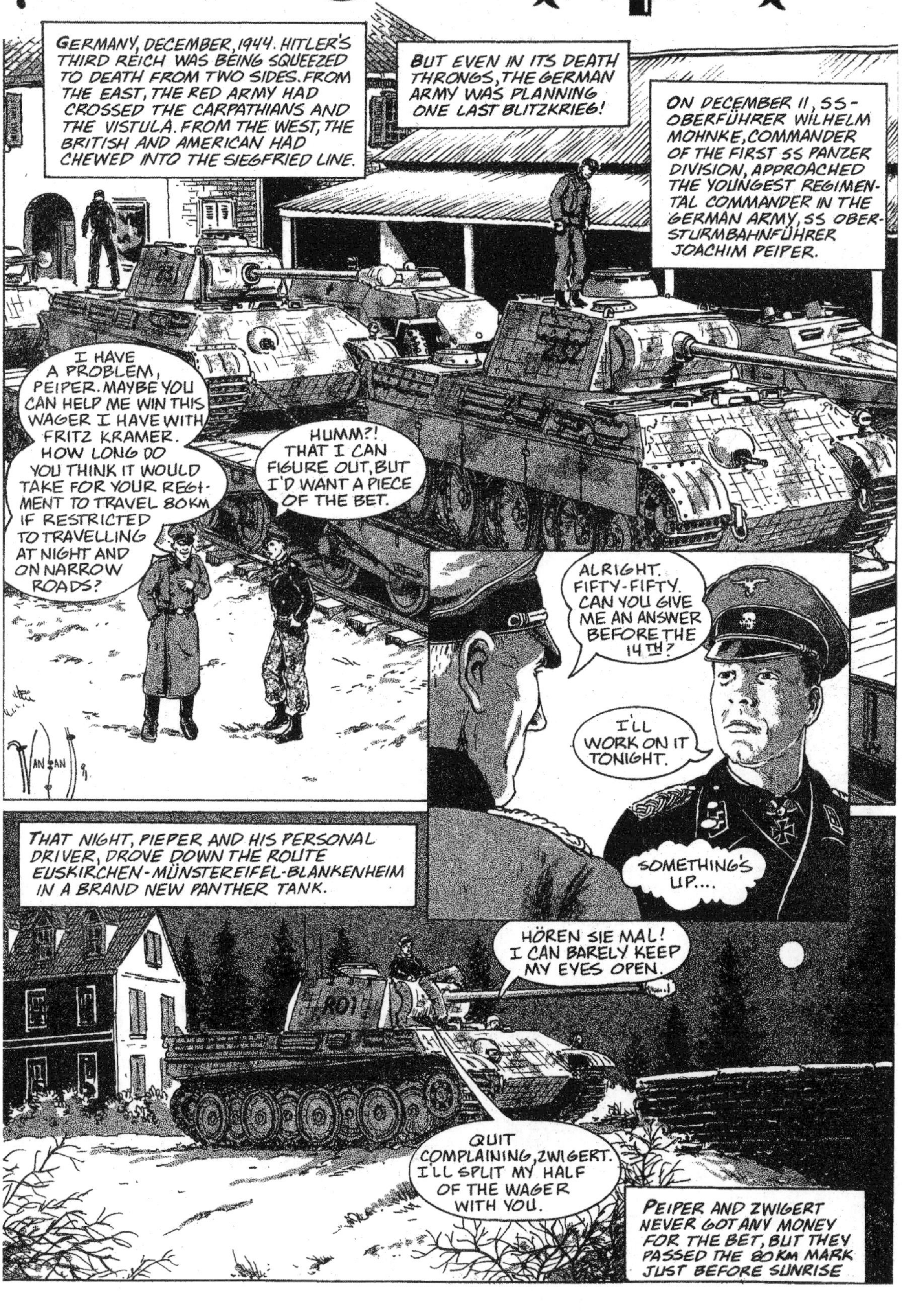
GERMANY, DECEMBER, 1944. HITLER'S THIRD REICH WAS BEING SQUEEZED TO DEATH FROM TWO SIDES. FROM THE EAST, THE RED ARMY HAD CROSSED THE CARPATHIANS AND THE VISTULA. FROM THE WEST, THE BRITISH AND AMERICAN HAD CHEWED INTO THE SIEGFRIED LINE.
BUT EVEN IN ITS DEATH THRONGS, THE GERMAN ARMY WAS PLANNING ONE LAST BLITZKRIEG!
ON DECEMBER 11, SS-OBERFÜHRER WILHELM MOHNKE, COMMANDER OF THE FIRST SS PANZER DIVISION, APPROACHED THE YOUNGEST REGIMENTAL COMMANDER IN THE GERMAN ARMY, SS OBERSTURMBAHNFÜHRER JOACHIM PEIPER.
I HAVE A PROBLEM, PEIPER. MAYBE YOU CAN HELP ME WIN THIS WAGER I HAVE WITH FRITZ KRAMER. HOW LONG DO YOU THINK IT WOULD TAKE FOR YOUR REGIMENT TO TRAVEL 80KM IF RESTRICTED TO TRAVELLING AT NIGHT AND ON NARROW ROADS?
HUMM?! THAT I CAN FIGURE OUT, BUT I'D WANT A PIECE OF THE BET.
ALRIGHT. FIFTY-FIFTY. CAN YOU GIVE ME AN ANSWER BEFORE THE 14TH?
I'LL WORK ON IT TONIGHT.
SOMETHING'S UP....
THAT NIGHT, PIEPER AND HIS PERSONAL DRIVER, DROVE DOWN THE ROUTE EUSKIRCHEN-MÜNSTEREIFEL-BLANKENHEIM IN A BRAND NEW PANTHER TANK.
HÖREN SIE MAL! I CAN BARELY KEEP MY EYES OPEN.
QUIT COMPLAINING, ZWIGERT. I'LL SPLIT MY HALF OF THE WAGER WITH YOU.
PEIPER AND ZWIGERT NEVER GOT ANY MONEY FOR THE BET, BUT THEY PASSED THE 80KM MARK JUST BEFORE SUNRISE

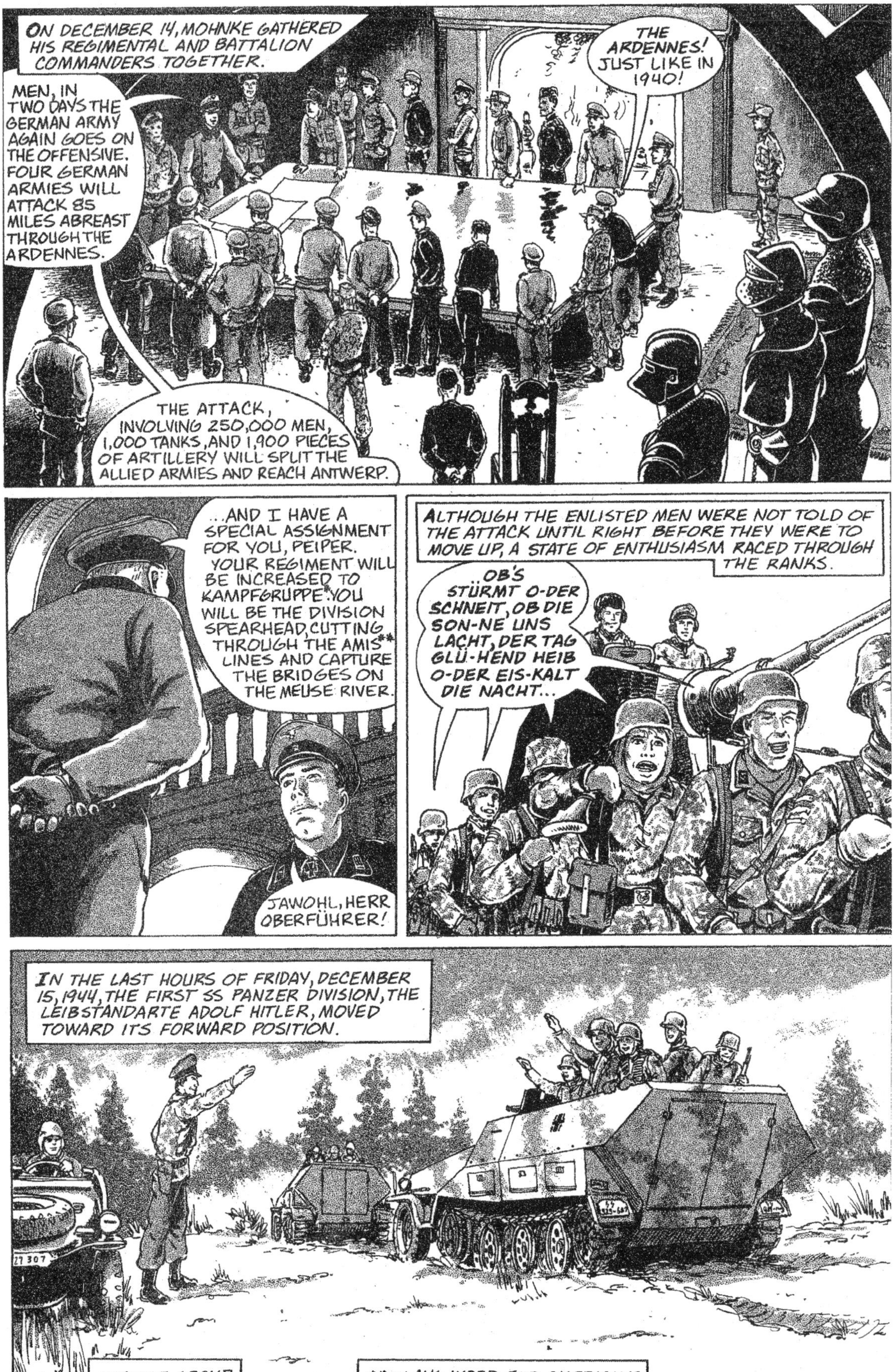
ON DECEMBER 14, MOHNKE GATHERED HIS REGIMENTAL AND BATTALION COMMANDERS TOGETHER.
MEN, IN TWO DAYS THE GERMAN ARMY AGAIN GOES ON THE OFFENSIVE. FOUR GERMAN ARMIES WILL ATTACK 85 MILES ABREAST THROUGH THE ARDENNES.
THE ARDENNES! JUST LIKE IN 1940!
THE ATTACK, INVOLVING 250,000 MEN, 1,000 TANKS, AND 1,900 PIECES OF ARTILLERY WILL SPLIT THE ALLIED ARMIES AND REACH ANTWERP.
...AND I HAVE A SPECIAL ASSIGNMENT FOR YOU, PEIPER. YOUR REGIMENT WILL BE INCREASED TO KAMPFGRUPPE*. YOU WILL BE THE DIVISION SPEARHEAD, CUTTING THROUGH THE AMIS** LINES AND CAPTURE THE BRIDGES ON THE MEUSE RIVER.
JAWOHL, HERR OBERFÜHRER!
ALTHOUGH THE ENLISTED MEN WERE NOT TOLD OF THE ATTACK UNTIL RIGHT BEFORE THEY WERE TO MOVE UP, A STATE OF ENTHUSIASM RACED THROUGH THE RANKS.
..OB'S STÜRMT O-DER SCHNEIT, OB DIE SON-NE UNS LACHT, DER TAG GLÜ-HEND HEIB O-DER EIS-KALT DIE NACHT...
IN THE LAST HOURS OF FRIDAY, DECEMBER 15, 1944, THE FIRST SS PANZER DIVISION, THE LEIBSTANDARTE ADOLF HITLER, MOVED TOWARD ITS FORWARD POSITION.
*BATTLE GROUP
**SLANG WORD FOR AMERICANS

The German Panzer Regiment of 1944 numbered 2,066 men. Since Battle Group Peiper did not go into the battle at full strength, and since numerous units were attached to them, it is impossible to say exactly how many took part. We can safely say there were at least 2,000. Below are shown the key types of armored vehicles that were a part of Battle Group Peiper.

THE PANTHER

The Panther medium tank is considered the finest tank design of World War II. With its 75mm main gun, slopped armor and 28 mph top speed, it could outfight any Russian, British or American tank. Peiper had 35 Panthers when he began the Ardennes offensive.

PANZERKAMPFWAGEN IV

The Panzerkampfwagen IV (called the Mark IV by is British and American enemies) was the work-horse of the German forces. First appearing in 1936, it was constantly updated by upgrading its guns and engine capacity, and by factory or field modified armor. Peiper had 35 Mark IV's.

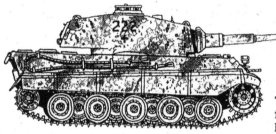

THE KING TIGER

The King Tiger (also called Tiger II and Royal Tiger) was without a doubt the mosty powerfull fighting vehicle to see service durning World War II. But its great weight (68 tons) and underpowered engine made it difficult to operate. 20 were assigned to Battle Group Peiper.

PANZERGRENADIER

Panzergrenadier companies were assigned to Peiper. These crack infantry units were carried into battle by SdKfz 251 half-tracks, reliable little vehicles that could be modified to be rocket launchers, mortar carriers, command vehicles, ambulances, bridge layers, flame-trowers, anti-aircraft gun platforms, and self propelled anti-tank guns.

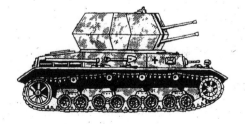

WIRBELWIND

Based on the Mark IV chassis, the Wirbelwind was a very effective mobile anti-aircraft platform to protect ground troops. And used against ground troops, it was extremely deadly.

THE ARDENNES OFFENSIVE

THE GERMAN PLAN - DEC. 1944

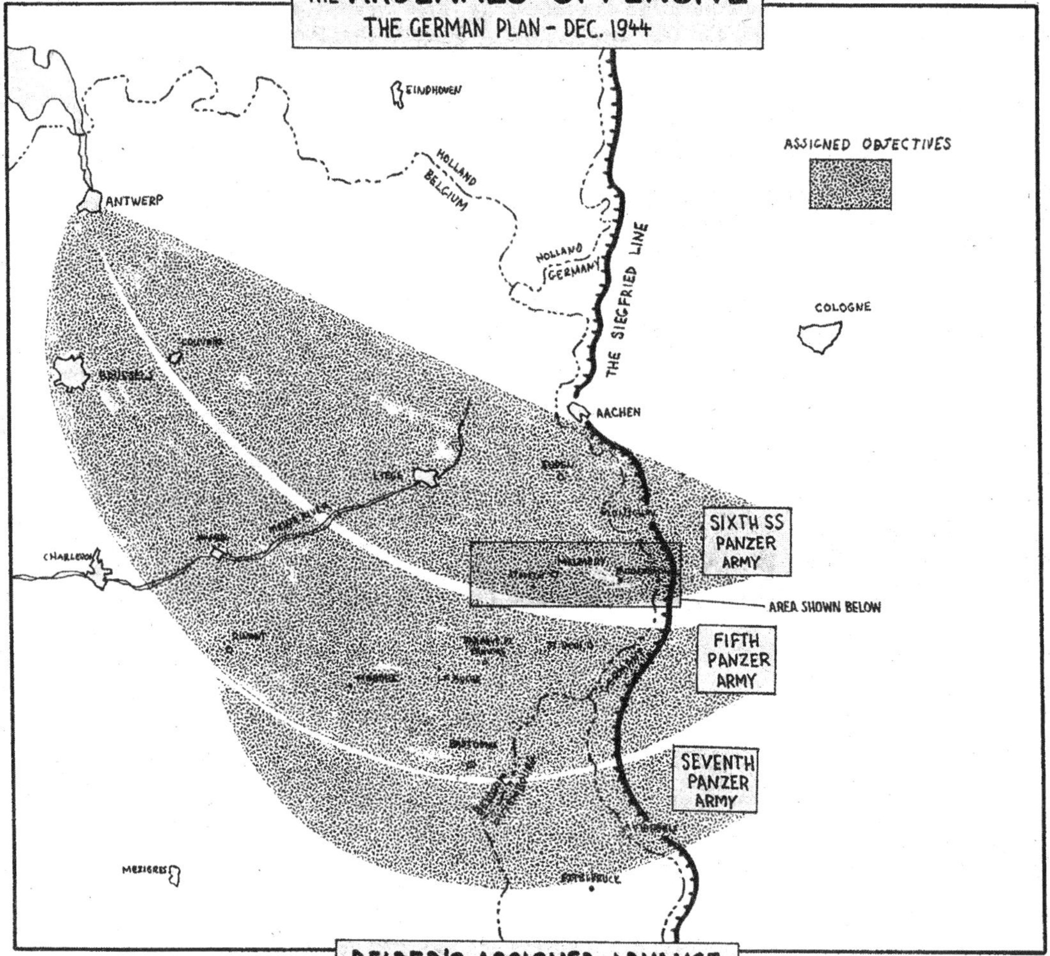

EINDHOVEN
HOLLAND
BELGIUM
ANTWERP
ASSIGNED OBJECTIVES
HOLLAND
GERMANY
THE SIEGFRIED LINE
COLOGNE
AACHEN
SIXTH SS
PANZER
ARMY
AREA SHOWN BELOW
FIFTH
PANZER
ARMY
SEVENTH
PANZER
ARMY
MEZIERES

PEIPER'S ASSIGNED ADVANCE

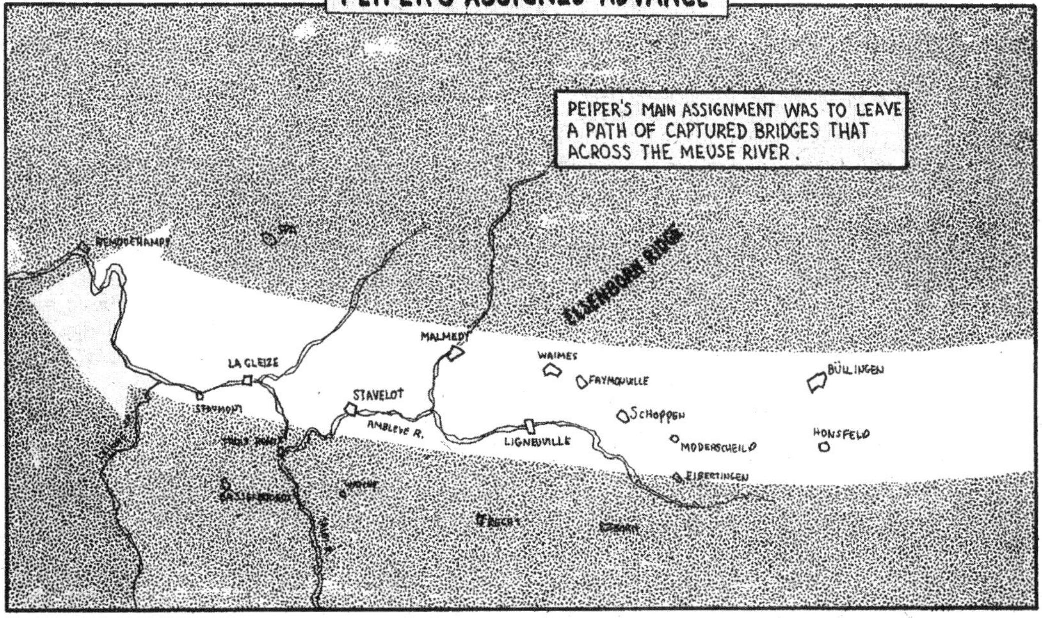

PEIPER'S MAIN ASSIGNMENT WAS TO LEAVE
A PATH OF CAPTURED BRIDGES THAT
ACROSS THE MEUSE RIVER.
ELSENBORN RIDGE
MALMEDY
WAIMES
FAYMONVILLE
BÜLLINGEN
LA GLEIZE
STAVELOT
SCHOPPEN
AMBLEVE R.
LIGNEUVILLE
HONSFELD
MODERSCHEID
EIBERTINGEN

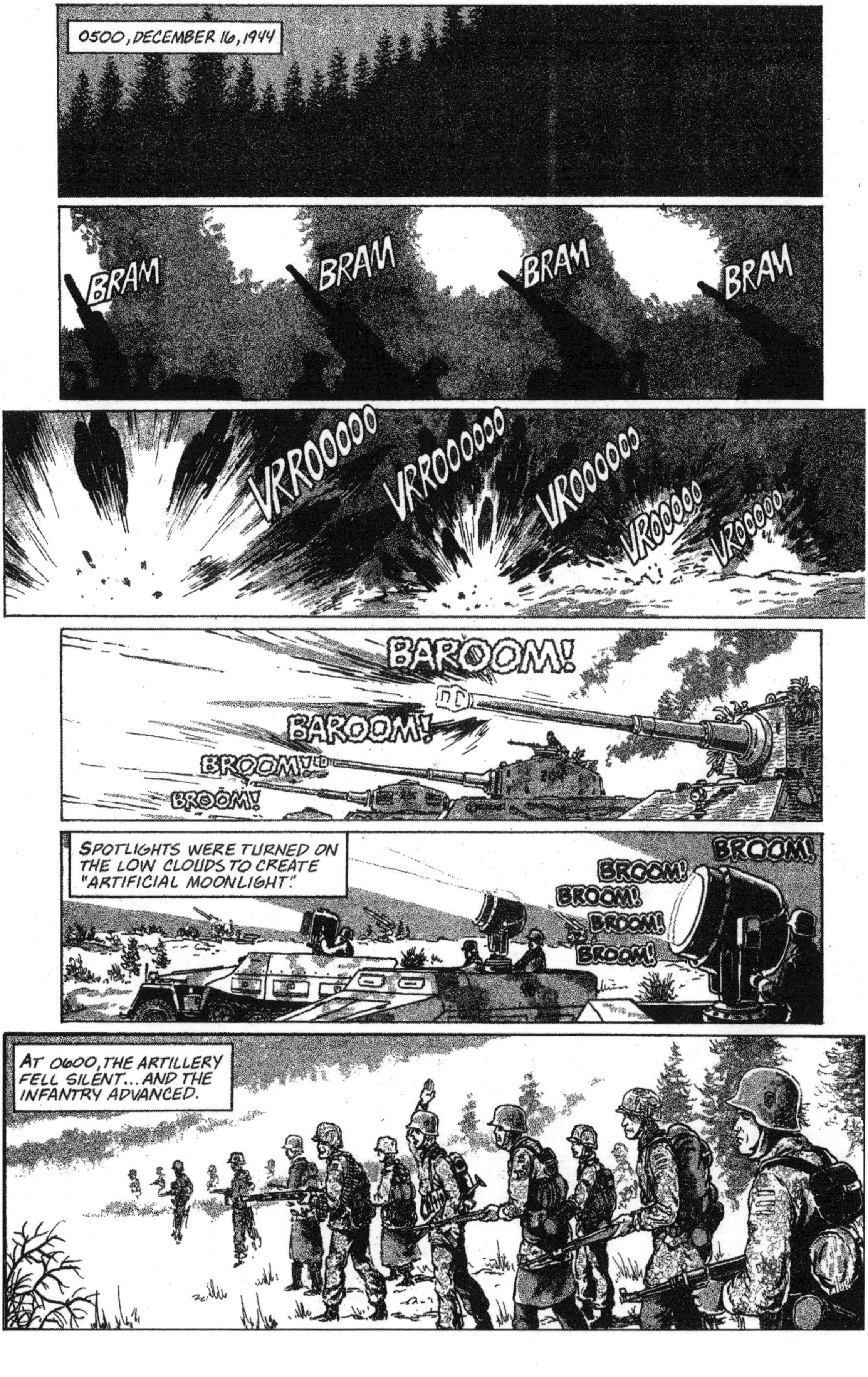
0500, DECEMBER 16, 1944
BRAM
BRAM
BRAM
BRAM
VRROOOOO
VRROOOOOO
VROOOOOO
VROOOOO
VROOOOO
BAROOM!
BAROOM!
BROOM!
BROOM!
SPOTLIGHTS WERE TURNED ON THE LOW CLOUDS TO CREATE "ARTIFICIAL MOONLIGHT."
BROOM!
BROOM!
BROOM!
BROOM!
BROOM!
AT 0600, THE ARTILLERY FELL SILENT... AND THE INFANTRY ADVANCED.

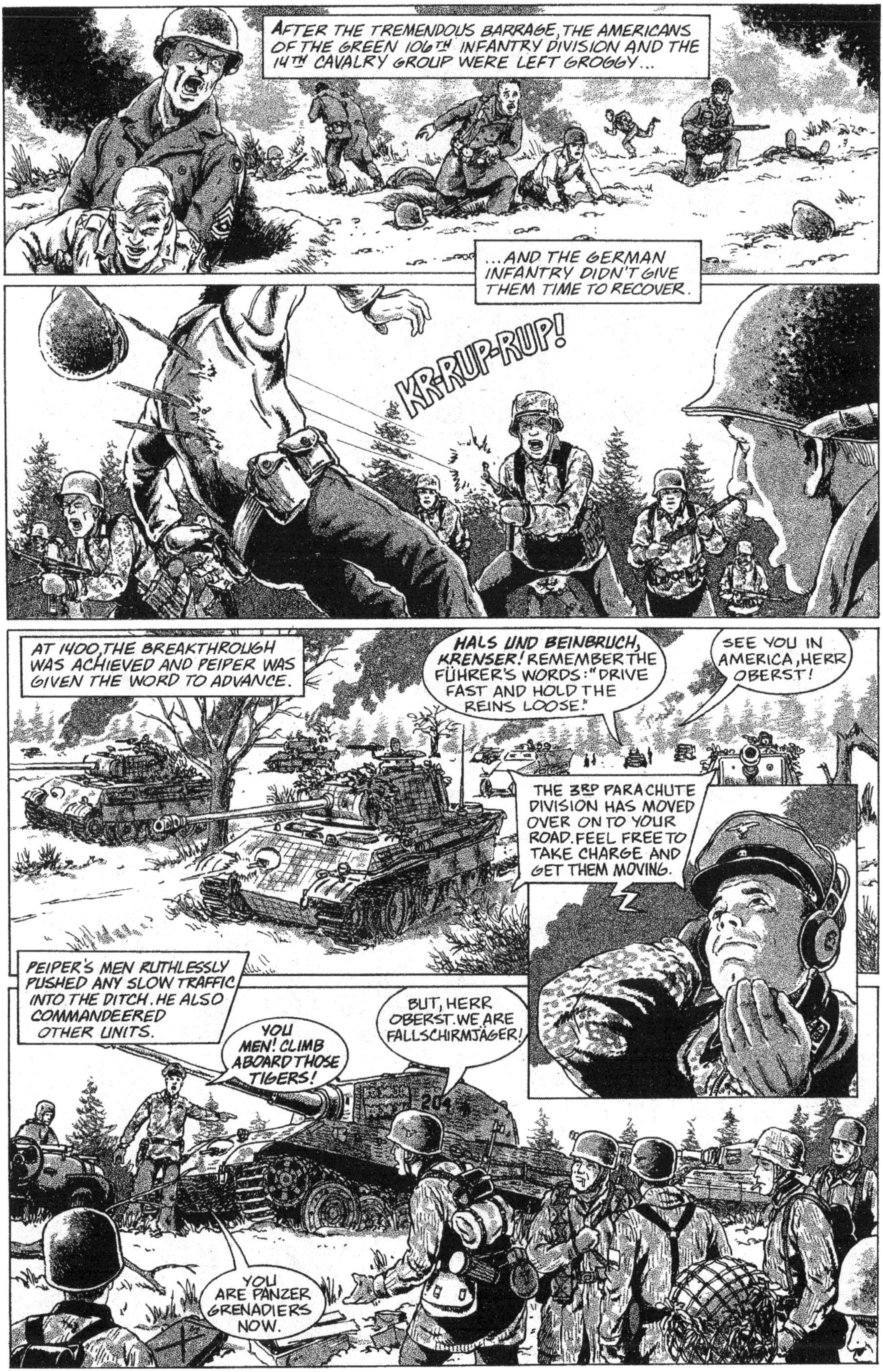
AFTER THE TREMENDOUS BARRAGE, THE AMERICANS OF THE GREEN 106TH INFANTRY DIVISION AND THE 14TH CAVALRY GROUP WERE LEFT GROGGY...
...AND THE GERMAN INFANTRY DIDN'T GIVE THEM TIME TO RECOVER.
KR-RUP-RUP!
AT 1400, THE BREAKTHROUGH WAS ACHIEVED AND PEIPER WAS GIVEN THE WORD TO ADVANCE.
HALS UND BEINBRUCH, KRENSER! REMEMBER THE FÜHRER'S WORDS: "DRIVE FAST AND HOLD THE REINS LOOSE."
SEE YOU IN AMERICA, HERR OBERST!
THE 3RD PARACHUTE DIVISION HAS MOVED OVER ON TO YOUR ROAD. FEEL FREE TO TAKE CHARGE AND GET THEM MOVING.
PEIPER'S MEN RUTHLESSLY PUSHED ANY SLOW TRAFFIC INTO THE DITCH. HE ALSO COMMANDEERED OTHER UNITS.
YOU MEN! CLIMB ABOARD THOSE TIGERS!
BUT, HERR OBERST. WE ARE FALLSCHIRMJÄGER!
YOU ARE PANZER GRENADIERS NOW.
204

Joachim Peiper was born on January 30, 1915, the son of a career German Army officer. Being raised in this setting, it seemed natural the he chose this career for himself. He graduated with honors from the SS training college at Brunswick, and in 1938 was posted as adjudent to the head of the SS, Heinrich Himmler.

In September, 1939, Peiper commanded Number 10 Company of the 1st SS Panzer Regiment in the invasion of Poland, and in the invasion of France the next summer, where he was awarded the Iron Crosses 1st and 2nd class. For his part in the recapture of Kharkov, Russia, he was awarded the Knight's Cross on March 9, 1943, and made a Battalion Commander. In November, 1943, he was made commander fo the 1st SS Panzer Regiment, the youngest regimental commander in the German Army.

On January 27, 1944, after his tanks destroyed 4 Russian Infantry Divisions, he received the Oak Leaves to his Knight's Cross.

His actions in the Ardennes would result in his receiving the Crossed Swords to his Knight's Cross...and lead to personal disaster.

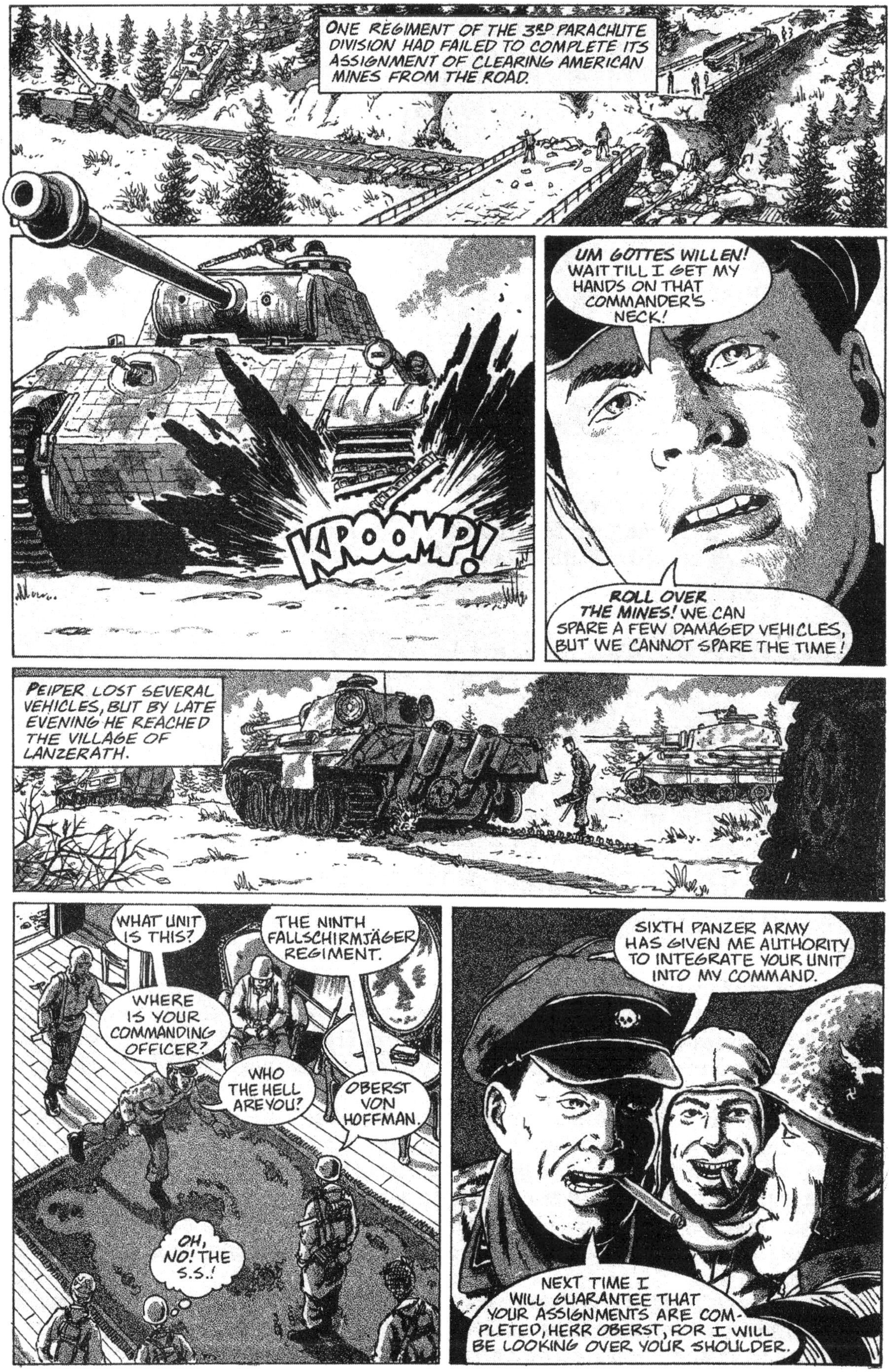
ONE REGIMENT OF THE 3RD PARACHUTE DIVISION HAD FAILED TO COMPLETE ITS ASSIGNMENT OF CLEARING AMERICAN MINES FROM THE ROAD.
KROOMP!
UM GOTTES WILLEN! WAIT TILL I GET MY HANDS ON THAT COMMANDER'S NECK!
ROLL OVER THE MINES! WE CAN SPARE A FEW DAMAGED VEHICLES, BUT WE CANNOT SPARE THE TIME!
PEIPER LOST SEVERAL VEHICLES, BUT BY LATE EVENING HE REACHED THE VILLAGE OF LANZERATH.
WHAT UNIT IS THIS?
THE NINTH FALLSCHIRMJÄGER REGIMENT.
WHERE IS YOUR COMMANDING OFFICER?
WHO THE HELL ARE YOU?
OBERST VON HOFFMAN.
OH, NO! THE S.S.!
SIXTH PANZER ARMY HAS GIVEN ME AUTHORITY TO INTEGRATE YOUR UNIT INTO MY COMMAND.
NEXT TIME I WILL GUARANTEE THAT YOUR ASSIGNMENTS ARE COMPLETED, HERR OBERST, FOR I WILL BE LOOKING OVER YOUR SHOULDER.

FROM D-DAY TO THE SIEGFRIED LINE

One June 6, 1944, British and American forces landed on the beaches of Normandy and began the long awaited liberation of Northwestern Europe. As hundreds of thousands of Allied troops poured ashore, Hitler held back his first-line Panzer forces, for he believed the landing was a ruse. He was convinced that the "real" invasion would come northeast of Normandy, at the Pas de Calais. By the time he was convinced otherwise, it was too late. The Allies were on the continent to stay, and were too strong to be pushed off again.

For the next two months, battle raged in the Normandy hedgerow country, and the German Army suffered terribly. At the Falaise Pocket, the Germans had 10,000 men killed, and 50,000 captured.

By mid-August the British and Americans had broken out of the beachhead and were driving across France and Belgium toward the German frontier. Paris was liberated, and American forces landed on the beaches of Southern France.

But as they neared the Rhine and into the defenses of the "Siegfried Line", the Western Allies found the resistance getting tougher. In September, an airborne assault in Holland failed. In October, the Americans took Aachen, the first German city to fall into their hands, but by November were haulted in the bloody battle for Hurtgen Forest.

The Supreme Commander, General Eisenhower, was having difficulty supplying and re-enforcing his troops along a front which stretched from Switzerland to the North Sea. He had to re-distribute his troops in order to keep greater pressure on key strong points. To do this he had to thin out his men in other areas. But where in the line was it safe to weaken their troop concentration? He decided on the Ardennes... and the very point where Hitler was planning his December offensive...

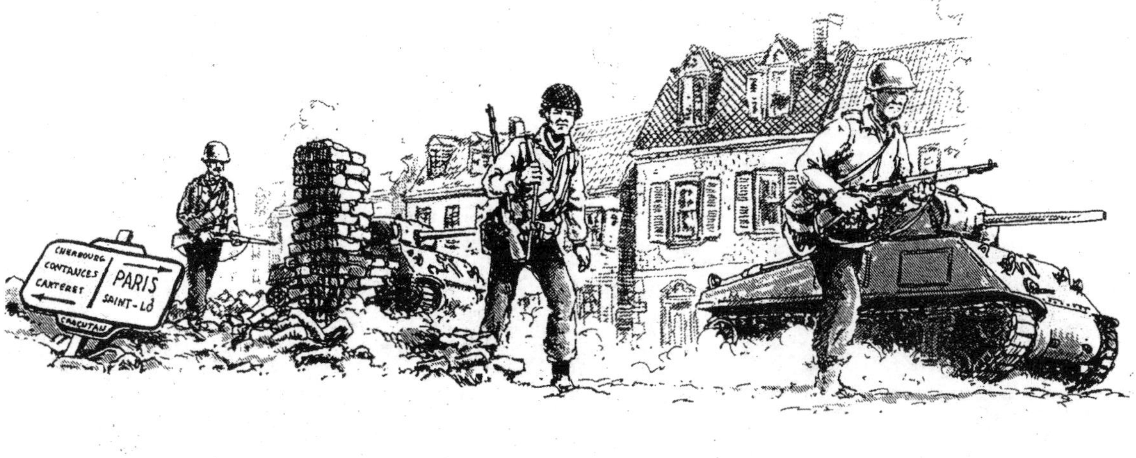
CHERBOURG
CONTANCES
CARTERET
PARIS
SAINT-LÔ

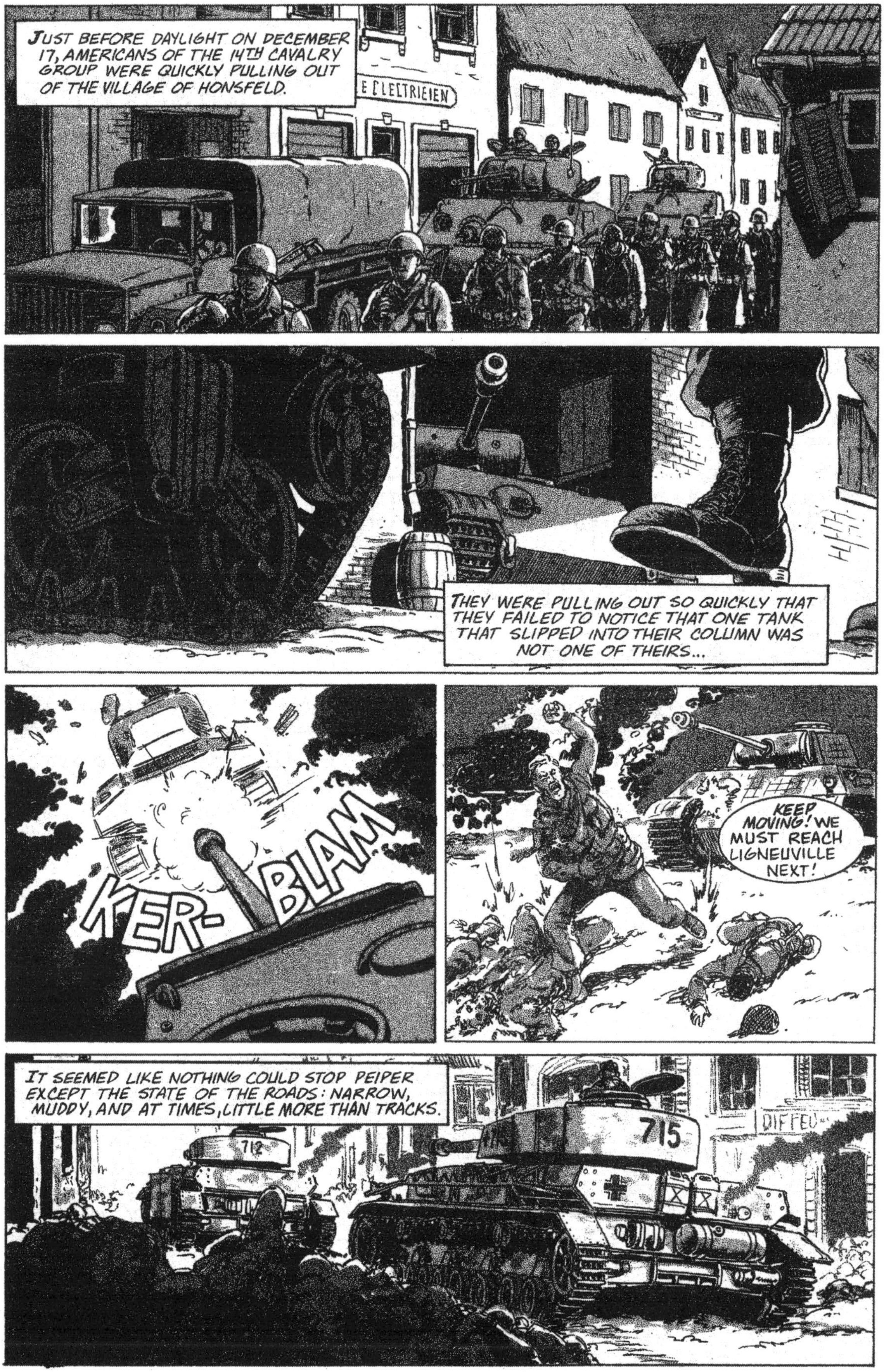

JUST BEFORE DAYLIGHT ON DECEMBER 17, AMERICANS OF THE 14TH CAVALRY GROUP WERE QUICKLY PULLING OUT OF THE VILLAGE OF HONSFELD.
E ELECTRIEIEN
THEY WERE PULLING OUT SO QUICKLY THAT THEY FAILED TO NOTICE THAT ONE TANK THAT SLIPPED INTO THEIR COLUMN WAS NOT ONE OF THEIRS...
KER-BLAM
KEEP MOVING! WE MUST REACH LIGNEUVILLE NEXT!
IT SEEMED LIKE NOTHING COULD STOP PEIPER EXCEPT THE STATE OF THE ROADS: NARROW, MUDDY, AND AT TIMES, LITTLE MORE THAN TRACKS.
712
715
DIFFEU

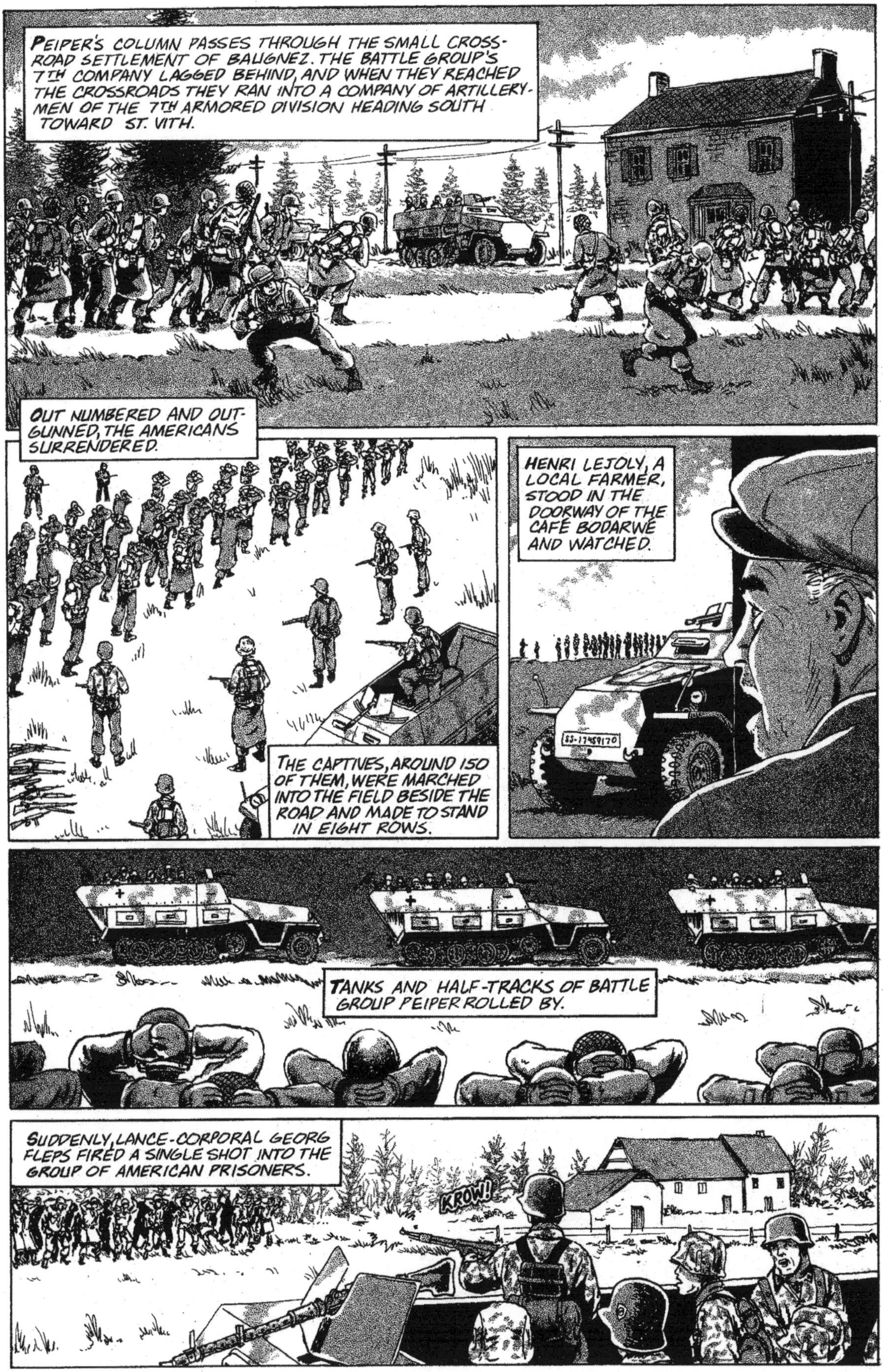
PEIPER'S COLUMN PASSES THROUGH THE SMALL CROSS-ROAD SETTLEMENT OF BAUGNEZ. THE BATTLE GROUP'S 7TH COMPANY LAGGED BEHIND, AND WHEN THEY REACHED THE CROSSROADS THEY RAN INTO A COMPANY OF ARTILLERY-MEN OF THE 7TH ARMORED DIVISION HEADING SOUTH TOWARD ST. VITH.
OUT NUMBERED AND OUT-GUNNED, THE AMERICANS SURRENDERED.
THE CAPTIVES, AROUND 150 OF THEM, WERE MARCHED INTO THE FIELD BESIDE THE ROAD AND MADE TO STAND IN EIGHT ROWS.
HENRI LEJOLY, A LOCAL FARMER, STOOD IN THE DOORWAY OF THE CAFÉ BODARWÉ AND WATCHED.
SS-17459170
TANKS AND HALF-TRACKS OF BATTLE GROUP PEIPER ROLLED BY.
SUDDENLY, LANCE-CORPORAL GEORG FLEPS FIRED A SINGLE SHOT INTO THE GROUP OF AMERICAN PRISONERS.
KROW!

OTHER SHOTS RANG OUT.

MACHINE-GUNS FROM PASSING TANKS OPENED UP.

BRATAT

BRA-TATAT

BRAT-TAT-AT

A HANDFUL OF PRISONERS MADE IT TO THE WOODS...

...BUT MOST OF THEM WERE CUT DOWN.

PEIPER'S SS TROOPSRS MOVED AMONG THE MEN IN THE FIELD, PUTTING BULLETS INTO THE HEAD OF ANYONE SHOWING SIGNS OF LIFE.

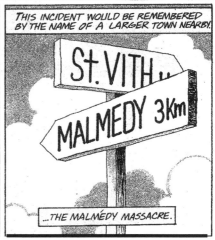

THIS INCIDENT WOULD BE REMEMBERED BY THE NAME OF A LARGER TOWN NEARBY.

St. VITH...

MALMEDY 3Km

...THE MALMEDY MASSACRE.

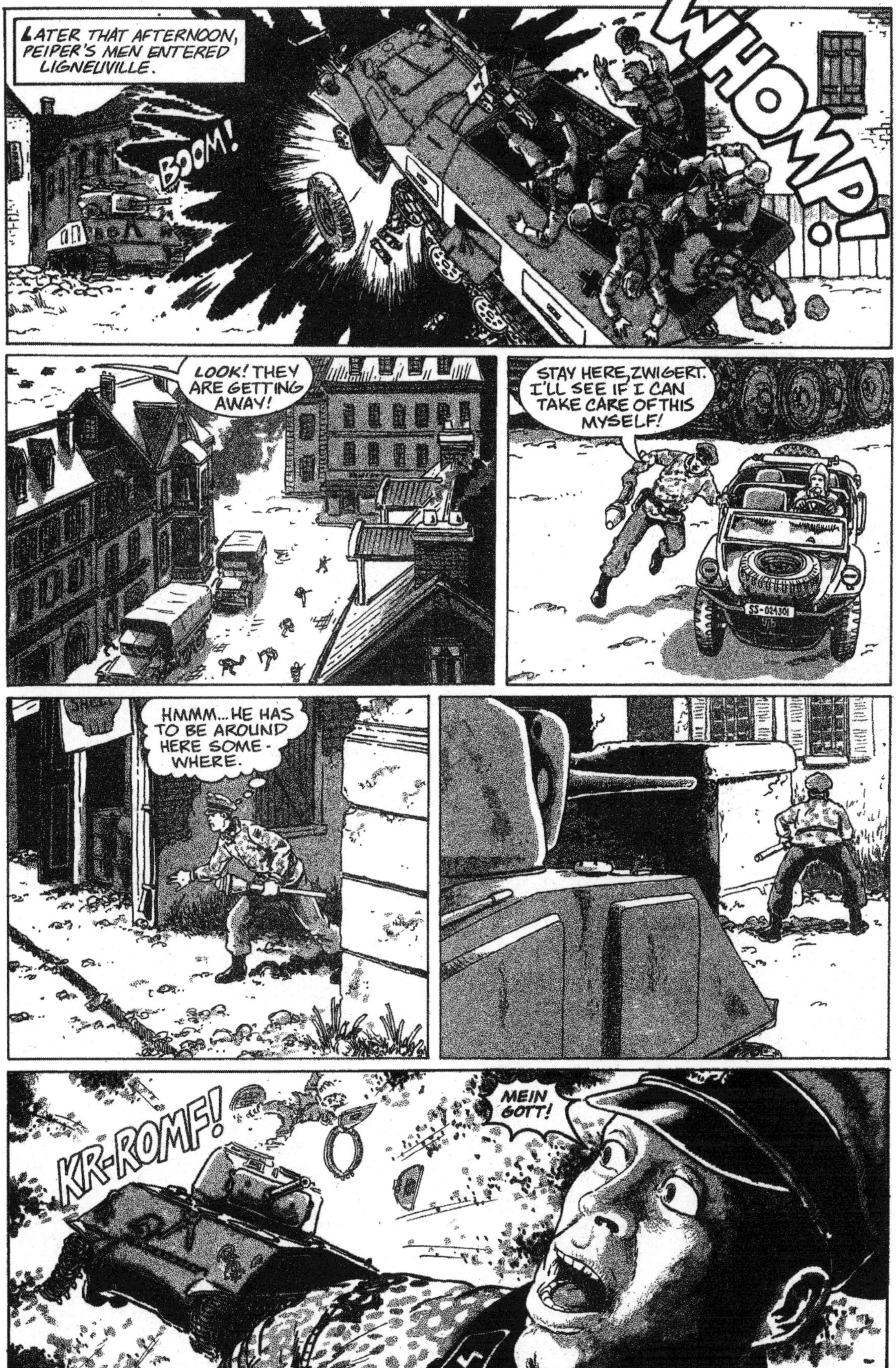
LATER THAT AFTERNOON, PEIPER'S MEN ENTERED LIGNEUVILLE.
WHOMP!
BOOM!
LOOK! THEY ARE GETTING AWAY!
STAY HERE, ZWIGERT. I'LL SEE IF I CAN TAKE CARE OF THIS MYSELF!
SS-024301
HMMM... HE HAS TO BE AROUND HERE SOME-WHERE.
KR-ROMF!
MEIN GOTT!

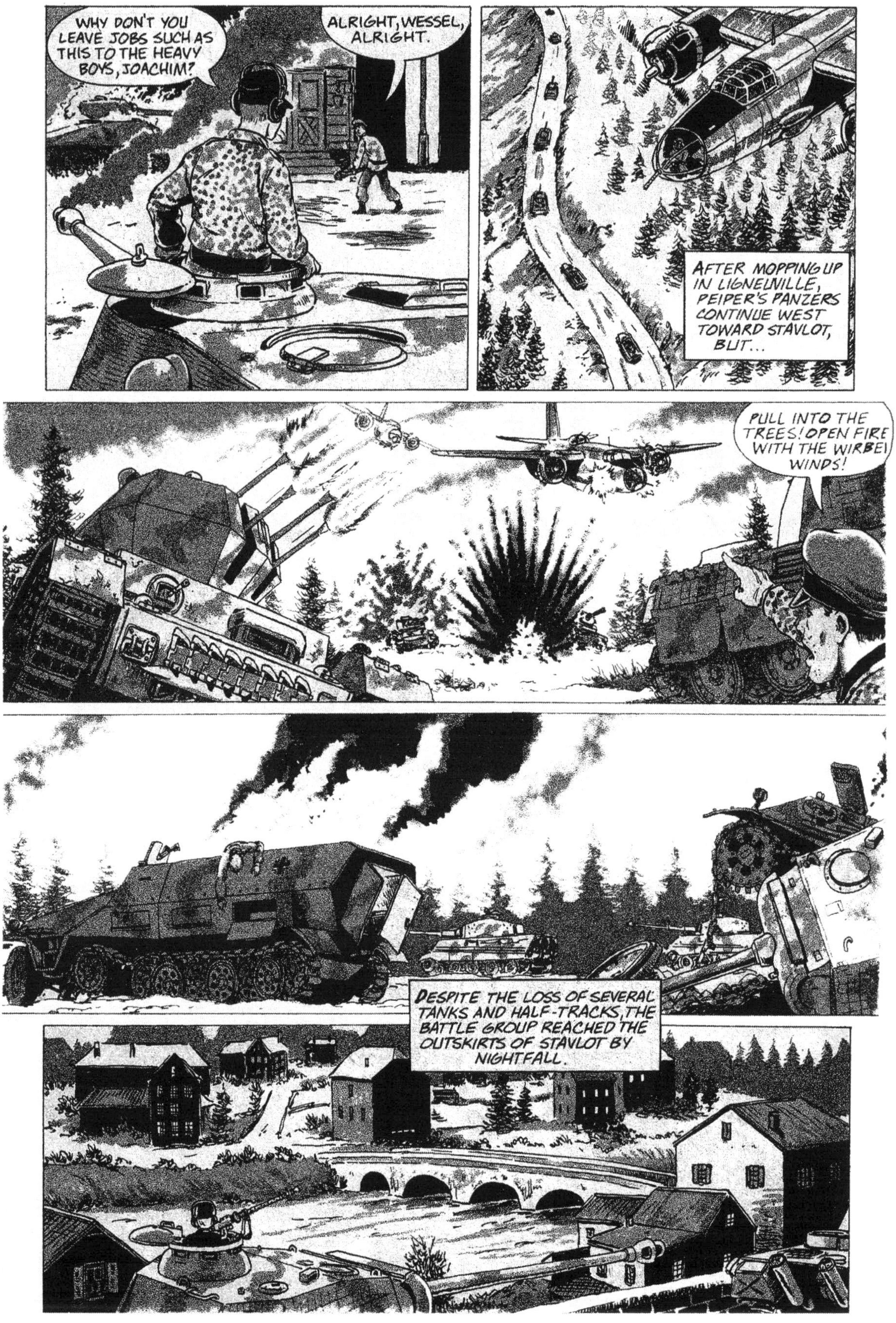
WHY DON'T YOU LEAVE JOBS SUCH AS THIS TO THE HEAVY BOYS, JOACHIM?
ALRIGHT, WESSEL, ALRIGHT.
AFTER MOPPING UP IN LIGNEUVILLE, PEIPER'S PANZERS CONTINUE WEST TOWARD STAVLOT, BUT...
PULL INTO THE TREES! OPEN FIRE WITH THE WIRBEL WINDS!
DESPITE THE LOSS OF SEVERAL TANKS AND HALF-TRACKS, THE BATTLE GROUP REACHED THE OUTSKIRTS OF STAVLOT BY NIGHTFALL.

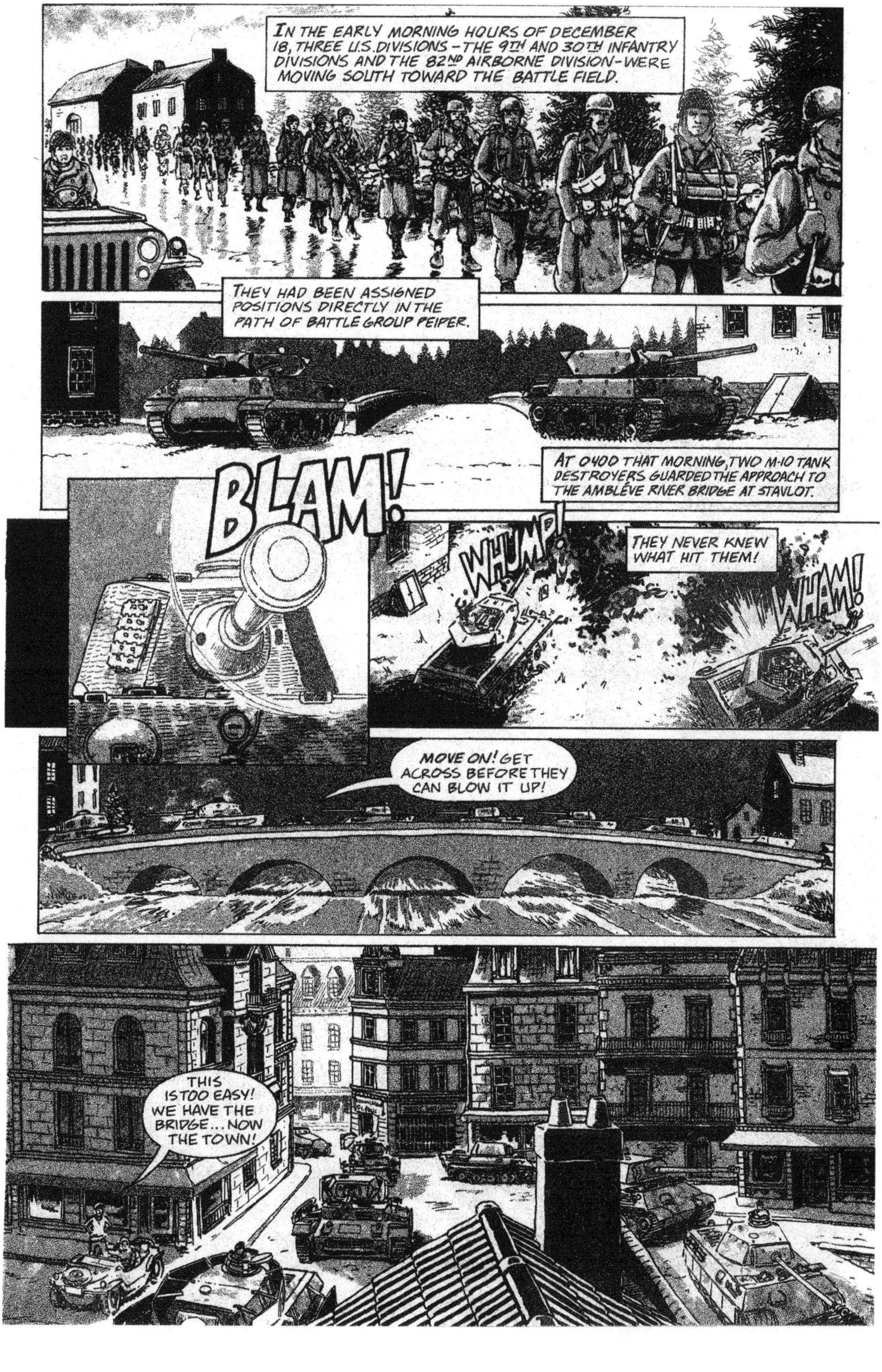
IN THE EARLY MORNING HOURS OF DECEMBER 18, THREE U.S. DIVISIONS – THE 9TH AND 30TH INFANTRY DIVISIONS AND THE 82ND AIRBORNE DIVISION – WERE MOVING SOUTH TOWARD THE BATTLE FIELD.
THEY HAD BEEN ASSIGNED POSITIONS DIRECTLY IN THE PATH OF BATTLE GROUP PEIPER.
AT 0400 THAT MORNING, TWO M-10 TANK DESTROYERS GUARDED THE APPROACH TO THE AMBLÈVE RIVER BRIDGE AT STAVLOT.
BLAM!
WHUMP!
THEY NEVER KNEW WHAT HIT THEM!
WHAM!
MOVE ON! GET ACROSS BEFORE THEY CAN BLOW IT UP!
THIS IS TOO EASY! WE HAVE THE BRIDGE... NOW THE TOWN!

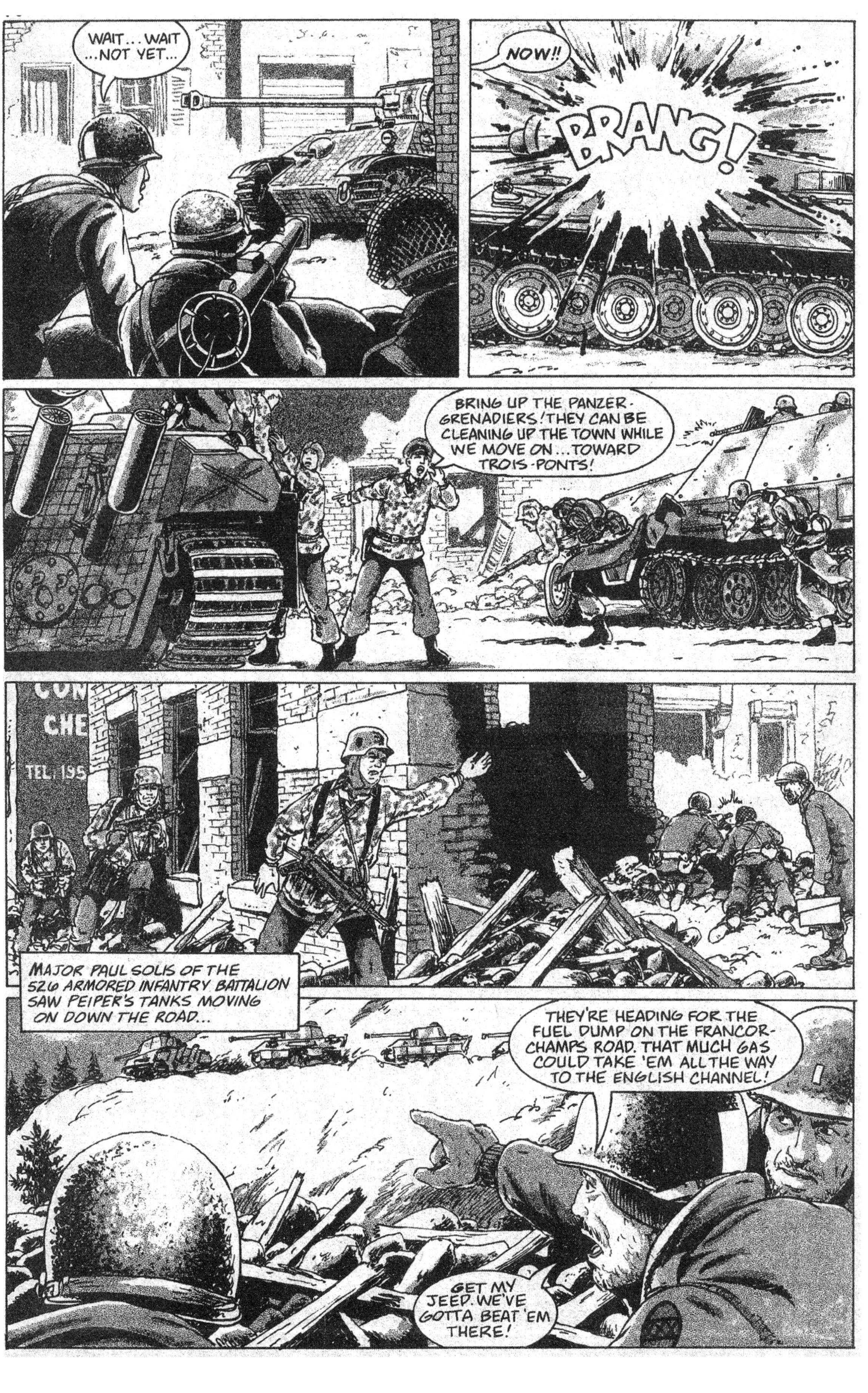
WAIT... WAIT ...NOT YET...
NOW!!
BRANG!
BRING UP THE PANZER-GRENADIERS! THEY CAN BE CLEANING UP THE TOWN WHILE WE MOVE ON...TOWARD TROIS-PONTS!
MAJOR PAUL SOLIS OF THE 526 ARMORED INFANTRY BATTALION SAW PEIPER'S TANKS MOVING ON DOWN THE ROAD...
THEY'RE HEADING FOR THE FUEL DUMP ON THE FRANCOR-CHAMPS ROAD. THAT MUCH GAS COULD TAKE 'EM ALL THE WAY TO THE ENGLISH CHANNEL!
GET MY JEEP. WE'VE GOTTA BEAT 'EM THERE!

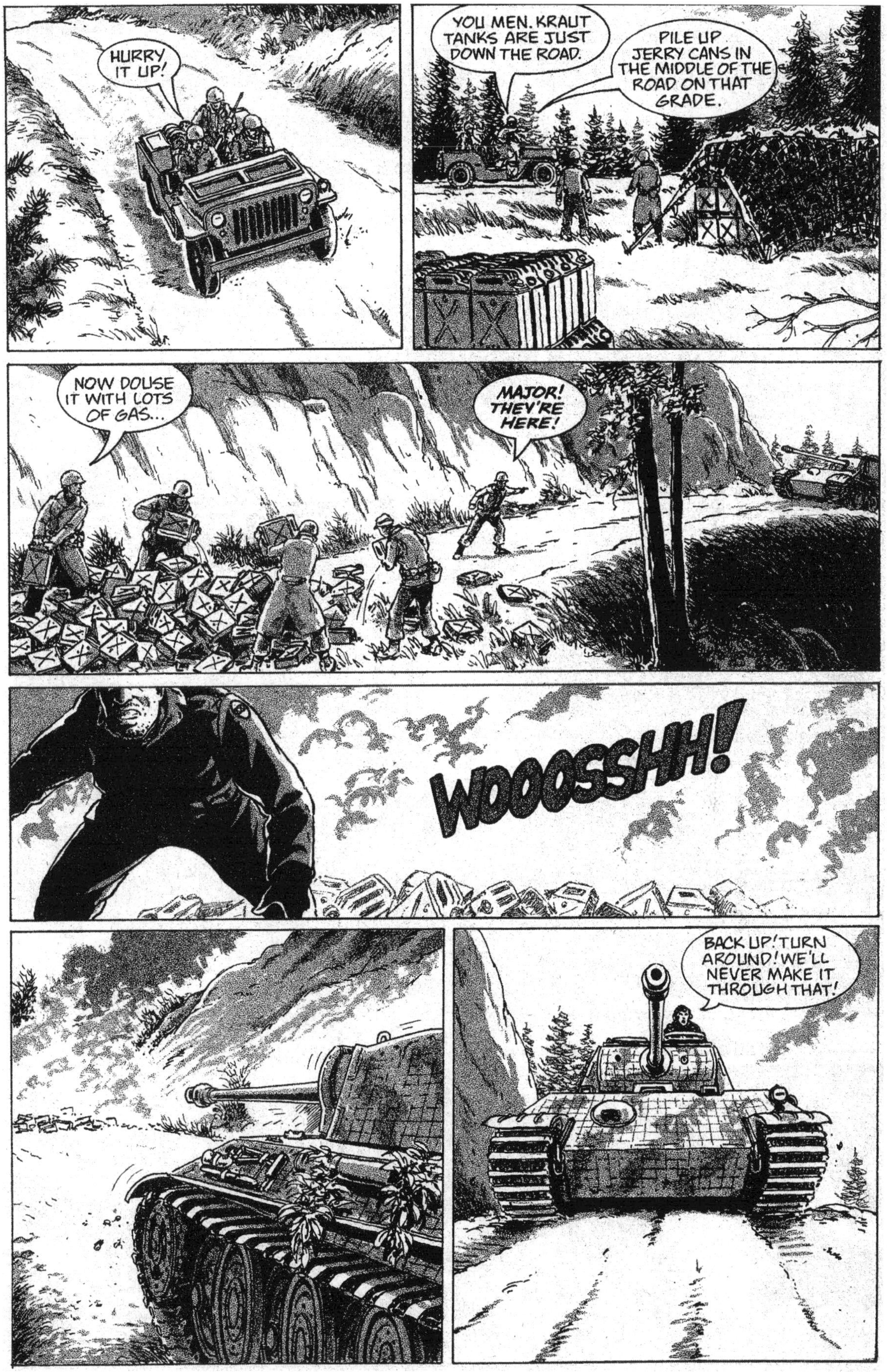
HURRY IT UP!
YOU MEN. KRAUT TANKS ARE JUST DOWN THE ROAD.
PILE UP JERRY CANS IN THE MIDDLE OF THE ROAD ON THAT GRADE.
NOW DOUSE IT WITH LOTS OF GAS...
MAJOR! THEY'RE HERE!
WOOOSSHH!
BACK UP! TURN AROUND! WE'LL NEVER MAKE IT THROUGH THAT!

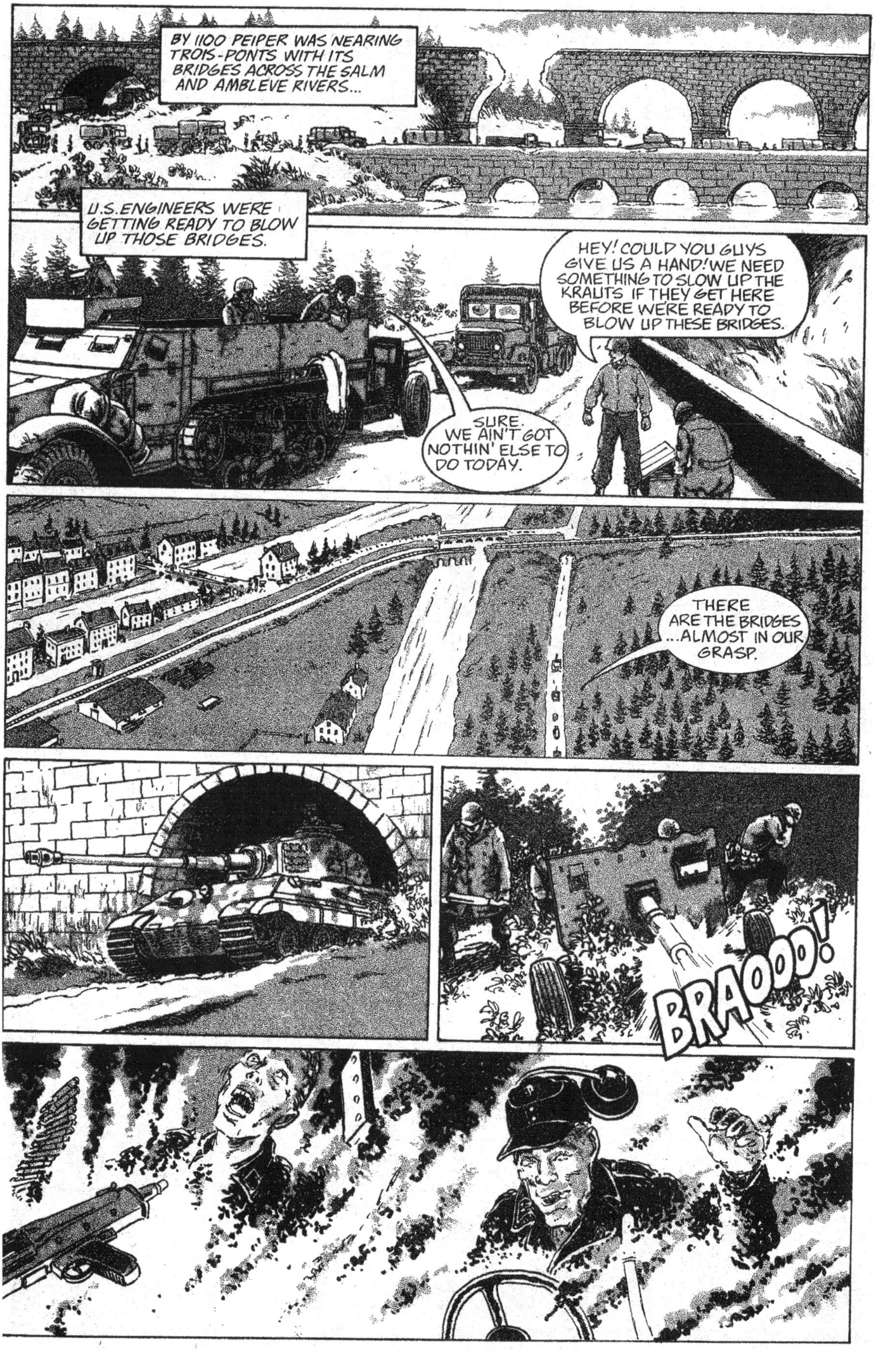
BY 1100 PEIPER WAS NEARING TROIS-PONTS WITH ITS BRIDGES ACROSS THE SALM AND AMBLEVE RIVERS...
U.S. ENGINEERS WERE GETTING READY TO BLOW UP THOSE BRIDGES.
HEY! COULD YOU GUYS GIVE US A HAND! WE NEED SOMETHING TO SLOW UP THE KRAUTS IF THEY GET HERE BEFORE WERE READY TO BLOW UP THESE BRIDGES.
SURE. WE AIN'T GOT NOTHIN' ELSE TO DO TODAY.
THERE ARE THE BRIDGES ...ALMOST IN OUR GRASP.
BRAOOO!

VERDAMMUNG! WHERE IS THAT ANTI-TANK GUN?

SUDDENLY, THE AMBLEVE RIVER BRIDGE BLEW...

VROOOM!

...THEN THE SALM BRIDGE WENT UP!

BOOOM!

THOSE DAMNED ENGINEERS! FIND THAT GUN! BLOW THEM UP! KILL THEM!

BLAM!

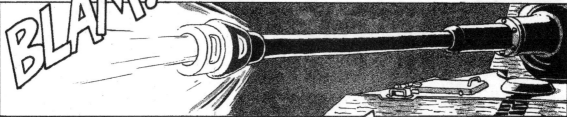

WRUMP!

FINALLY, THE GERMAN GUNNERS FOUND THEIR MARK. THE FOUR MEN OF THE ANTI-TANK GUN CREW — McCOLLUM, HOLLEN-BECK, BUCHANAN AND HIGGINS — WERE ALL KILLED IN A SINGLE BLAST.

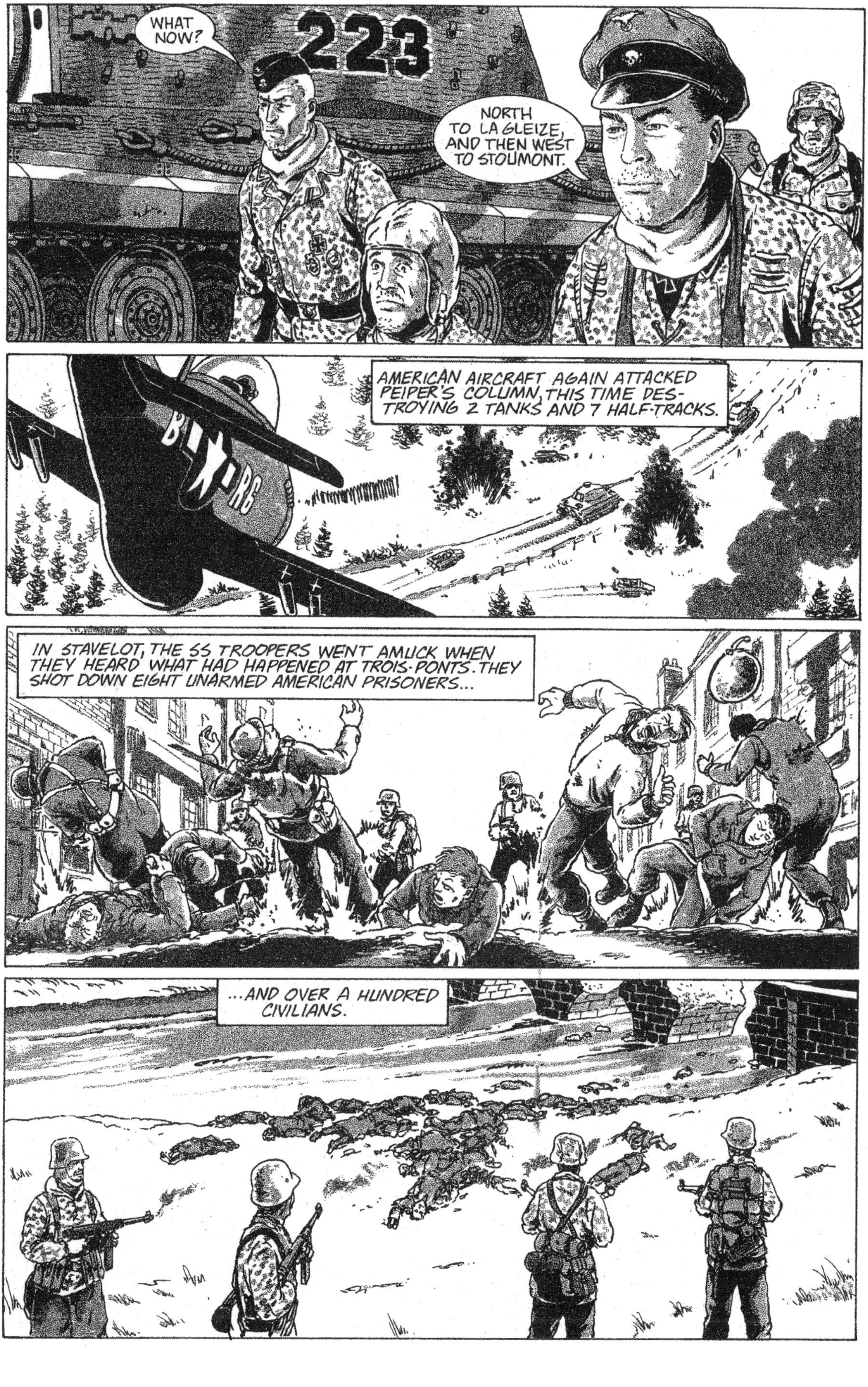
223
WHAT NOW?
NORTH TO LA GLEIZE, AND THEN WEST TO STOUMONT.
AMERICAN AIRCRAFT AGAIN ATTACKED PEIPER'S COLUMN, THIS TIME DESTROYING 2 TANKS AND 7 HALF-TRACKS.
IN STAVELOT, THE SS TROOPERS WENT AMUCK WHEN THEY HEARD WHAT HAD HAPPENED AT TROIS-PONTS. THEY SHOT DOWN EIGHT UNARMED AMERICAN PRISONERS...
...AND OVER A HUNDRED CIVILIANS.

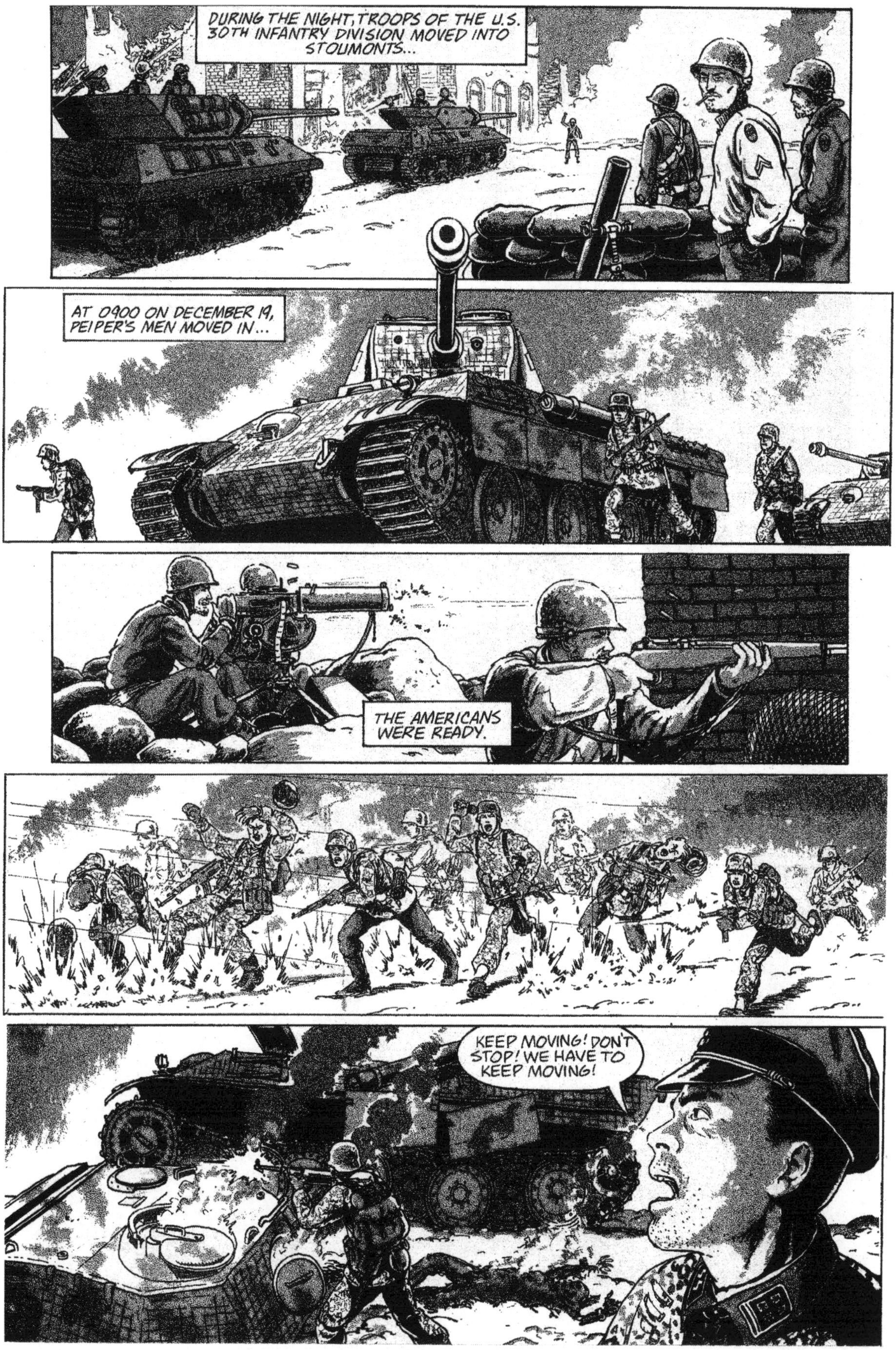
DURING THE NIGHT, TROOPS OF THE U.S. 30TH INFANTRY DIVISION MOVED INTO STOUMONTS...
AT 0900 ON DECEMBER 19, PEIPER'S MEN MOVED IN...
THE AMERICANS WERE READY.
KEEP MOVING! DON'T STOP! WE HAVE TO KEEP MOVING!

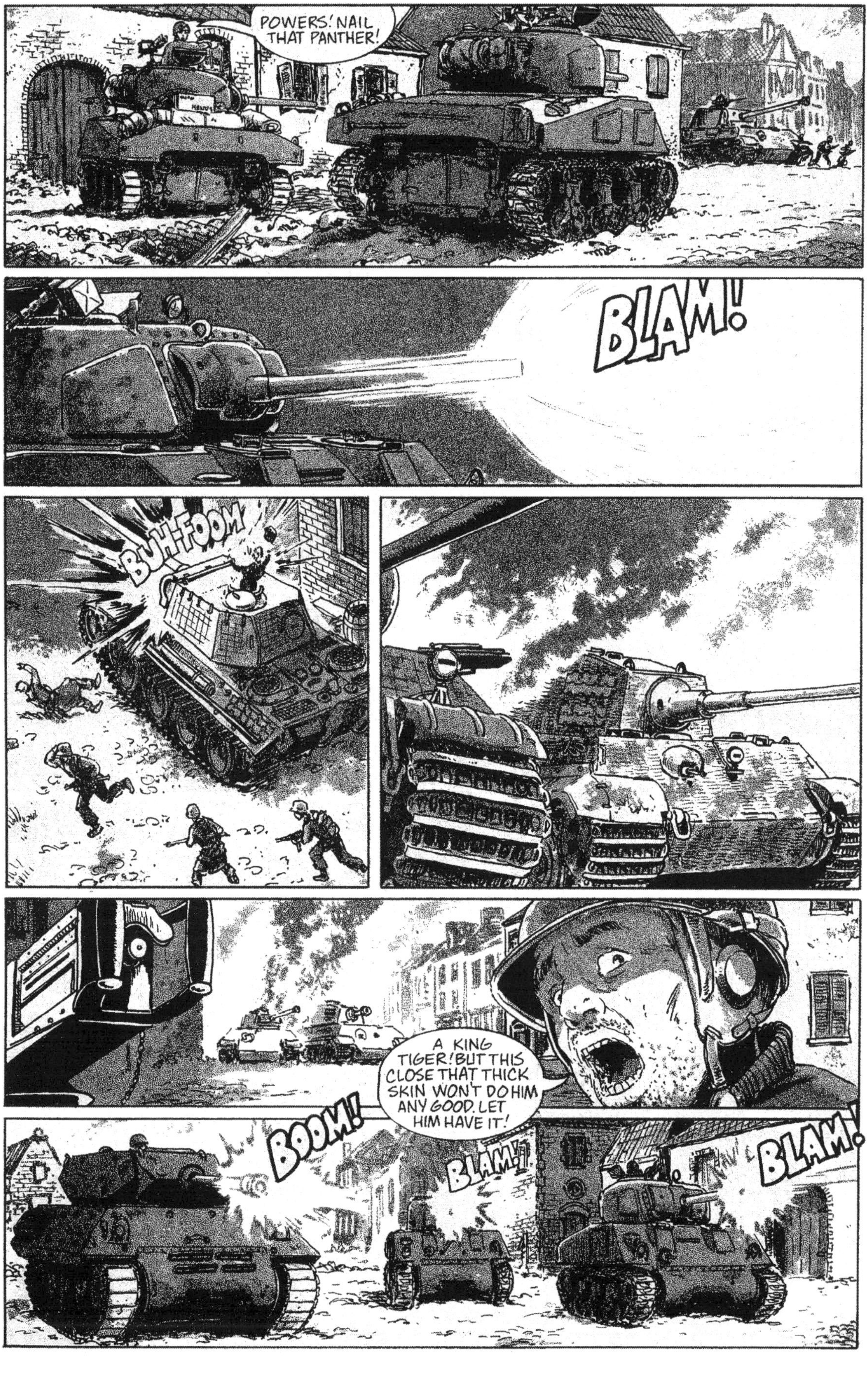
POWERS! NAIL THAT PANTHER!
BLAM!
BUH-FOOM
A KING TIGER! BUT THIS CLOSE THAT THICK SKIN WON'T DO HIM ANY GOOD. LET HIM HAVE IT!
BOOM!
BLAM!
BLAM!

THE FIRE LAID DOWN BY THE 30TH DIVISION MEN AND TANKS WAS DEVASTATING. THE SUPERIOR ARMOR OF THE TIGER AND PANTHER TANKS WAS NOT AN ADVANTAGE AT THIS CLOSE RANGE.

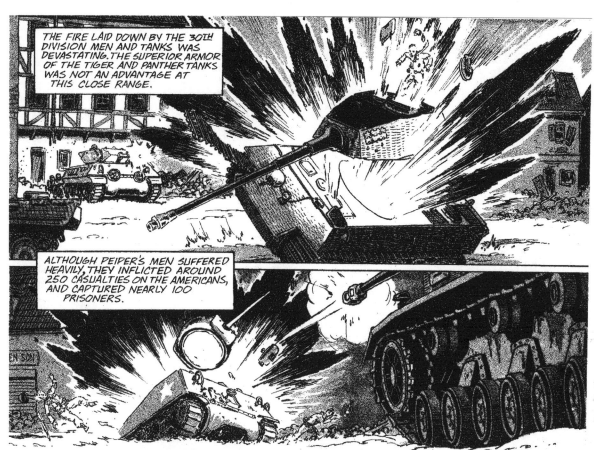

ALTHOUGH PEIPER'S MEN SUFFERED HEAVILY, THEY INFLICTED AROUND 250 CASUALTIES ON THE AMERICANS, AND CAPTURED NEARLY 100 PRISONERS.

WE'RE GETTING LOW ON AMMO, AND WE CAN'T KEEP UP THE PRESSURE LIKE THIS WITHOUT MORE.

PULL BACK AND FORM A DEFENSIVE PERIMETER UNTIL OUR SUPPLIES CATCH UP WITH US. WE'LL USE THAT BUILDING AS A COMMAND POST.

BUT BATTLE GROUP PEIPER WOULDN'T BE GETTING ANY SUPPLIES. FOR IN STAVELOT, THE 30TH DIVISION HAD MANAGED TO PUSH THE SS TROOPERS OUT OF THE TOWN AND BACK ACROSS THE AMBLEVE RIVER.

BATTLE GROUP PEIPER WAS NOW CUT OFF.

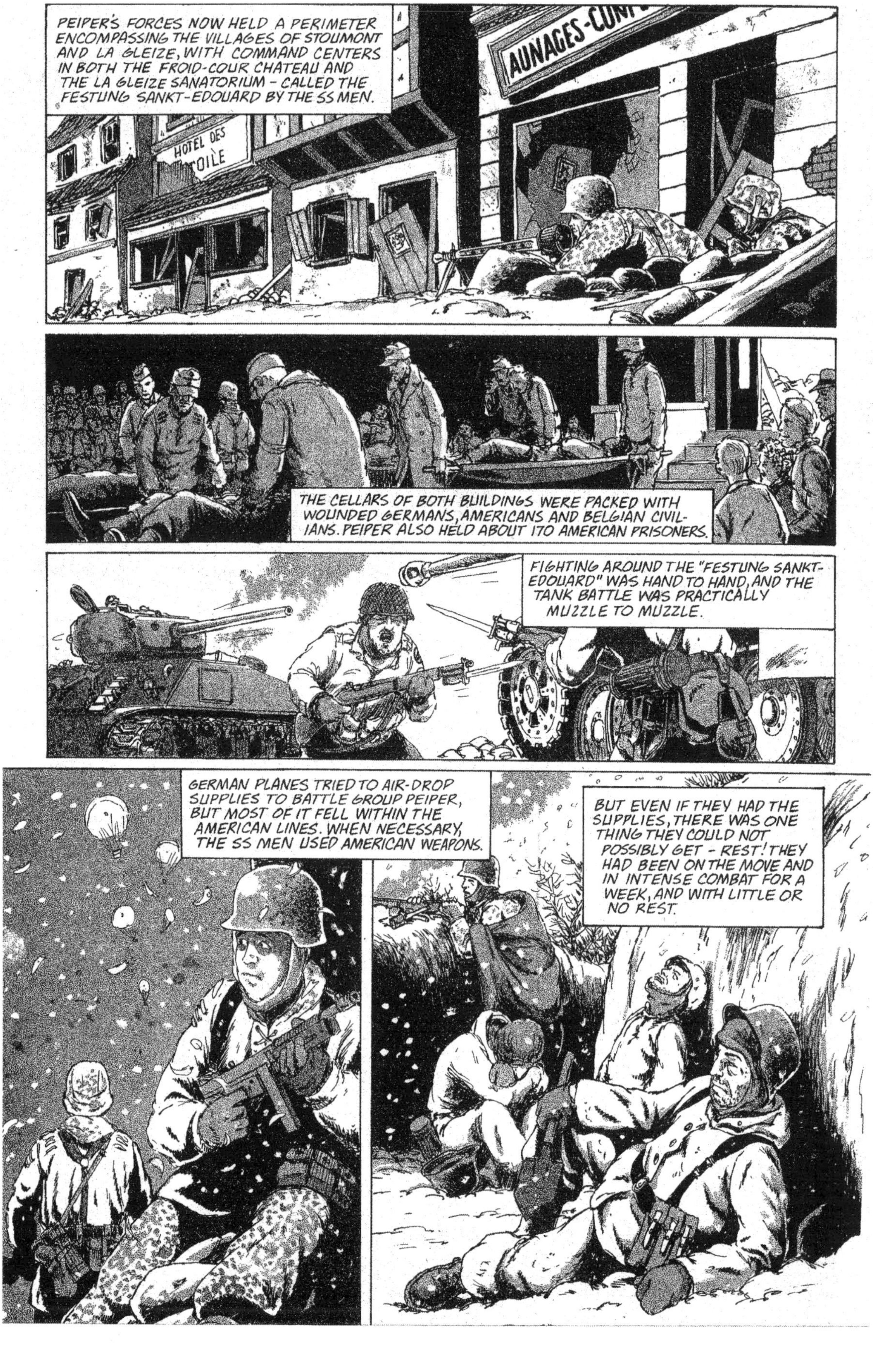
PEIPER'S FORCES NOW HELD A PERIMETER ENCOMPASSING THE VILLAGES OF STOUMONT AND LA GLEIZE, WITH COMMAND CENTERS IN BOTH THE FROID-COUR CHATEAU AND THE LA GLEIZE SANATORIUM - CALLED THE FESTUNG SANKT-EDOUARD BY THE SS MEN.
HOTEL DES
THE CELLARS OF BOTH BUILDINGS WERE PACKED WITH WOUNDED GERMANS, AMERICANS AND BELGIAN CIVILIANS. PEIPER ALSO HELD ABOUT 170 AMERICAN PRISONERS.
FIGHTING AROUND THE "FESTUNG SANKT-EDOUARD" WAS HAND TO HAND, AND THE TANK BATTLE WAS PRACTICALLY MUZZLE TO MUZZLE.
GERMAN PLANES TRIED TO AIR-DROP SUPPLIES TO BATTLE GROUP PEIPER, BUT MOST OF IT FELL WITHIN THE AMERICAN LINES. WHEN NECESSARY, THE SS MEN USED AMERICAN WEAPONS.
BUT EVEN IF THEY HAD THE SUPPLIES, THERE WAS ONE THING THEY COULD NOT POSSIBLY GET - REST! THEY HAD BEEN ON THE MOVE AND IN INTENSE COMBAT FOR A WEEK, AND WITH LITTLE OR NO REST.

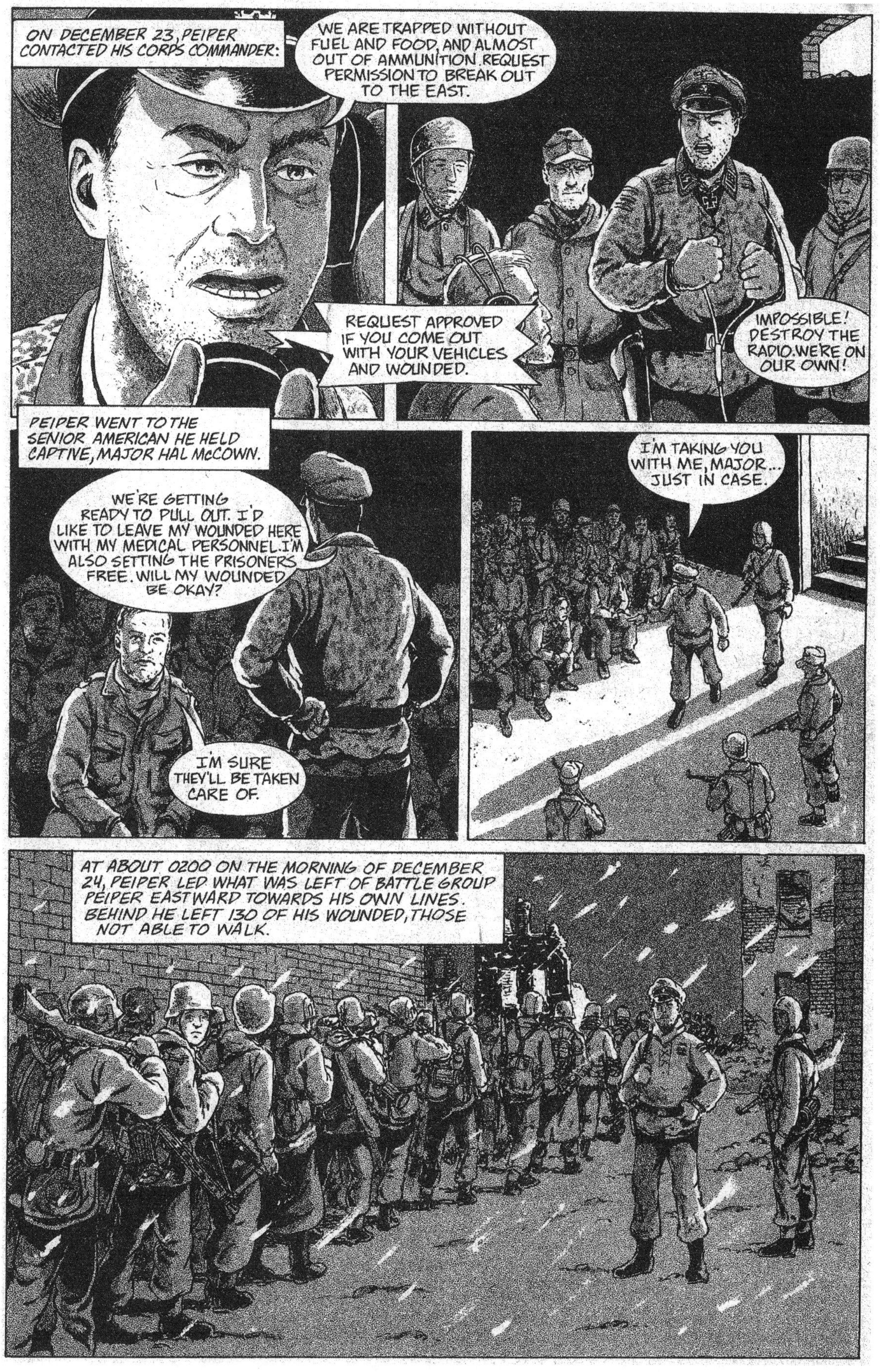
ON DECEMBER 23, PEIPER CONTACTED HIS CORPS COMMANDER:
WE ARE TRAPPED WITHOUT FUEL AND FOOD, AND ALMOST OUT OF AMMUNITION. REQUEST PERMISSION TO BREAK OUT TO THE EAST.
REQUEST APPROVED IF YOU COME OUT WITH YOUR VEHICLES AND WOUNDED.
IMPOSSIBLE! DESTROY THE RADIO. WE'RE ON OUR OWN!
PEIPER WENT TO THE SENIOR AMERICAN HE HELD CAPTIVE, MAJOR HAL McCOWN.
WE'RE GETTING READY TO PULL OUT. I'D LIKE TO LEAVE MY WOUNDED HERE WITH MY MEDICAL PERSONNEL. I'M ALSO SETTING THE PRISONERS FREE. WILL MY WOUNDED BE OKAY?
I'M SURE THEY'LL BE TAKEN CARE OF.
I'M TAKING YOU WITH ME, MAJOR... JUST IN CASE.
AT ABOUT 0200 ON THE MORNING OF DECEMBER 24, PEIPER LED WHAT WAS LEFT OF BATTLE GROUP PEIPER EASTWARD TOWARDS HIS OWN LINES. BEHIND HE LEFT 130 OF HIS WOUNDED, THOSE NOT ABLE TO WALK.

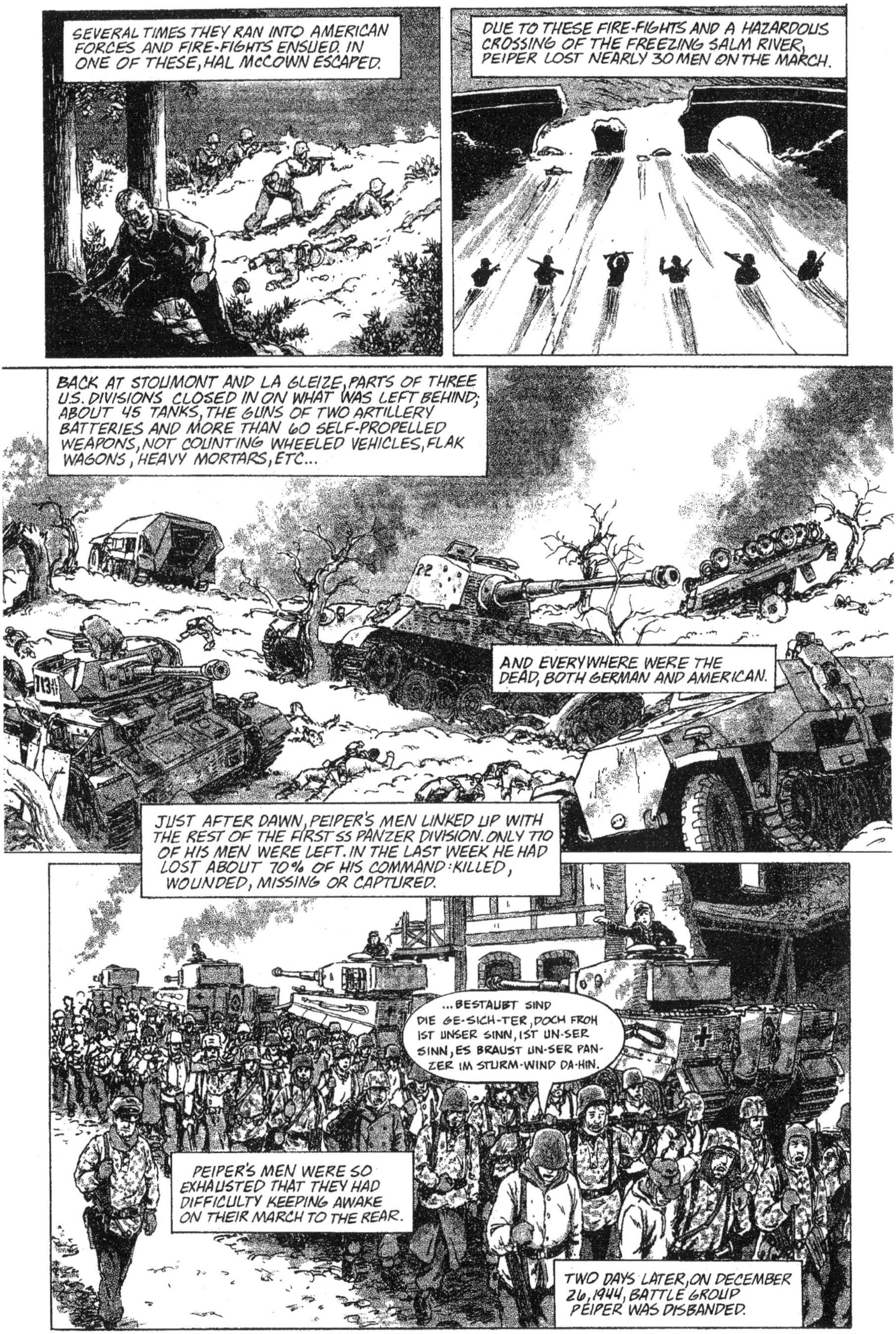
SEVERAL TIMES THEY RAN INTO AMERICAN FORCES AND FIRE-FIGHTS ENSUED. IN ONE OF THESE, HAL McCOWN ESCAPED.
DUE TO THESE FIRE-FIGHTS AND A HAZARDOUS CROSSING OF THE FREEZING SALM RIVER, PEIPER LOST NEARLY 30 MEN ON THE MARCH.
BACK AT STOUMONT AND LA GLEIZE, PARTS OF THREE U.S. DIVISIONS CLOSED IN ON WHAT WAS LEFT BEHIND; ABOUT 45 TANKS, THE GUNS OF TWO ARTILLERY BATTERIES AND MORE THAN 60 SELF-PROPELLED WEAPONS, NOT COUNTING WHEELED VEHICLES, FLAK WAGONS, HEAVY MORTARS, ETC...
AND EVERYWHERE WERE THE DEAD, BOTH GERMAN AND AMERICAN.
JUST AFTER DAWN, PEIPER'S MEN LINKED UP WITH THE REST OF THE FIRST SS PANZER DIVISION. ONLY 770 OF HIS MEN WERE LEFT. IN THE LAST WEEK HE HAD LOST ABOUT 70% OF HIS COMMAND: KILLED, WOUNDED, MISSING OR CAPTURED.
...BESTAUBT SIND DIE GE-SICH-TER, DOCH FROH IST UNSER SINN, IST UN-SER SINN, ES BRAUST UN-SER PAN-ZER IM STURM-WIND DA-HIN.
PEIPER'S MEN WERE SO EXHAUSTED THAT THEY HAD DIFFICULTY KEEPING AWAKE ON THEIR MARCH TO THE REAR.
TWO DAYS LATER, ON DECEMBER 26, 1944, BATTLE GROUP PEIPER WAS DISBANDED.

JUDGEMENT AT DACHAU

When the war in Europe ended on May 7, 1945, and evidence of Nazi brutality made clear, the Allied forces wasted no time in bringing those guilty to justice. This included those accused of murder on the battlefield. Crimes in combat situations cannot always be easily solved. For in war, killing and murder are not easily separated.

On May 16, 1946, seventy-four former Waffen-SS troopers were brought to trial for the massacre of American prisoners-of-war at the Baugnez crossroads near Malmedy. The trial was held at the former concentration camp at Dachau.

Joachim Peiper (#42 in picture) was the "star" of the trial. He was accused of putting out written orders for the execution of American prisoners, but no such written order was produced by the prosecution. He was accused of ordering the killings of prisoners at la Gleize, but the town's Mayor and Major Hal McCown testified that no such massacre took place (NOTE: After the Malmedy massacre, several U.S. units did put out written orders that no SS prisoners were to be taken). Belgian farmer Henri Lejoly, who witnessed the massacre, stated he saw no one at the sight that looked lilke Peiper.

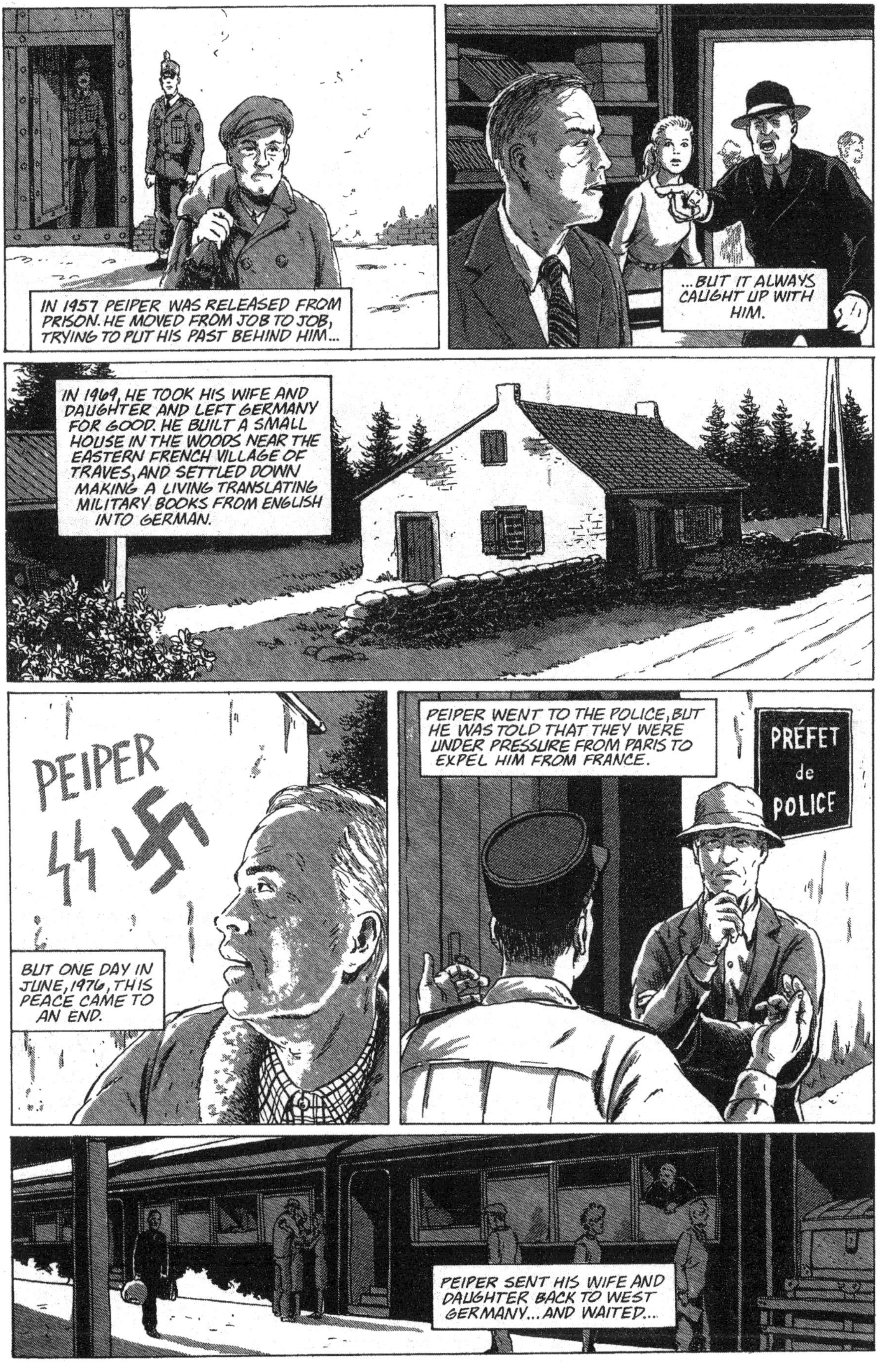
IN 1957 PEIPER WAS RELEASED FROM PRISON. HE MOVED FROM JOB TO JOB, TRYING TO PUT HIS PAST BEHIND HIM...
...BUT IT ALWAYS CAUGHT UP WITH HIM.
IN 1969, HE TOOK HIS WIFE AND DAUGHTER AND LEFT GERMANY FOR GOOD. HE BUILT A SMALL HOUSE IN THE WOODS NEAR THE EASTERN FRENCH VILLAGE OF TRAVES, AND SETTLED DOWN MAKING A LIVING TRANSLATING MILITARY BOOKS FROM ENGLISH INTO GERMAN.
PEIPER
BUT ONE DAY IN JUNE, 1976, THIS PEACE CAME TO AN END.
PEIPER WENT TO THE POLICE, BUT HE WAS TOLD THAT THEY WERE UNDER PRESSURE FROM PARIS TO EXPEL HIM FROM FRANCE.
PRÉFET de POLICE
PEIPER SENT HIS WIFE AND DAUGHTER BACK TO WEST GERMANY... AND WAITED...

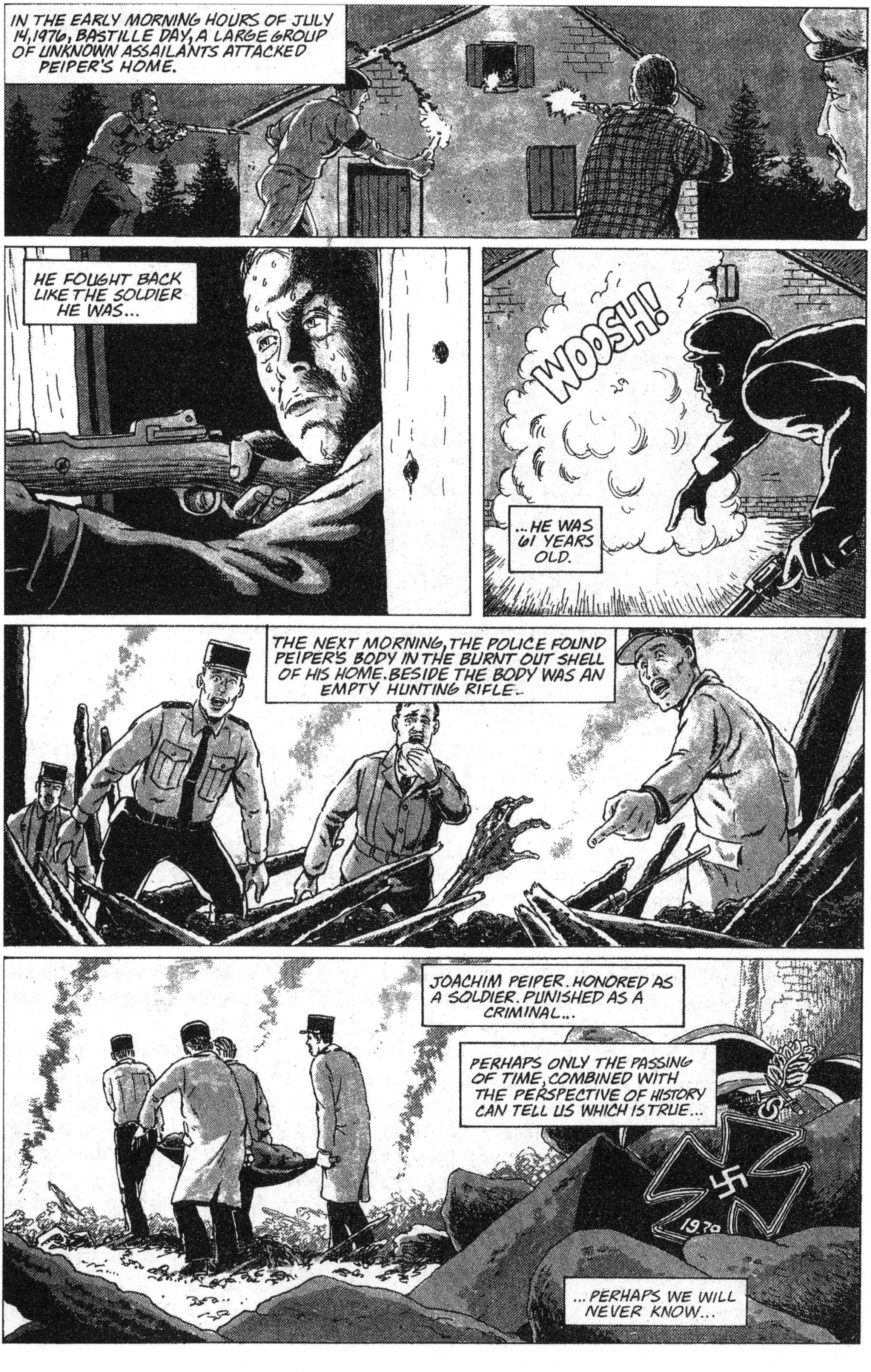
IN THE EARLY MORNING HOURS OF JULY 14, 1976, BASTILLE DAY, A LARGE GROUP OF UNKNOWN ASSAILANTS ATTACKED PEIPER'S HOME.
HE FOUGHT BACK LIKE THE SOLDIER HE WAS...
WOOSH!
...HE WAS 61 YEARS OLD.
THE NEXT MORNING, THE POLICE FOUND PEIPER'S BODY IN THE BURNT OUT SHELL OF HIS HOME. BESIDE THE BODY WAS AN EMPTY HUNTING RIFLE.
JOACHIM PEIPER. HONORED AS A SOLDIER. PUNISHED AS A CRIMINAL...
PERHAPS ONLY THE PASSING OF TIME, COMBINED WITH THE PERSPECTIVE OF HISTORY CAN TELL US WHICH IS TRUE...
1970
...PERHAPS WE WILL NEVER KNOW...

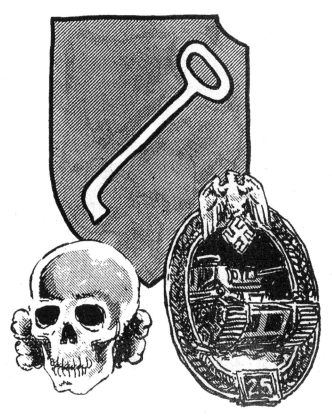

THE BLACK BAND

In March 1923, 200 men were formed into a group who swore to preserve the life of one man no matter what the cost to themselves. The man was Adolph Hitler. And this group, called the *Leibstandarte* (Bodyguard) *Adolph Hitler,* later became the 1st SS Panzer Division.

The SS itself was the creation of the scrawny son of a Munich school teacher, Heinrich Himmler. The SS became Hitler's physical instrument for gaining power in Germany. It was his political force and weapon of revenge.

As armed combat troops, the *Leibstandarte Adolph Hitler* were ruthless, and they were responsible for the first recorded atrocity of the armed SS in World War II, when their artillary company massacred 50 Jews who had been herded into a synagogue. The Army protested to Hitler, but he gave the SS freedom from Wehrmacht jurisdiction. This served to aggravate the suspicion and dislike with which the Waffen SS was regarded by the regular German Army.

But in the end, the Waffen SS was to show disregard and contempt for their own creator. When, in one of his frequent shows of temper, Hitler slurringly questioned their bravery, the officers of the Leibstandarte returned their medals to him in a chamber pot.

BLUNTING THE BULGE

Hitler's Ardennes Offensive failed. Althought his troops performed incredibly, the odds were stacked against them from the start.

The American forces just had too much- too many men, too may planes and tanks, too much of everything- for the Germans to succeed.

Few of the German objectives were taken, and those that were, were too far behind schedule to do them any good. Patton's 3rd Army, driving up on their southern flank, made it necessary to pull troops out of the attack and defend against this unexpected threat. When the skies cleared, American fighter- bombers straffed the columns of German tanks and infantry, bringing the drive to a halt. The offensive was finally stopped by the 2nd Armored Division only four miles from the Meuse River.

But the real cause for the German defeat in the Battle of the Bulge was the common American soldier. After three years of war, this citizen soldier had finally become a professional.

In the Bulge the G. I.'s was frequently cut off from his command structure in small but fierce battle that determined great issues. Platoons, squads, or sometimes one or two men took on superior numbers. Men like Major Paul Solis at Stavelot. The Anti- tank crew at Trois- Ponts. And the American tanks at Stoumonts.

In this, the greatest American battle ever fought, it is fitting the HE gets the credit.

KNIGHTS OF THE SKULL

Three Tales Originally Appearing in Negative Burn

"Tank Killers"
"A Boy and His Dog"
"The Bloody Youth"

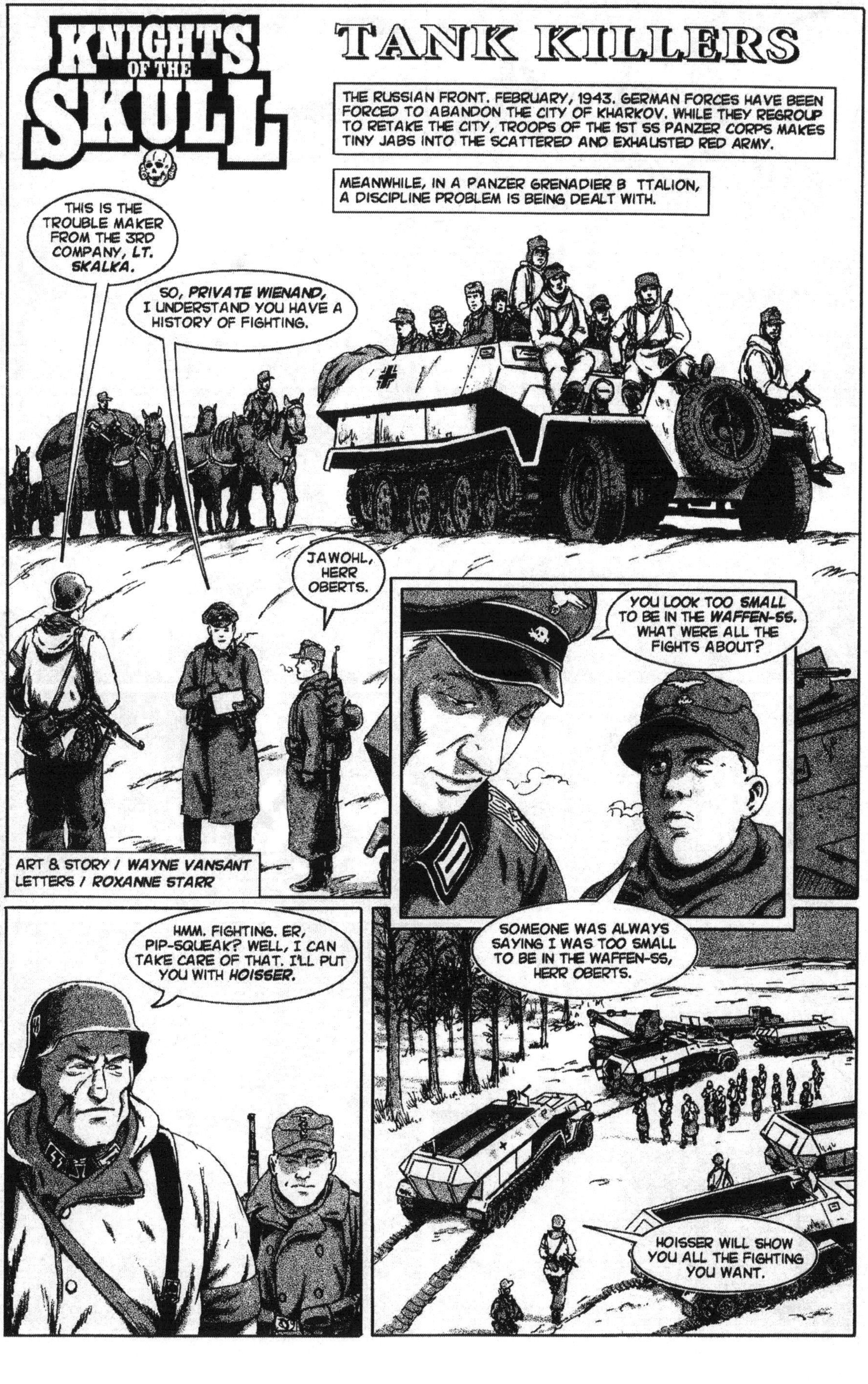

KNIGHTS OF THE SKULL
TANK KILLERS
THE RUSSIAN FRONT. FEBRUARY, 1943. GERMAN FORCES HAVE BEEN FORCED TO ABANDON THE CITY OF KHARKOV. WHILE THEY REGROUP TO RETAKE THE CITY, TROOPS OF THE 1ST SS PANZER CORPS MAKES TINY JABS INTO THE SCATTERED AND EXHAUSTED RED ARMY.
MEANWHILE, IN A PANZER GRENADIER B TTALION, A DISCIPLINE PROBLEM IS BEING DEALT WITH.
THIS IS THE TROUBLE MAKER FROM THE 3RD COMPANY, LT. SKALKA.
SO, PRIVATE WIENAND, I UNDERSTAND YOU HAVE A HISTORY OF FIGHTING.
JAWOHL, HERR OBERTS.
ART & STORY / WAYNE VANSANT
LETTERS / ROXANNE STARR
YOU LOOK TOO SMALL TO BE IN THE WAFFEN-SS. WHAT WERE ALL THE FIGHTS ABOUT?
SOMEONE WAS ALWAYS SAYING I WAS TOO SMALL TO BE IN THE WAFFEN-SS, HERR OBERTS.
HMM. FIGHTING. ER, PIP-SQUEAK? WELL, I CAN TAKE CARE OF THAT. I'LL PUT YOU WITH HOISSER.
HOISSER WILL SHOW YOU ALL THE FIGHTING YOU WANT.

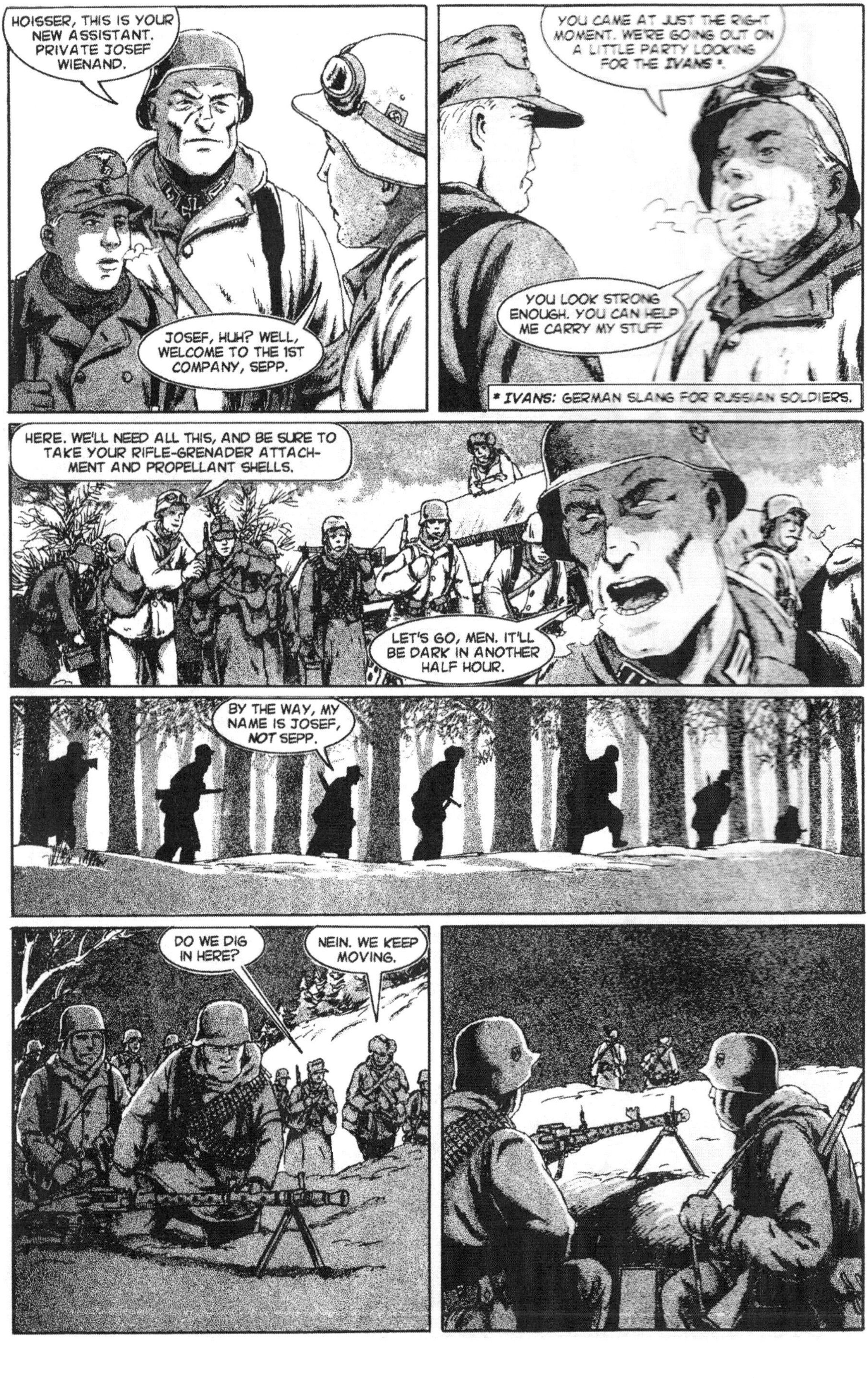
HOISSER, THIS IS YOUR NEW ASSISTANT. PRIVATE JOSEF WIENAND.
JOSEF, HUH? WELL, WELCOME TO THE 1ST COMPANY, SEPP.
YOU CAME AT JUST THE RIGHT MOMENT. WE'RE GOING OUT ON A LITTLE PARTY LOOKING FOR THE IVANS *.
YOU LOOK STRONG ENOUGH. YOU CAN HELP ME CARRY MY STUFF
* IVANS: GERMAN SLANG FOR RUSSIAN SOLDIERS.
HERE. WE'LL NEED ALL THIS, AND BE SURE TO TAKE YOUR RIFLE-GRENADER ATTACHMENT AND PROPELLANT SHELLS.
LET'S GO, MEN. IT'LL BE DARK IN ANOTHER HALF HOUR.
BY THE WAY, MY NAME IS JOSEF, NOT SEPP.
DO WE DIG IN HERE?
NEIN. WE KEEP MOVING.

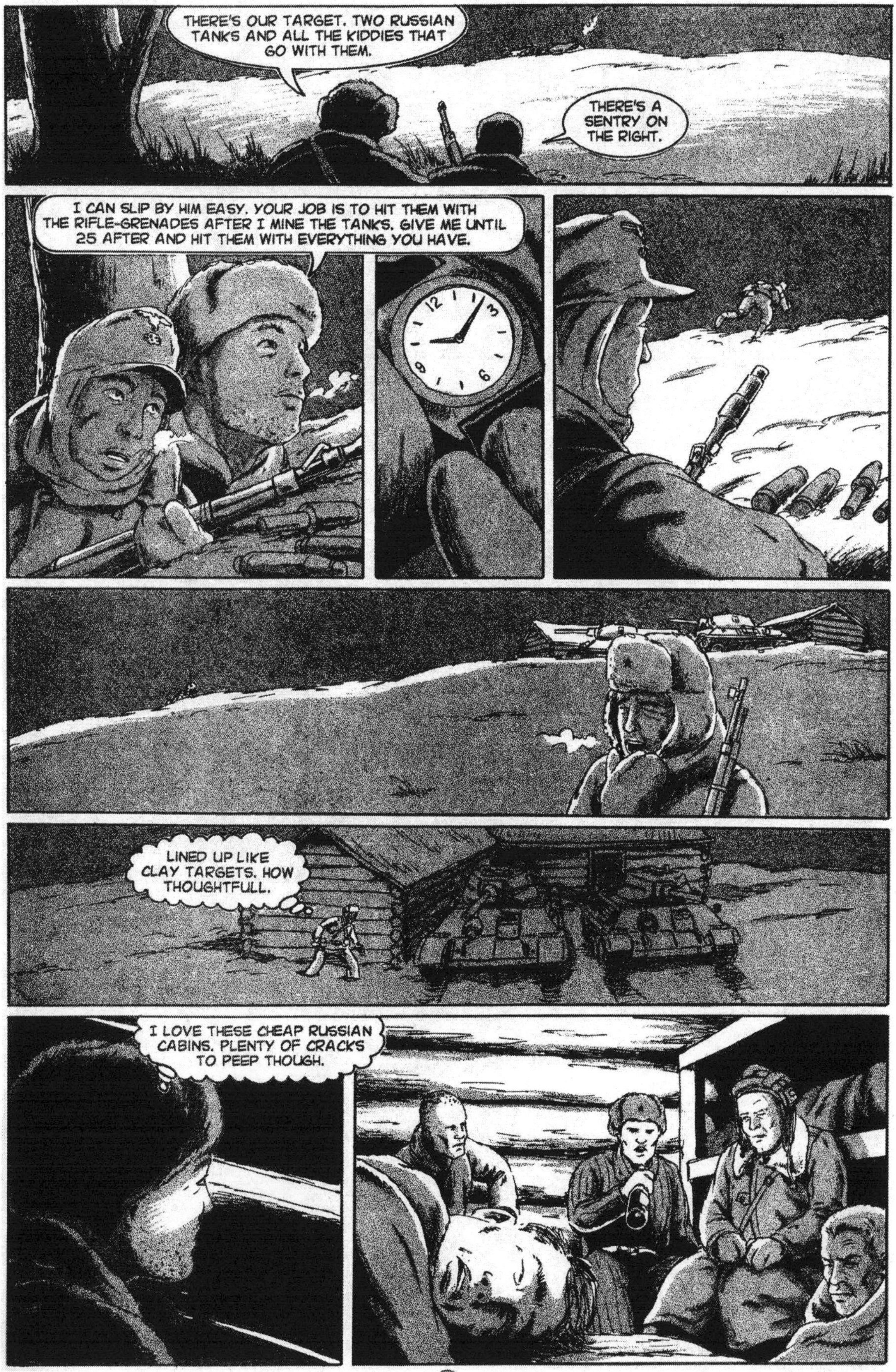
THERE'S OUR TARGET. TWO RUSSIAN TANKS AND ALL THE KIDDIES THAT GO WITH THEM.
THERE'S A SENTRY ON THE RIGHT.
I CAN SLIP BY HIM EASY. YOUR JOB IS TO HIT THEM WITH THE RIFLE-GRENADES AFTER I MINE THE TANKS. GIVE ME UNTIL 25 AFTER AND HIT THEM WITH EVERYTHING YOU HAVE.
LINED UP LIKE CLAY TARGETS. HOW THOUGHTFULL.
I LOVE THESE CHEAP RUSSIAN CABINS. PLENTY OF CRACKS TO PEEP THOUGH.

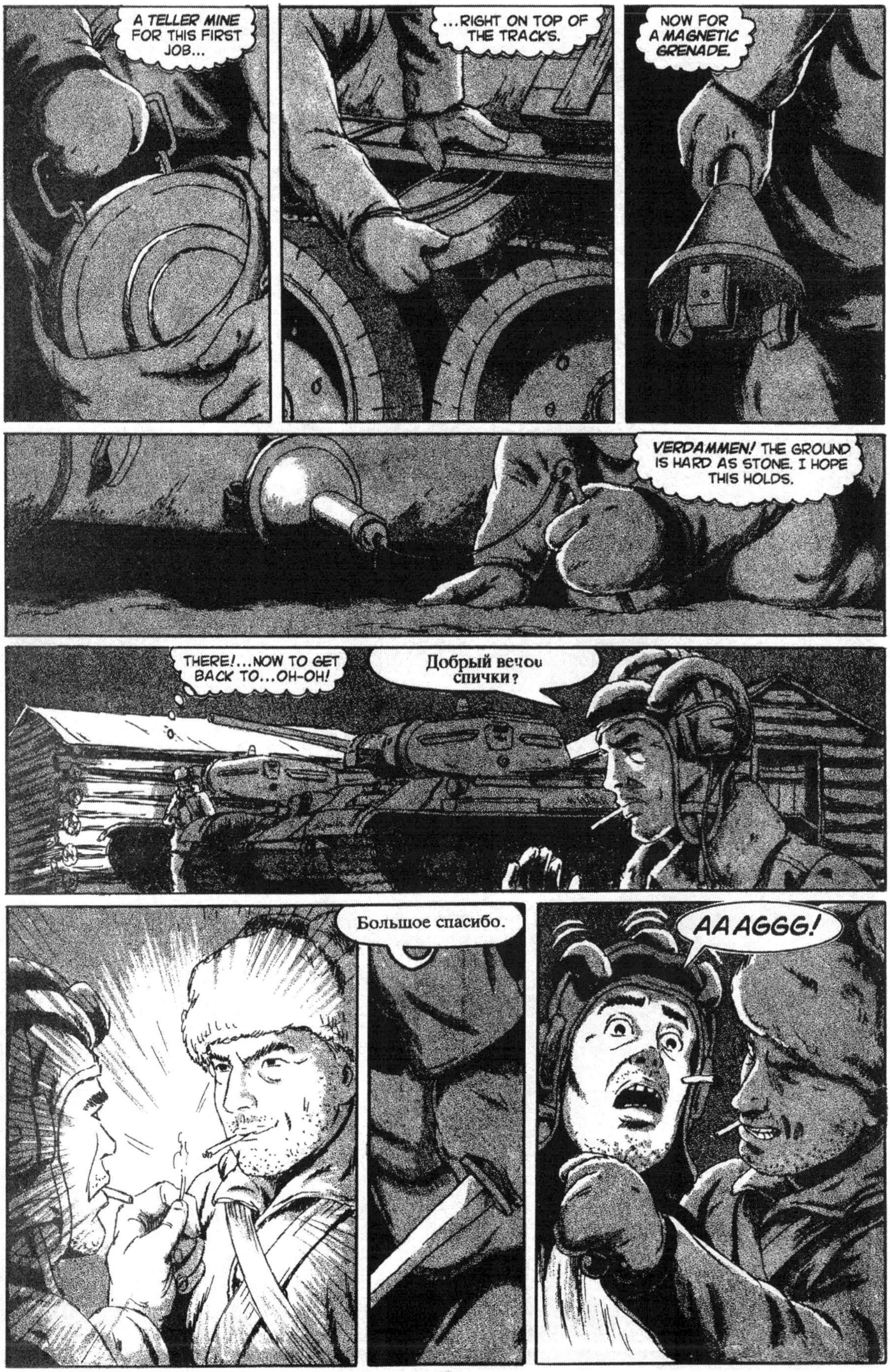
A TELLER MINE FOR THIS FIRST JOB...
...RIGHT ON TOP OF THE TRACKS.
NOW FOR A MAGNETIC GRENADE.
VERDAMMEN! THE GROUND IS HARD AS STONE. I HOPE THIS HOLDS.
THERE!...NOW TO GET BACK TO...OH-OH!
Добрый вечоu спички?
Большое спасибо.
AAAGGG!

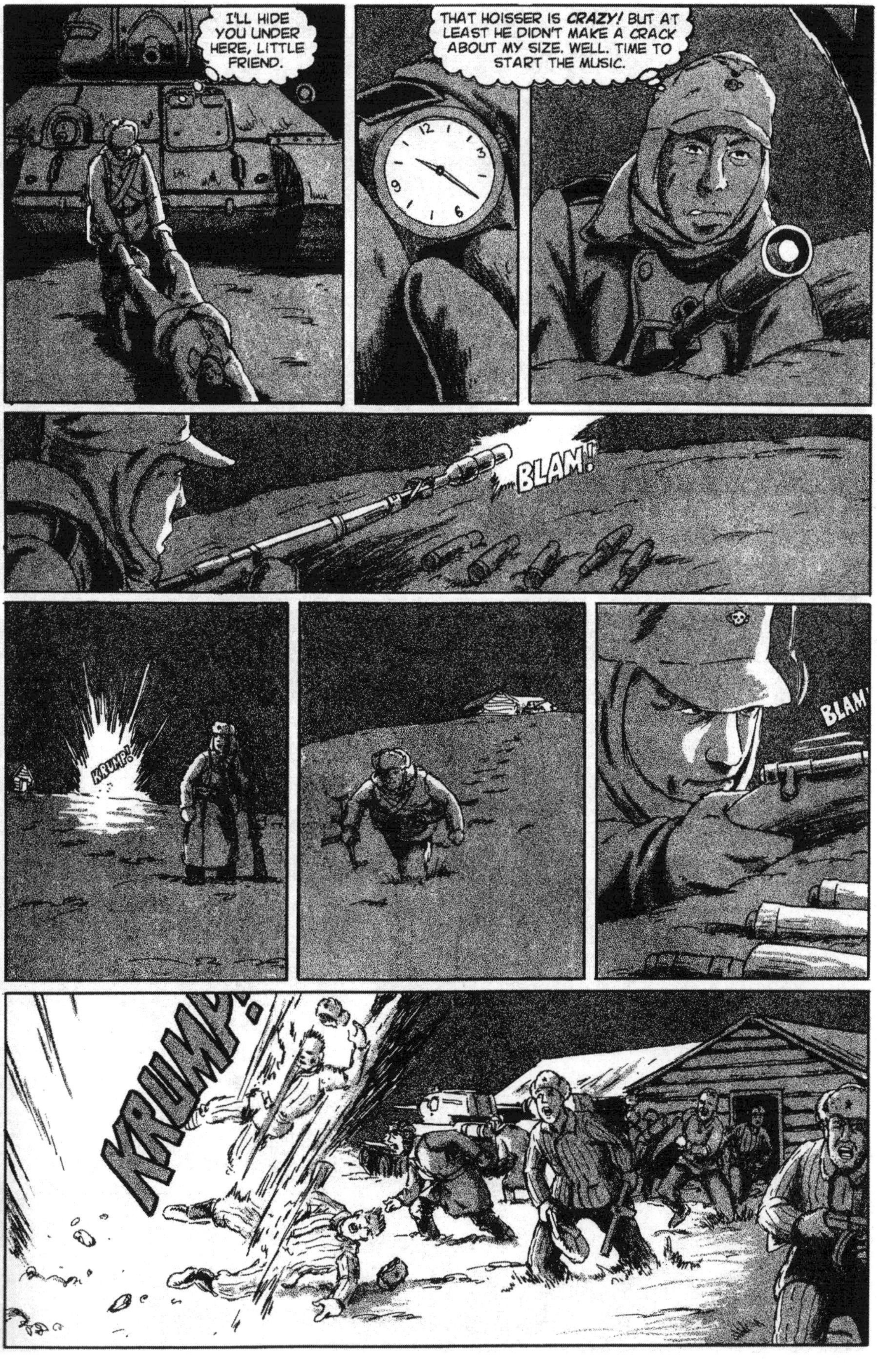
I'LL HIDE YOU UNDER HERE, LITTLE FRIEND.
THAT HOISSER IS *CRAZY!* BUT AT LEAST HE DIDN'T MAKE A *CRACK* ABOUT MY SIZE. WELL. TIME TO START THE MUSIC.
BLAM!
KRUMP!
BLAM!
KRUMP!

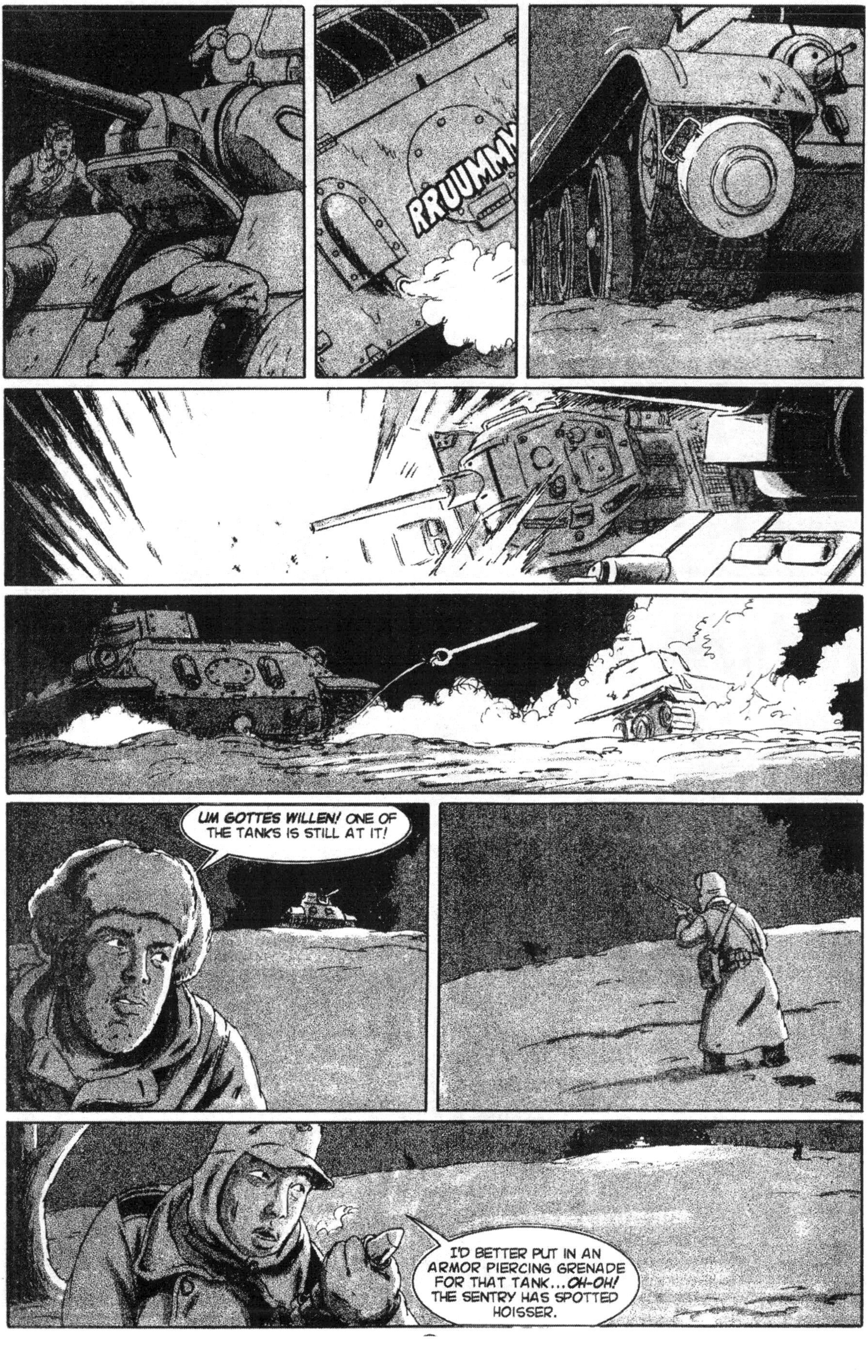
RRUUMMM
UM GOTTES WILLEN! ONE OF THE TANKS IS STILL AT IT!
I'D BETTER PUT IN AN ARMOR PIERCING GRENADE FOR THAT TANK... OH-OH! THE SENTRY HAS SPOTTED HOISSER.

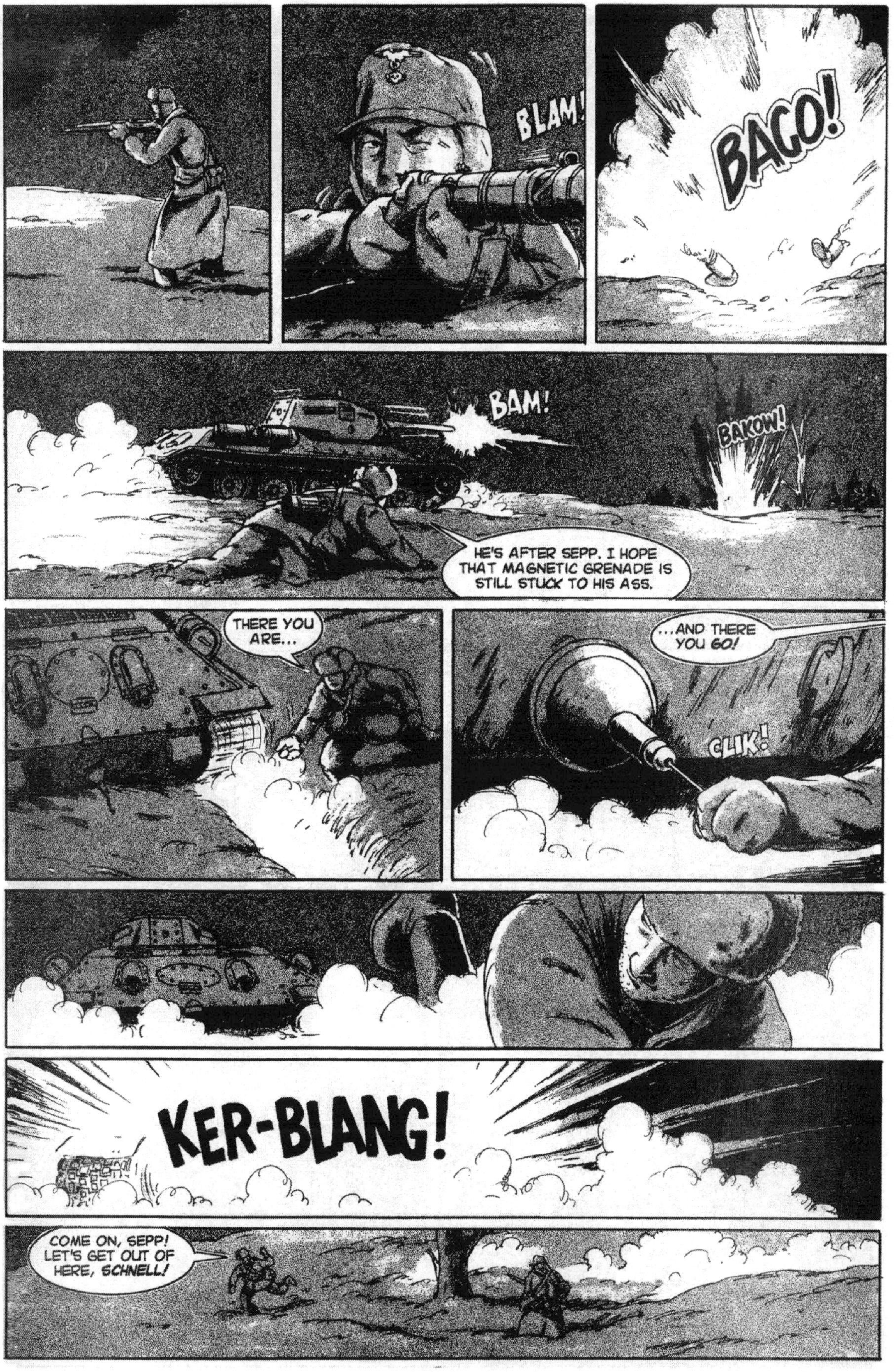
BLAM!
BAGO!
BAM!
BAKOW!
HE'S AFTER SEPP. I HOPE THAT MAGNETIC GRENADE IS STILL STUCK TO HIS ASS.
THERE YOU ARE...
...AND THERE YOU GO!
CLIK!
KER-BLANG!
COME ON, SEPP! LET'S GET OUT OF HERE, SCHNELL!

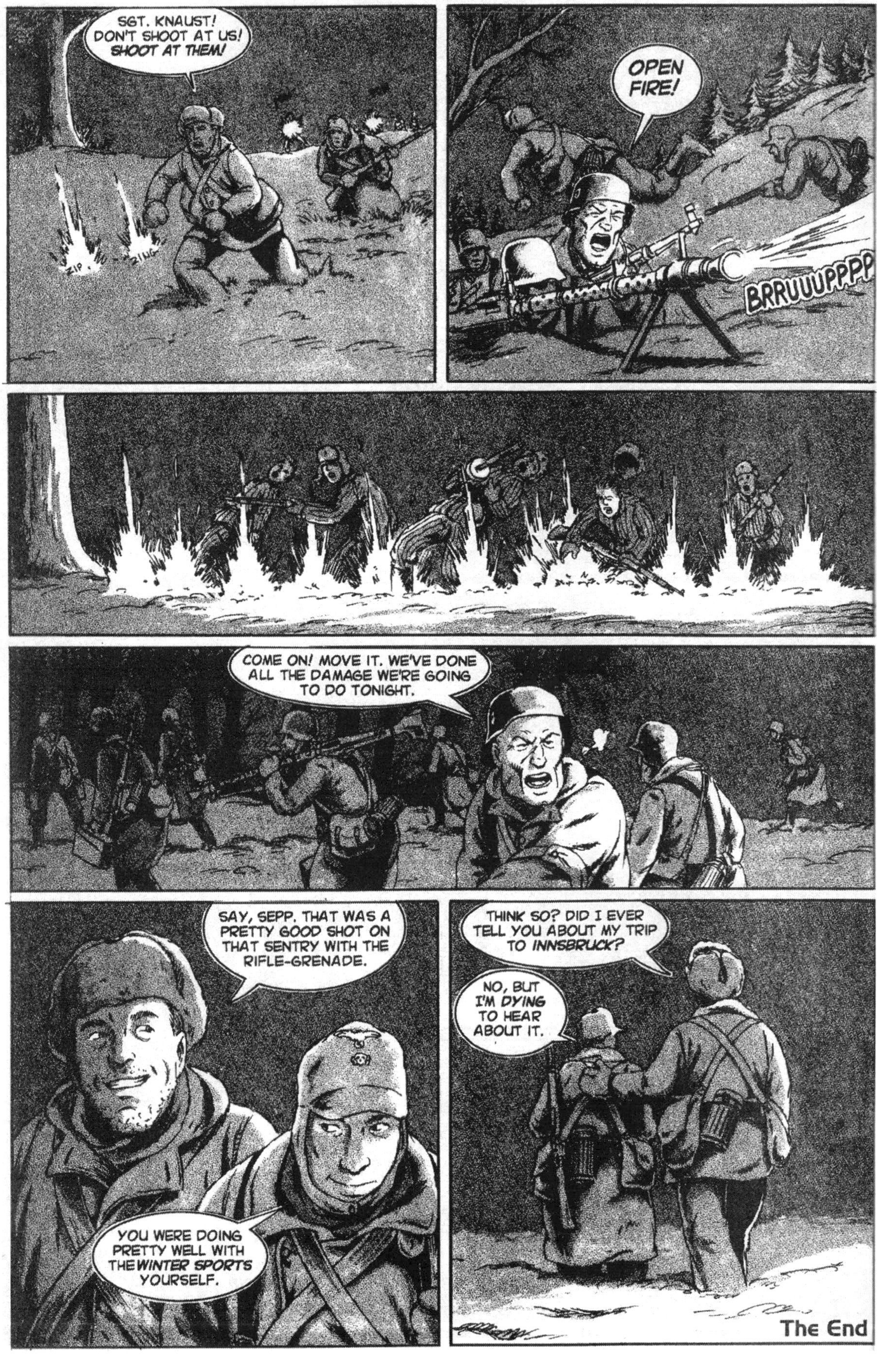
SGT. KNAUST! DON'T SHOOT AT US! SHOOT AT THEM!
ZIP
ZING
OPEN FIRE!
BRRUUUPPPP
COME ON! MOVE IT. WE'VE DONE ALL THE DAMAGE WE'RE GOING TO DO TONIGHT.
SAY, SEPP. THAT WAS A PRETTY GOOD SHOT ON THAT SENTRY WITH THE RIFLE-GRENADE.
YOU WERE DOING PRETTY WELL WITH THE WINTER SPORTS YOURSELF.
THINK SO? DID I EVER TELL YOU ABOUT MY TRIP TO INNSBRUCK?
NO, BUT I'M DYING TO HEAR ABOUT IT.
The End

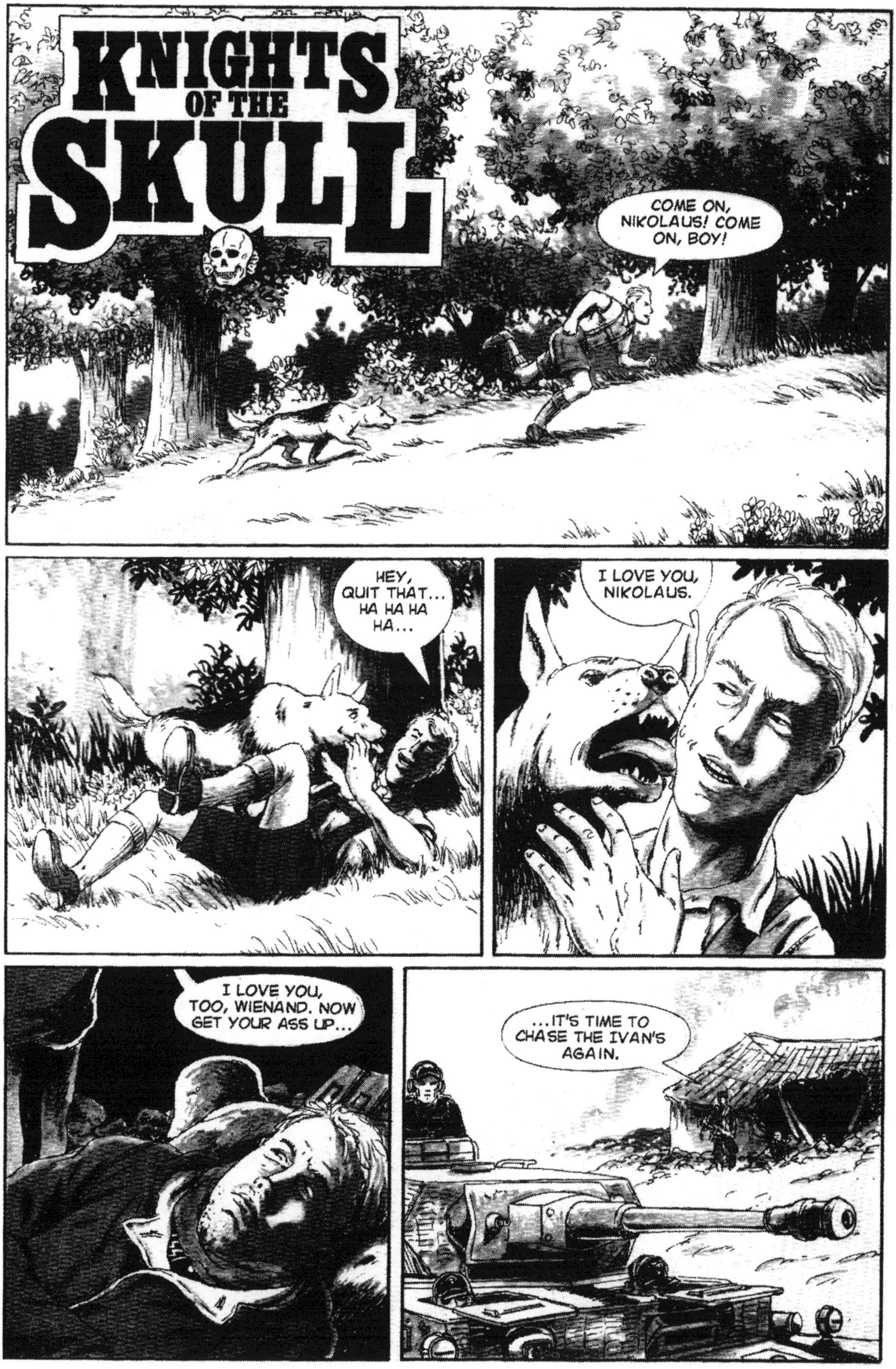
KNIGHTS OF THE SKULL
COME ON, NIKOLAUS! COME ON, BOY!
HEY, QUIT THAT... HA HA HA HA...
I LOVE YOU, NIKOLAUS.
I LOVE YOU, TOO, WIENAND. NOW GET YOUR ASS UP...
...IT'S TIME TO CHASE THE IVAN'S AGAIN.

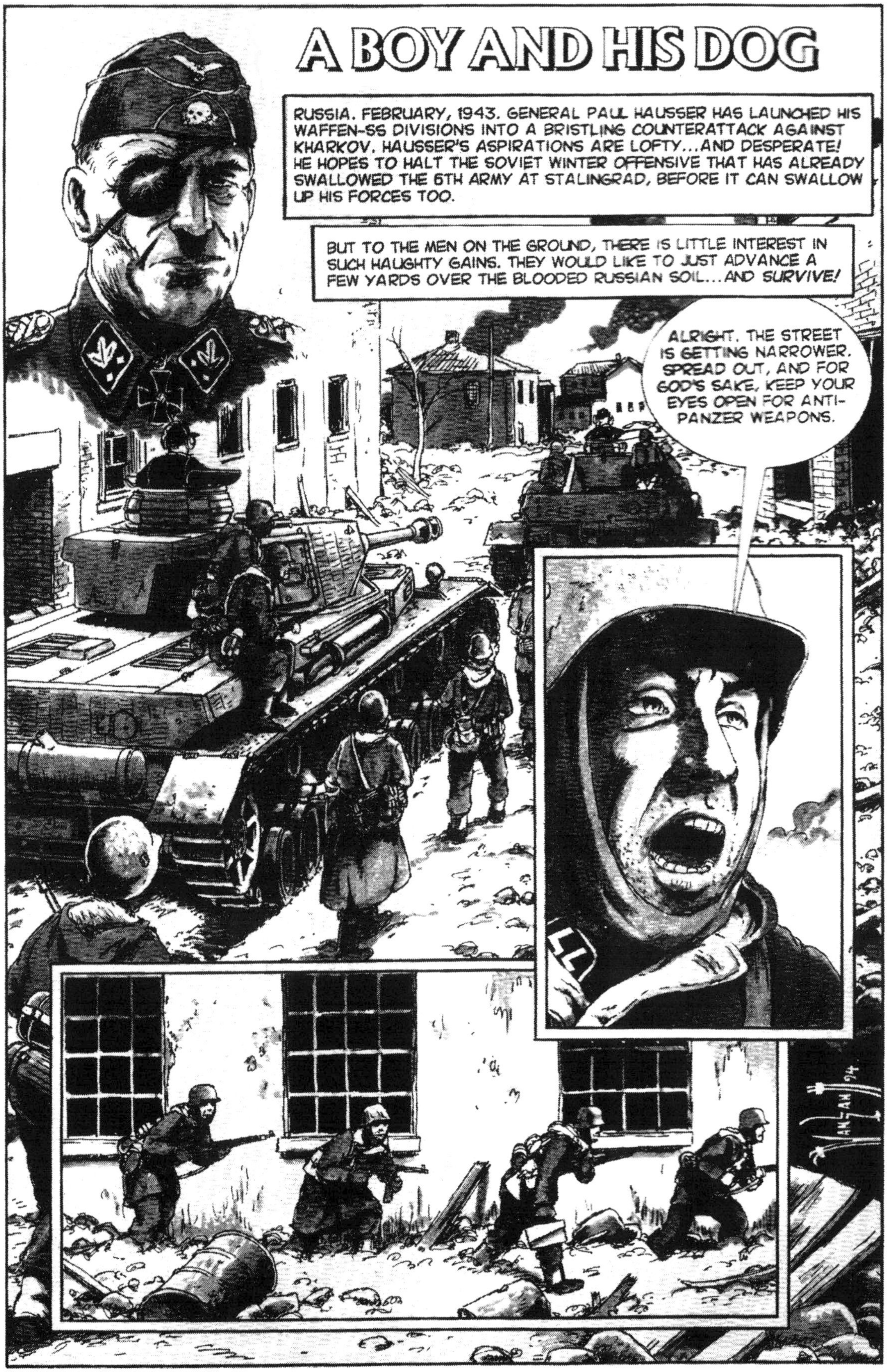
A BOY AND HIS DOG
RUSSIA. FEBRUARY, 1943. GENERAL PAUL HAUSSER HAS LAUNCHED HIS WAFFEN-SS DIVISIONS INTO A BRISTLING COUNTERATTACK AGAINST KHARKOV. HAUSSER'S ASPIRATIONS ARE LOFTY...AND DESPERATE! HE HOPES TO HALT THE SOVIET WINTER OFFENSIVE THAT HAS ALREADY SWALLOWED THE 6TH ARMY AT STALINGRAD, BEFORE IT CAN SWALLOW UP HIS FORCES TOO.
BUT TO THE MEN ON THE GROUND, THERE IS LITTLE INTEREST IN SUCH HAUGHTY GAINS. THEY WOULD LIKE TO JUST ADVANCE A FEW YARDS OVER THE BLOODED RUSSIAN SOIL...AND SURVIVE!
ALRIGHT. THE STREET IS GETTING NARROWER. SPREAD OUT, AND FOR GOD'S SAKE, KEEP YOUR EYES OPEN FOR ANTI-PANZER WEAPONS.

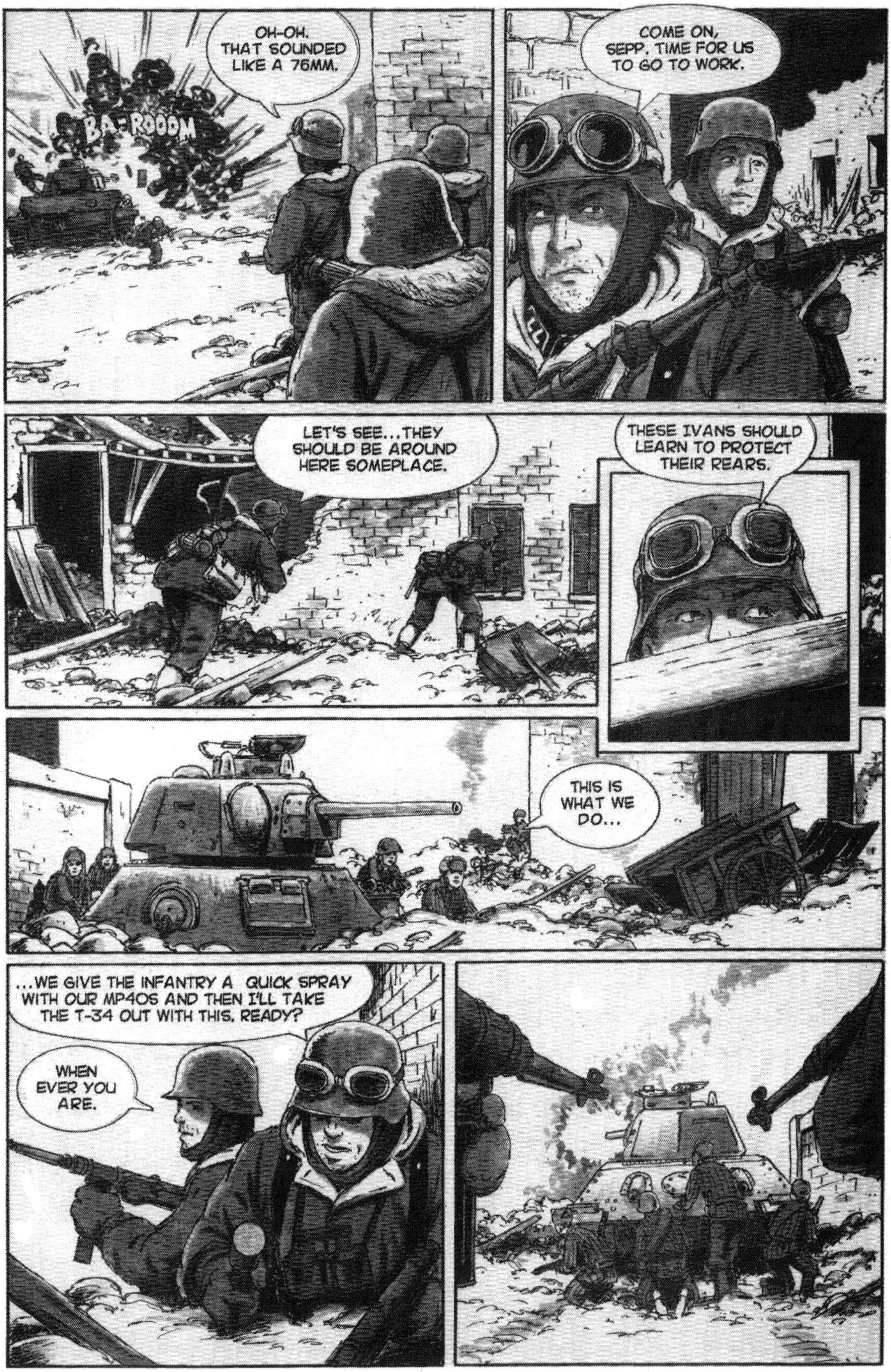
OH-OH. THAT SOUNDED LIKE A 76MM.
BA-ROOM
COME ON, SEPP. TIME FOR US TO GO TO WORK.
LET'S SEE...THEY SHOULD BE AROUND HERE SOMEPLACE.
THESE IVANS SHOULD LEARN TO PROTECT THEIR REARS.
THIS IS WHAT WE DO...
...WE GIVE THE INFANTRY A QUICK SPRAY WITH OUR MP40S AND THEN I'LL TAKE THE T-34 OUT WITH THIS. READY?
WHEN EVER YOU ARE.

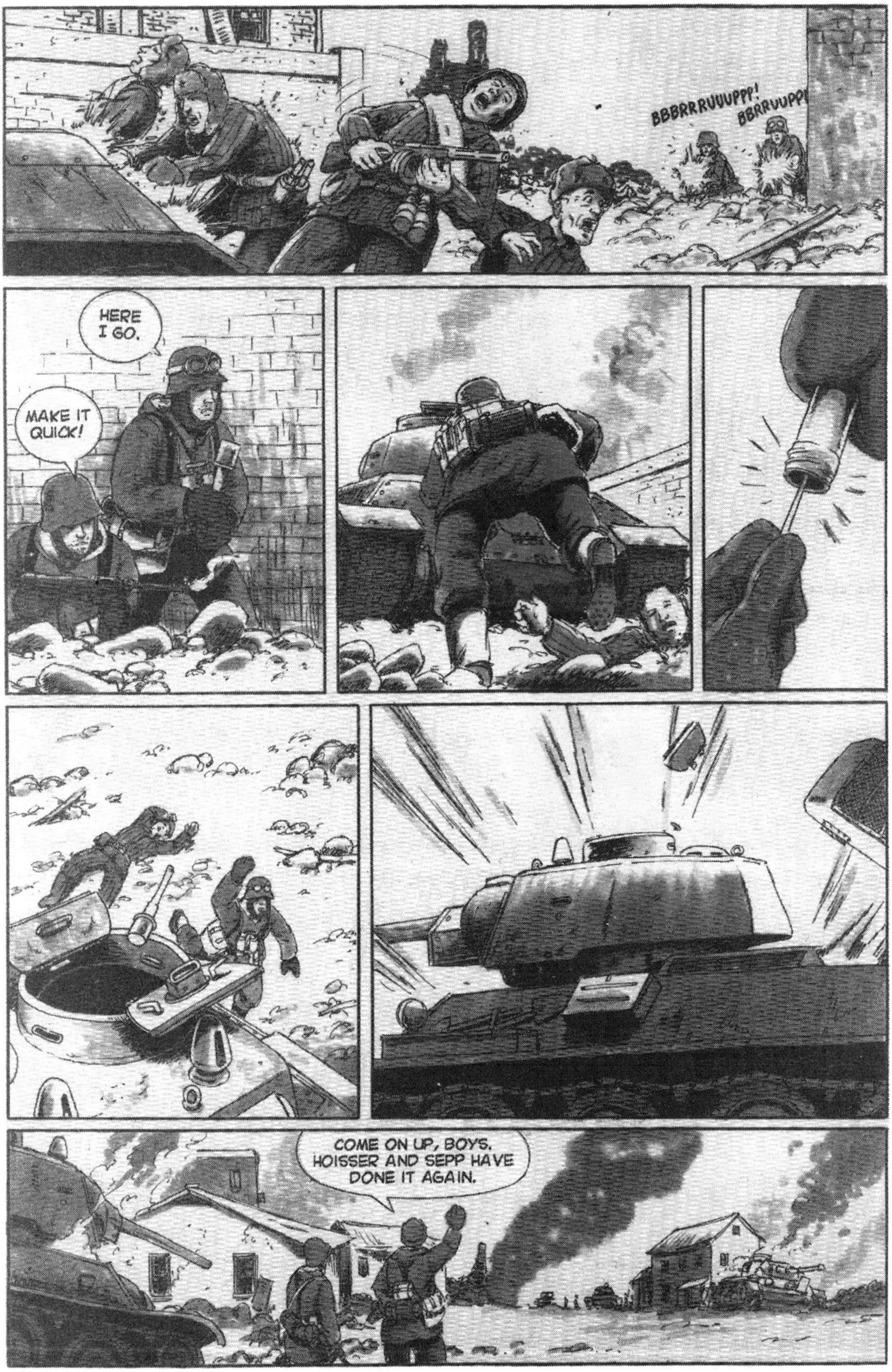
BBBRRRUUUPPP!
BBRRUUPP!
HERE I GO.
MAKE IT QUICK!
COME ON UP, BOYS. HOISSER AND SEPP HAVE DONE IT AGAIN.

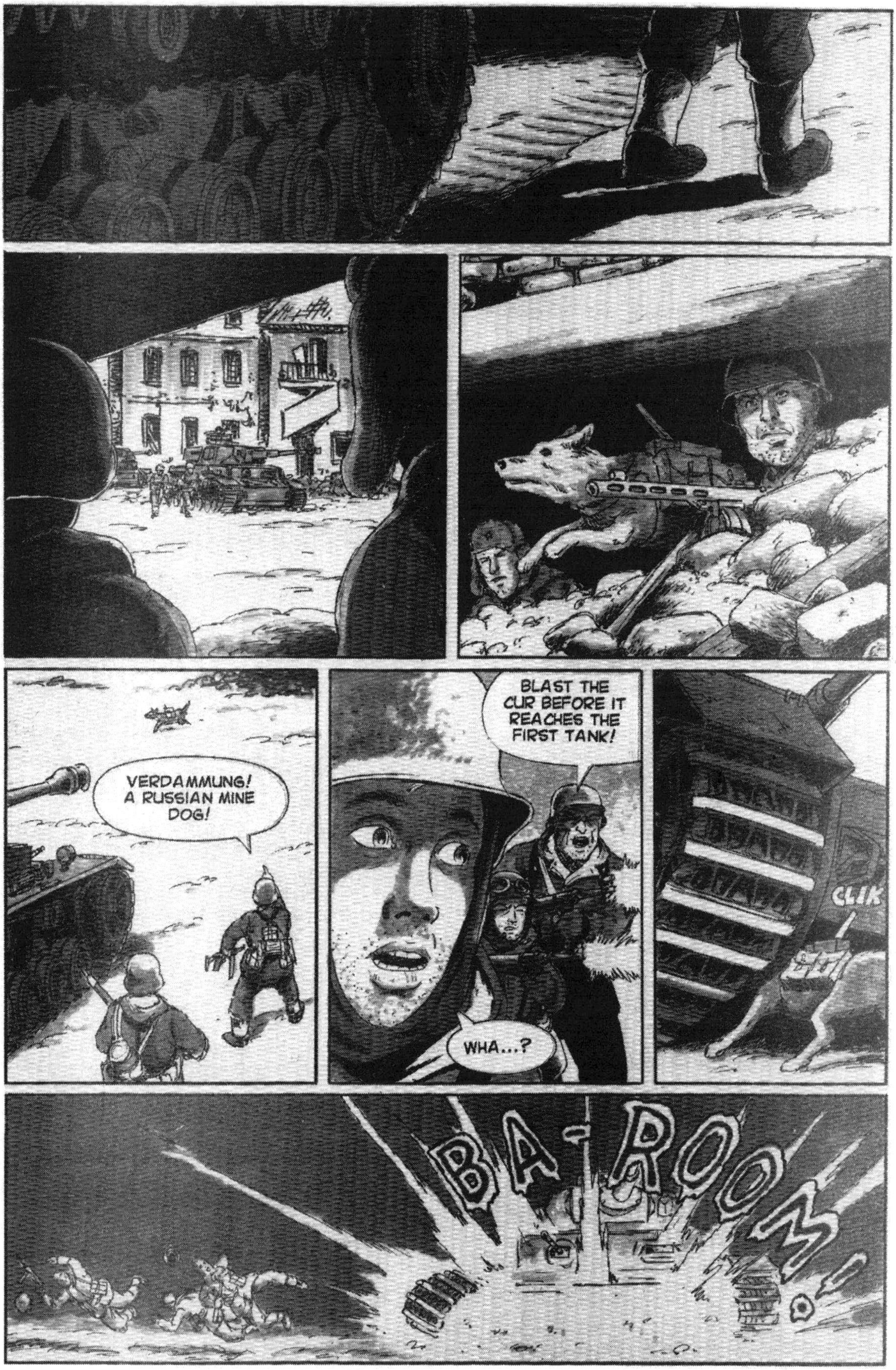
VERDAMMUNG! A RUSSIAN MINE DOG!
BLAST THE CUR BEFORE IT REACHES THE FIRST TANK!
WHA...?
CLIK
BA-ROOM!

OH... MY HEAD ...

LOOKOUT! THERE'S ANOTHER! SHOOT THE BITCH!

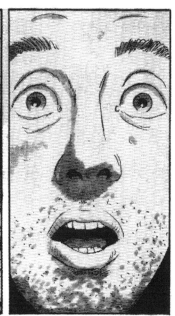

NO! NO! NO, GIRL, EH, BOY.

HOISSER, WHAT IN HELL IS THAT PARTNER OF YOURS THINK HE'S DOING? THERE'S HALF A POUND OF EXPLOSIVES ON THAT MANGY MONGREL!

COME ON, PUP. YOU JUST WANT SOMETHING TO EAT. THERE'S NOTHING FOR YOU UNDER THAT PANZER.

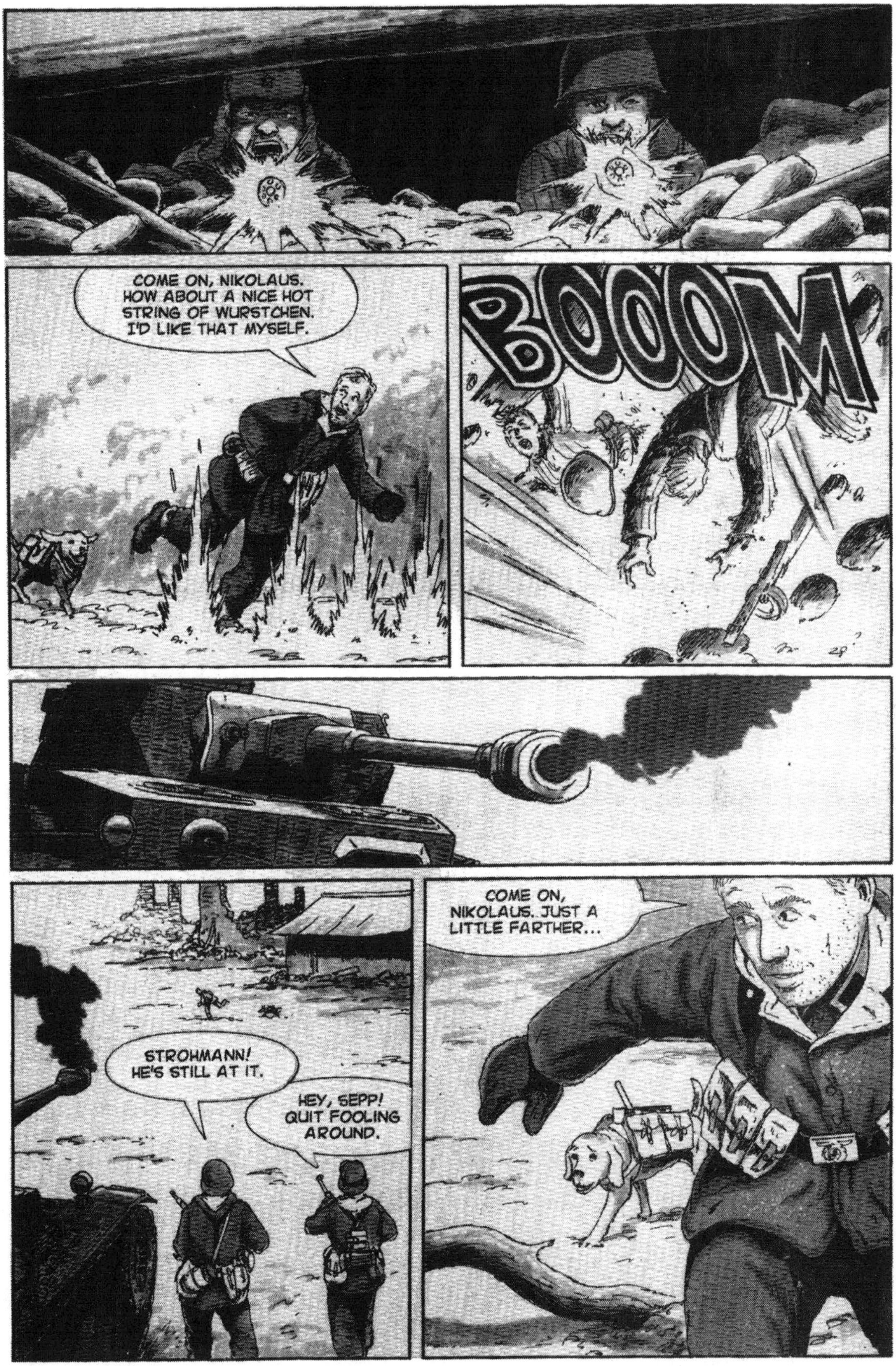
COME ON, NIKOLAUS. HOW ABOUT A NICE HOT STRING OF WURSTCHEN. I'D LIKE THAT MYSELF.
BOOOOM
STROHMANN! HE'S STILL AT IT.
HEY, SEPP! QUIT FOOLING AROUND.
COME ON, NIKOLAUS. JUST A LITTLE FARTHER...

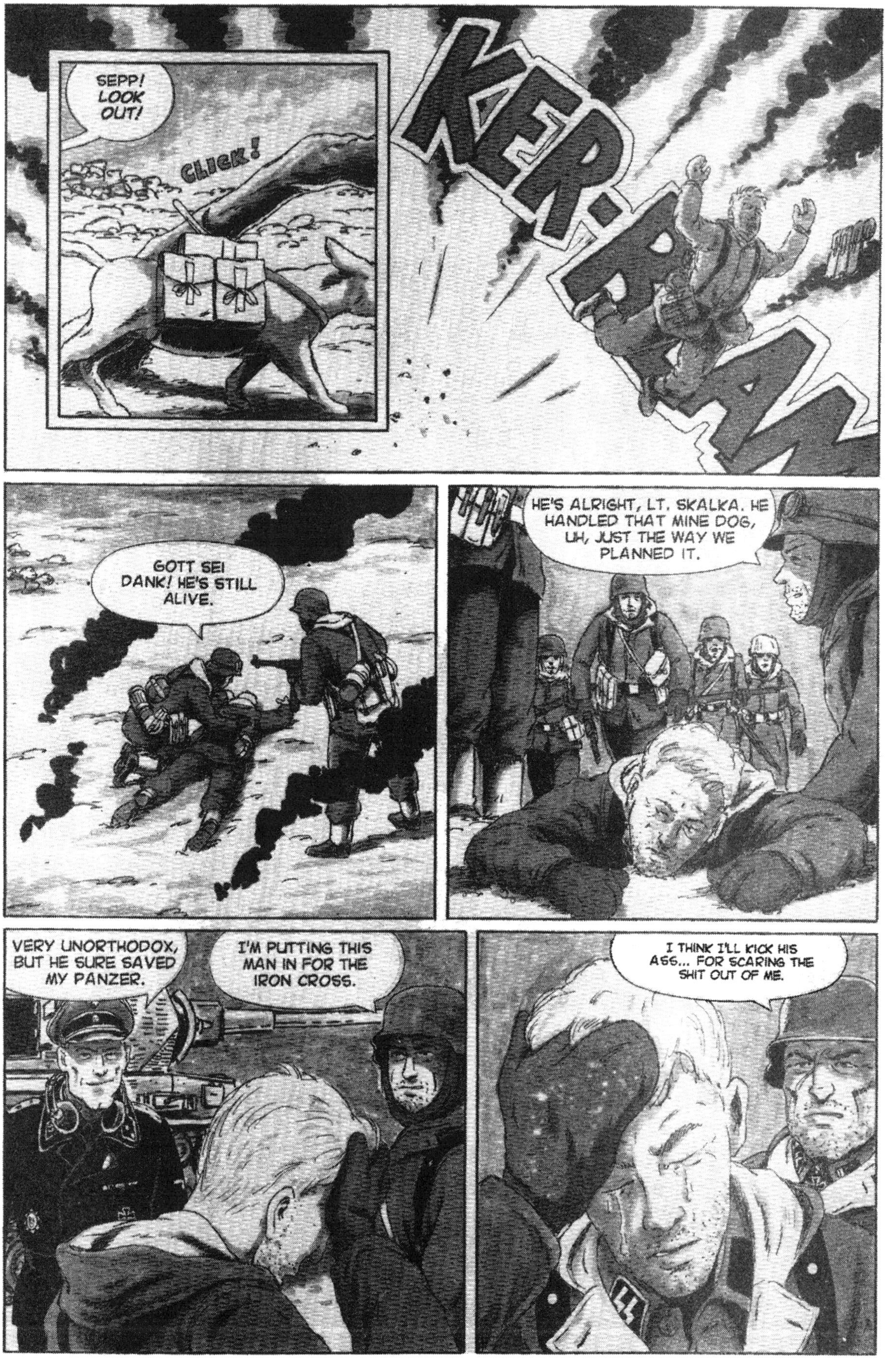
SEPP! LOOK OUT!
CLICK!
KER-BLAM
GOTT SEI DANK! HE'S STILL ALIVE.
HE'S ALRIGHT, LT. SKALKA. HE HANDLED THAT MINE DOG, UH, JUST THE WAY WE PLANNED IT.
VERY UNORTHODOX, BUT HE SURE SAVED MY PANZER.
I'M PUTTING THIS MAN IN FOR THE IRON CROSS.
I THINK I'LL KICK HIS ASS... FOR SCARING THE SHIT OUT OF ME.

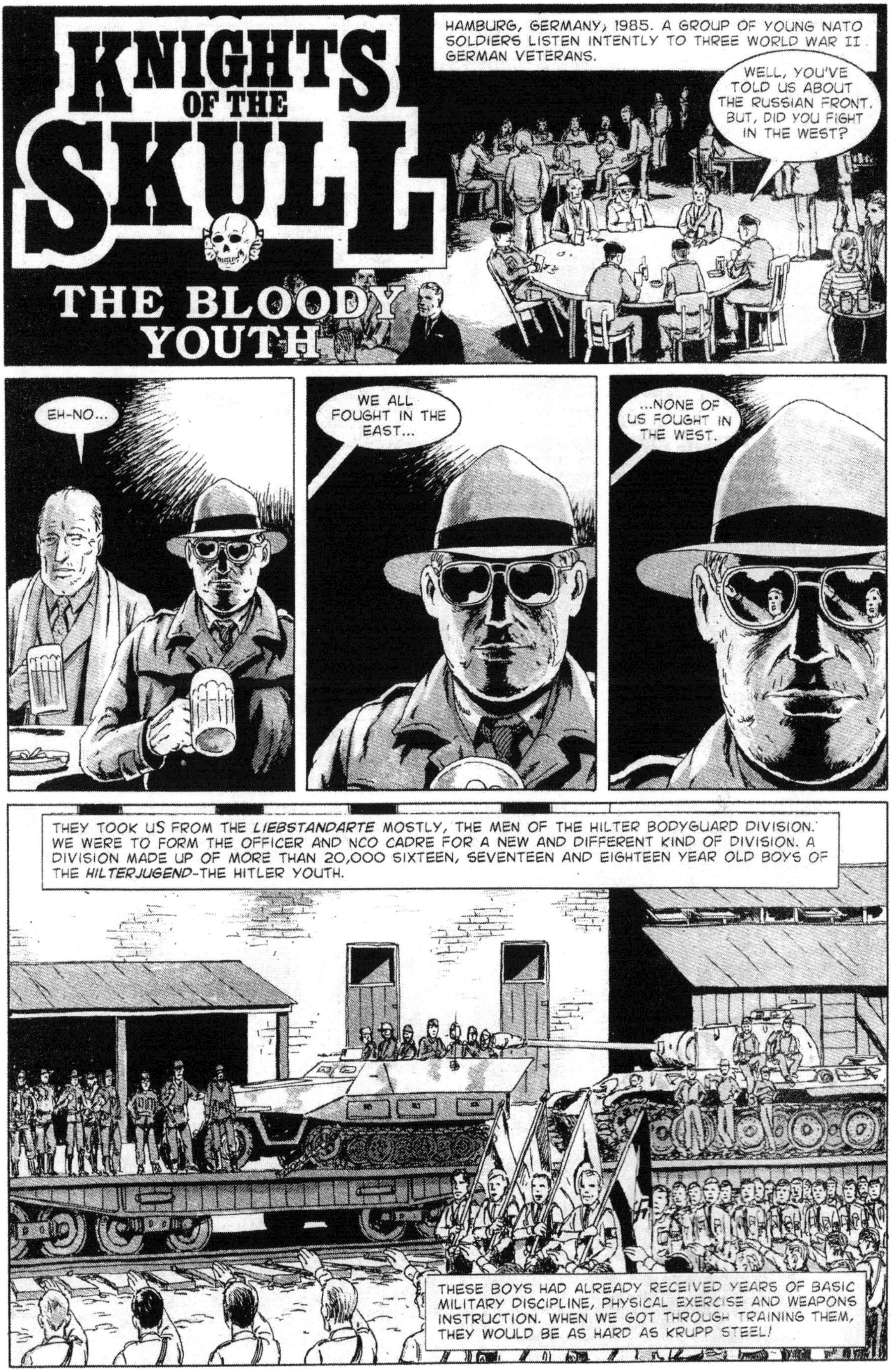
KNIGHTS OF THE SKULL
THE BLOODY YOUTH
HAMBURG, GERMANY, 1985. A GROUP OF YOUNG NATO SOLDIERS LISTEN INTENTLY TO THREE WORLD WAR II GERMAN VETERANS.
WELL, YOU'VE TOLD US ABOUT THE RUSSIAN FRONT. BUT, DID YOU FIGHT IN THE WEST?
EH-NO...
WE ALL FOUGHT IN THE EAST...
...NONE OF US FOUGHT IN THE WEST.
THEY TOOK US FROM THE LIEBSTANDARTE MOSTLY, THE MEN OF THE HILTER BODYGUARD DIVISION. WE WERE TO FORM THE OFFICER AND NCO CADRE FOR A NEW AND DIFFERENT KIND OF DIVISION. A DIVISION MADE UP OF MORE THAN 20,000 SIXTEEN, SEVENTEEN AND EIGHTEEN YEAR OLD BOYS OF THE HILTERJUGEND-THE HITLER YOUTH.
THESE BOYS HAD ALREADY RECEIVED YEARS OF BASIC MILITARY DISCIPLINE, PHYSICAL EXERCISE AND WEAPONS INSTRUCTION. WHEN WE GOT THROUGH TRAINING THEM, THEY WOULD BE AS HARD AS KRUPP STEEL!

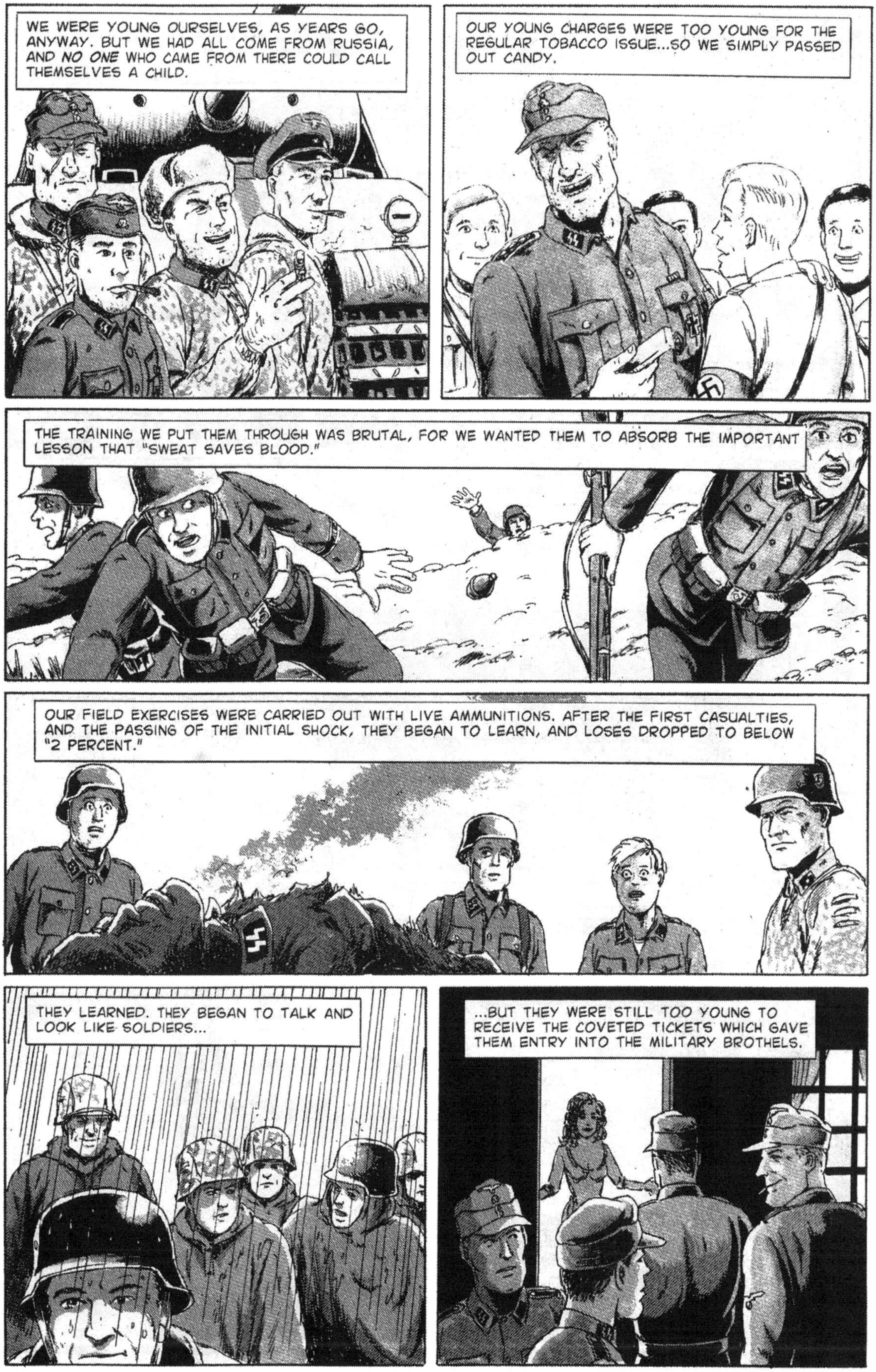
WE WERE YOUNG OURSELVES, AS YEARS GO, ANYWAY. BUT WE HAD ALL COME FROM RUSSIA, AND *NO ONE* WHO CAME FROM THERE COULD CALL THEMSELVES A CHILD.
OUR YOUNG CHARGES WERE TOO YOUNG FOR THE REGULAR TOBACCO ISSUE...SO WE SIMPLY PASSED OUT CANDY.
THE TRAINING WE PUT THEM THROUGH WAS BRUTAL, FOR WE WANTED THEM TO ABSORB THE IMPORTANT LESSON THAT "SWEAT SAVES BLOOD."
OUR FIELD EXERCISES WERE CARRIED OUT WITH LIVE AMMUNITIONS. AFTER THE FIRST CASUALTIES, AND THE PASSING OF THE INITIAL SHOCK, THEY BEGAN TO LEARN, AND LOSES DROPPED TO BELOW "2 PERCENT."
THEY LEARNED. THEY BEGAN TO TALK AND LOOK LIKE SOLDIERS...
...BUT THEY WERE STILL TOO YOUNG TO RECEIVE THE COVETED TICKETS WHICH GAVE THEM ENTRY INTO THE MILITARY BROTHELS.

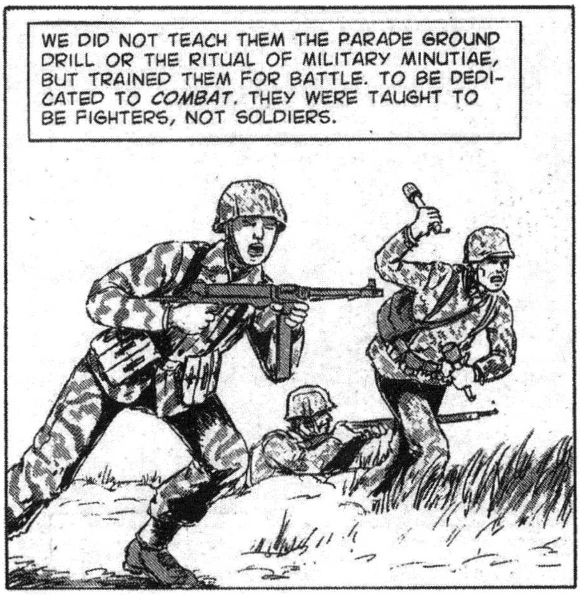
WE DID NOT TEACH THEM THE PARADE GROUND DRILL OR THE RITUAL OF MILITARY MINUTIAE, BUT TRAINED THEM FOR BATTLE. TO BE DEDICATED TO *COMBAT*. THEY WERE TAUGHT TO BE FIGHTERS, NOT SOLDIERS.

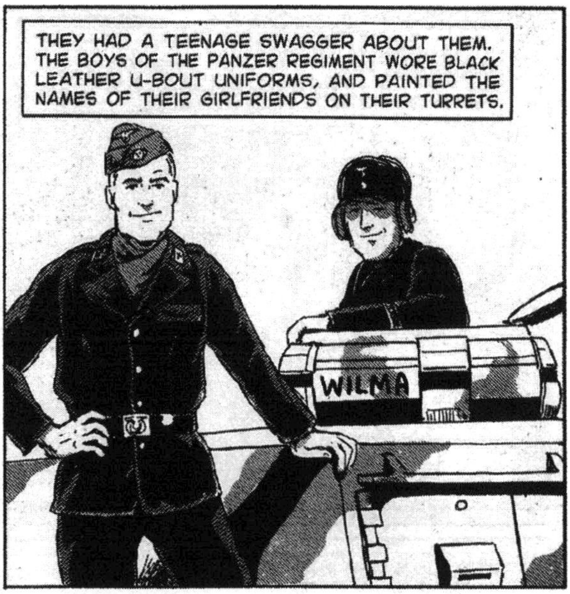
THEY HAD A TEENAGE SWAGGER ABOUT THEM. THE BOYS OF THE PANZER REGIMENT WORE BLACK LEATHER U-BOUT UNIFORMS, AND PAINTED THE NAMES OF THEIR GIRLFRIENDS ON THEIR TURRETS.
WILMA

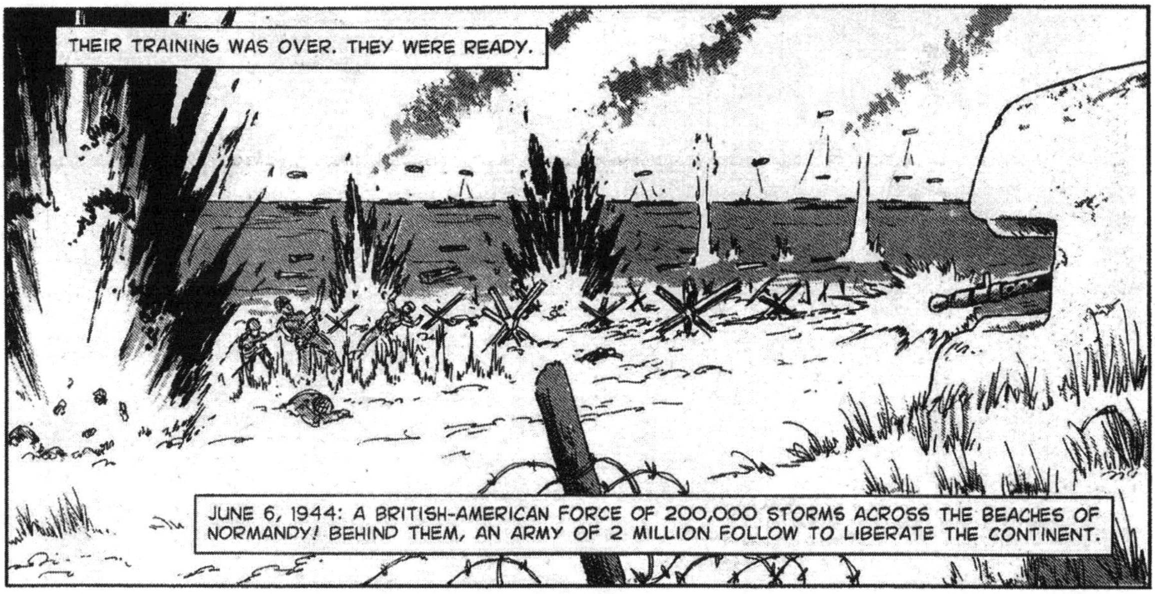
THEIR TRAINING WAS OVER. THEY WERE READY.
JUNE 6, 1944: A BRITISH-AMERICAN FORCE OF 200,000 STORMS ACROSS THE BEACHES OF NORMANDY! BEHIND THEM, AN ARMY OF 2 MILLION FOLLOW TO LIBERATE THE CONTINENT.

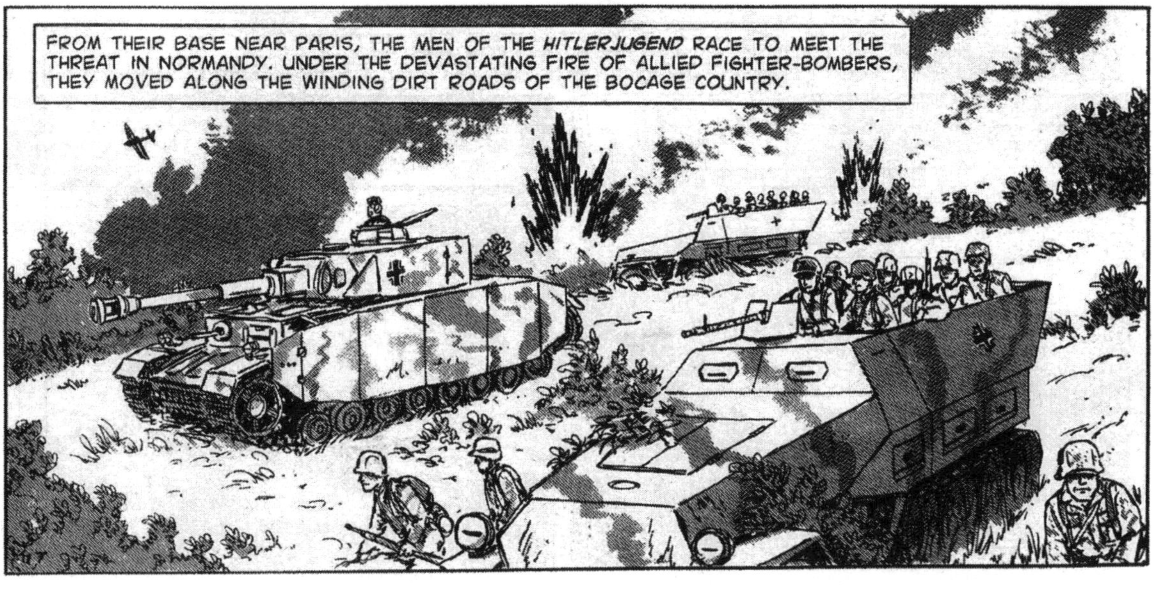
FROM THEIR BASE NEAR PARIS, THE MEN OF THE *HITLERJUGEND* RACE TO MEET THE THREAT IN NORMANDY. UNDER THE DEVASTATING FIRE OF ALLIED FIGHTER-BOMBERS, THEY MOVED ALONG THE WINDING DIRT ROADS OF THE BOCAGE COUNTRY.

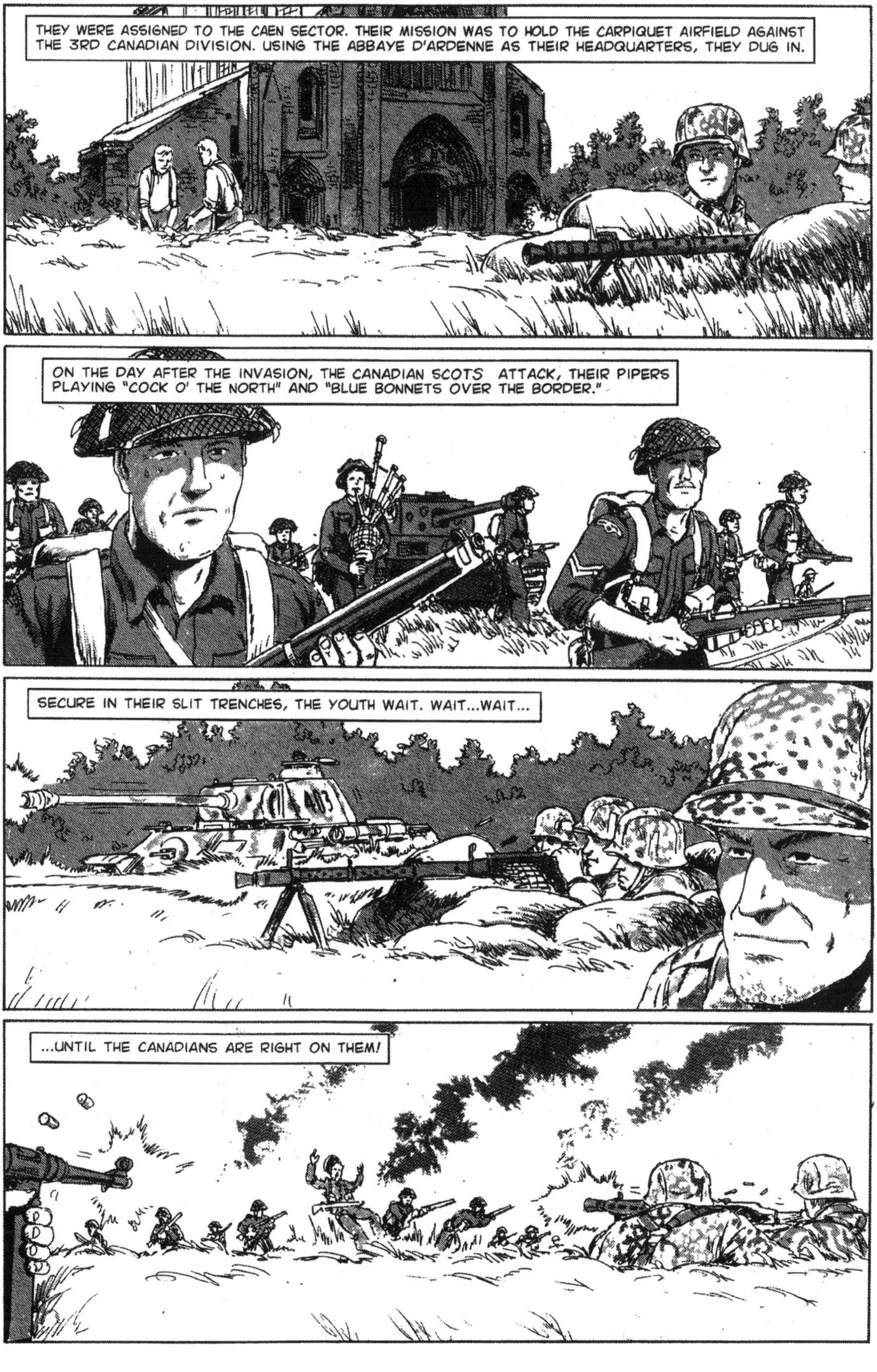
THEY WERE ASSIGNED TO THE CAEN SECTOR. THEIR MISSION WAS TO HOLD THE CARPIQUET AIRFIELD AGAINST THE 3RD CANADIAN DIVISION. USING THE ABBAYE D'ARDENNE AS THEIR HEADQUARTERS, THEY DUG IN.
ON THE DAY AFTER THE INVASION, THE CANADIAN SCOTS ATTACK, THEIR PIPERS PLAYING "COCK O' THE NORTH" AND "BLUE BONNETS OVER THE BORDER."
SECURE IN THEIR SLIT TRENCHES, THE YOUTH WAIT. WAIT...WAIT...
...UNTIL THE CANADIANS ARE RIGHT ON THEM!

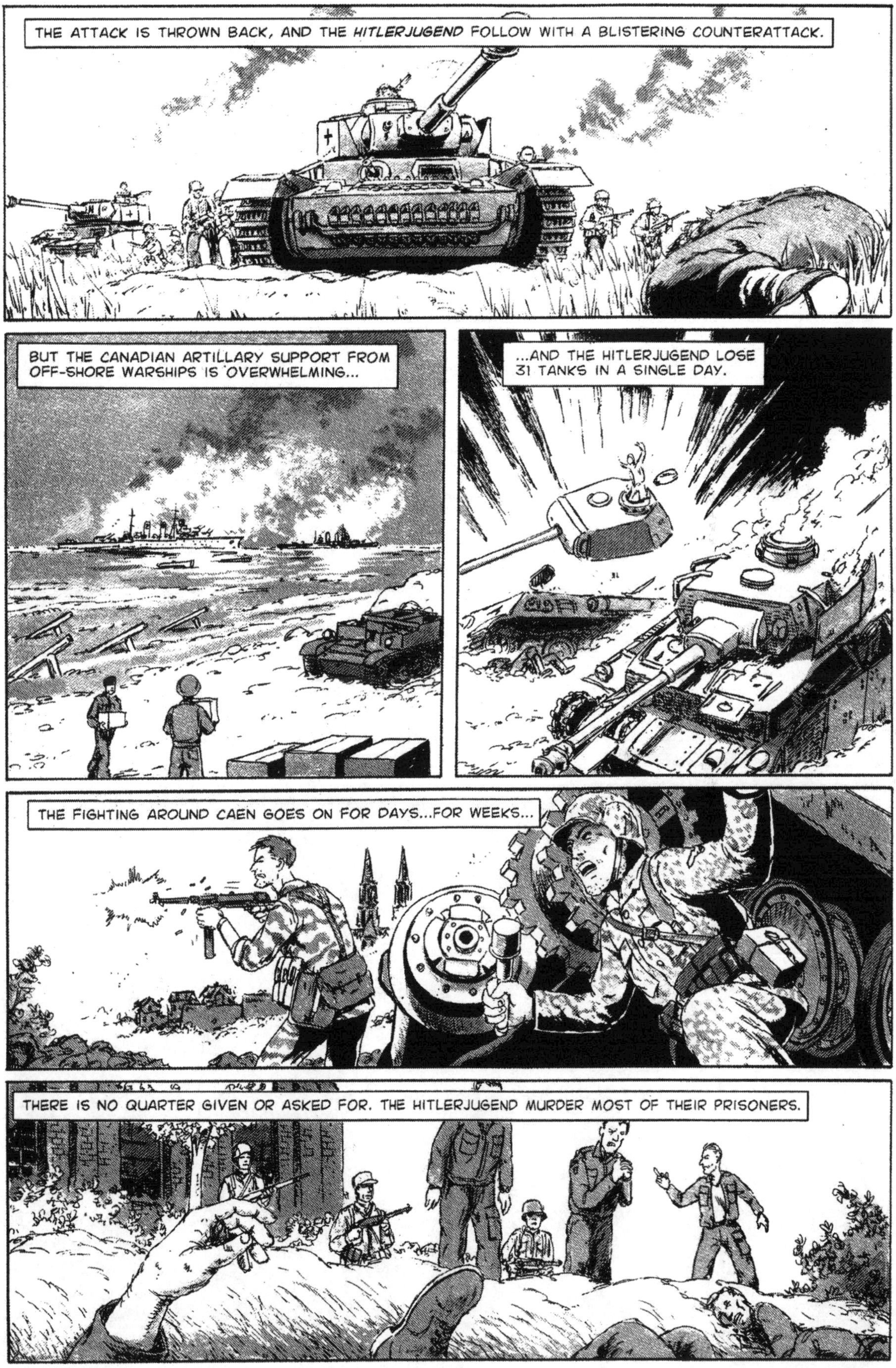
THE ATTACK IS THROWN BACK, AND THE *HITLERJUGEND* FOLLOW WITH A BLISTERING COUNTERATTACK.
BUT THE CANADIAN ARTILLARY SUPPORT FROM OFF-SHORE WARSHIPS IS OVERWHELMING...
...AND THE HITLERJUGEND LOSE 31 TANKS IN A SINGLE DAY.
THE FIGHTING AROUND CAEN GOES ON FOR DAYS...FOR WEEKS...
THERE IS NO QUARTER GIVEN OR ASKED FOR. THE HITLERJUGEND MURDER MOST OF THEIR PRISONERS.

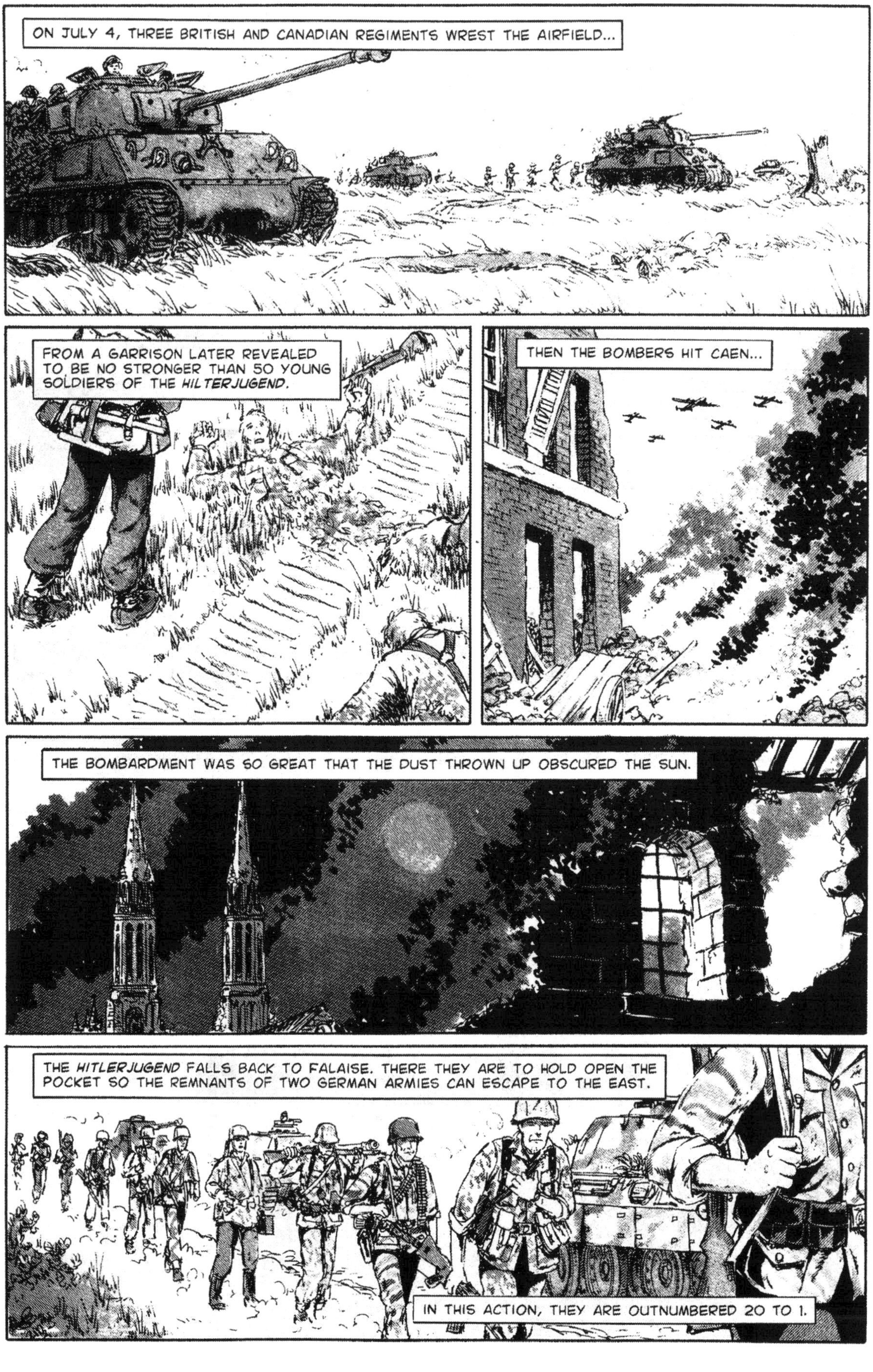
ON JULY 4, THREE BRITISH AND CANADIAN REGIMENTS WREST THE AIRFIELD...
FROM A GARRISON LATER REVEALED TO BE NO STRONGER THAN 50 YOUNG SOLDIERS OF THE *HILTERJUGEND*.
THEN THE BOMBERS HIT CAEN...
THE BOMBARDMENT WAS SO GREAT THAT THE DUST THROWN UP OBSCURED THE SUN.
THE *HITLERJUGEND* FALLS BACK TO FALAISE. THERE THEY ARE TO HOLD OPEN THE POCKET SO THE REMNANTS OF TWO GERMAN ARMIES CAN ESCAPE TO THE EAST.
IN THIS ACTION, THEY ARE OUTNUMBERED 20 TO 1.

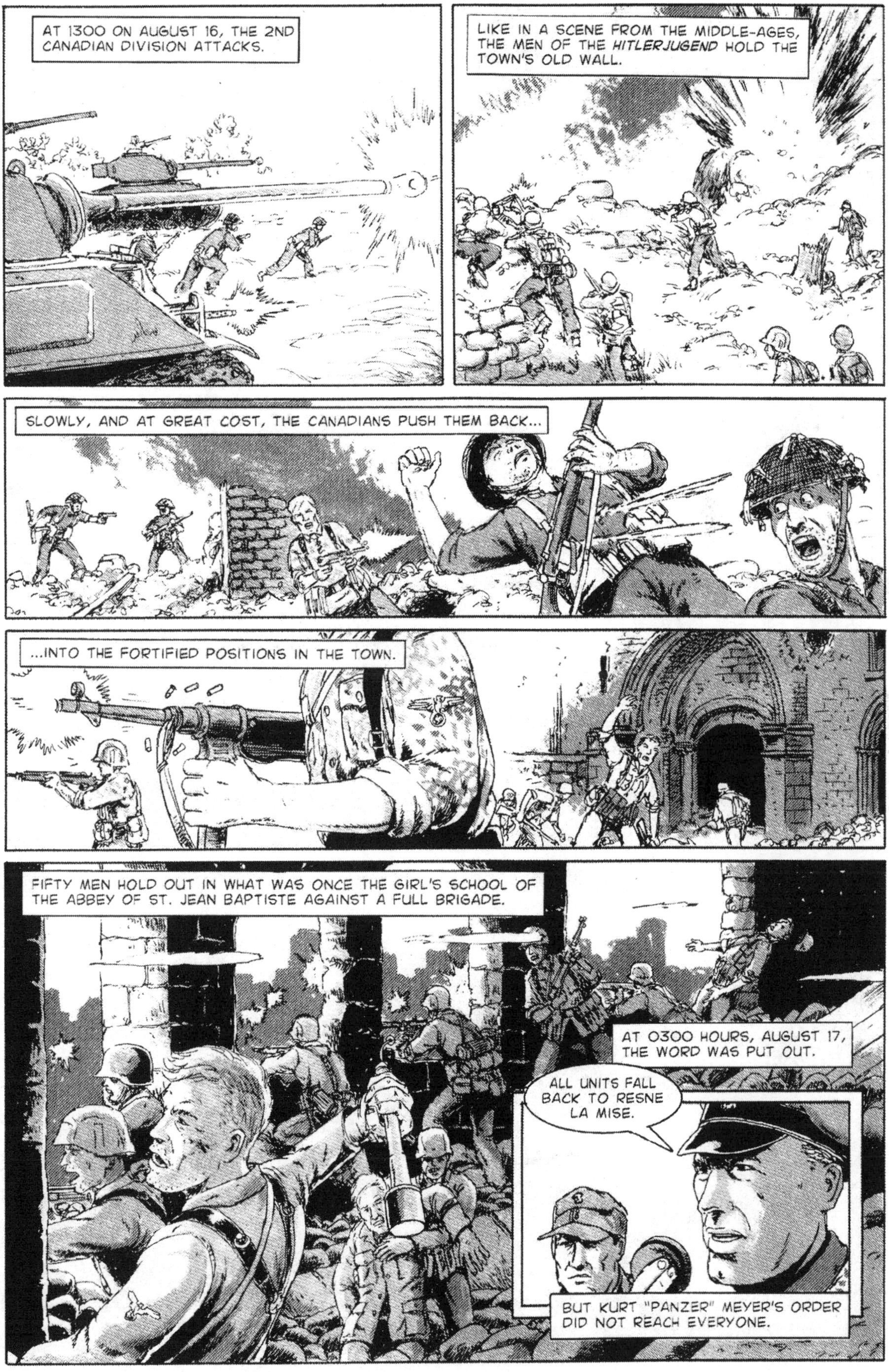
AT 1300 ON AUGUST 16, THE 2ND CANADIAN DIVISION ATTACKS.
LIKE IN A SCENE FROM THE MIDDLE-AGES, THE MEN OF THE *HITLERJUGEND* HOLD THE TOWN'S OLD WALL.
SLOWLY, AND AT GREAT COST, THE CANADIANS PUSH THEM BACK...
...INTO THE FORTIFIED POSITIONS IN THE TOWN.
FIFTY MEN HOLD OUT IN WHAT WAS ONCE THE GIRL'S SCHOOL OF THE ABBEY OF ST. JEAN BAPTISTE AGAINST A FULL BRIGADE.
AT 0300 HOURS, AUGUST 17, THE WORD WAS PUT OUT.
ALL UNITS FALL BACK TO RESNE LA MISE.
BUT KURT "PANZER" MEYER'S ORDER DID NOT REACH EVERYONE.

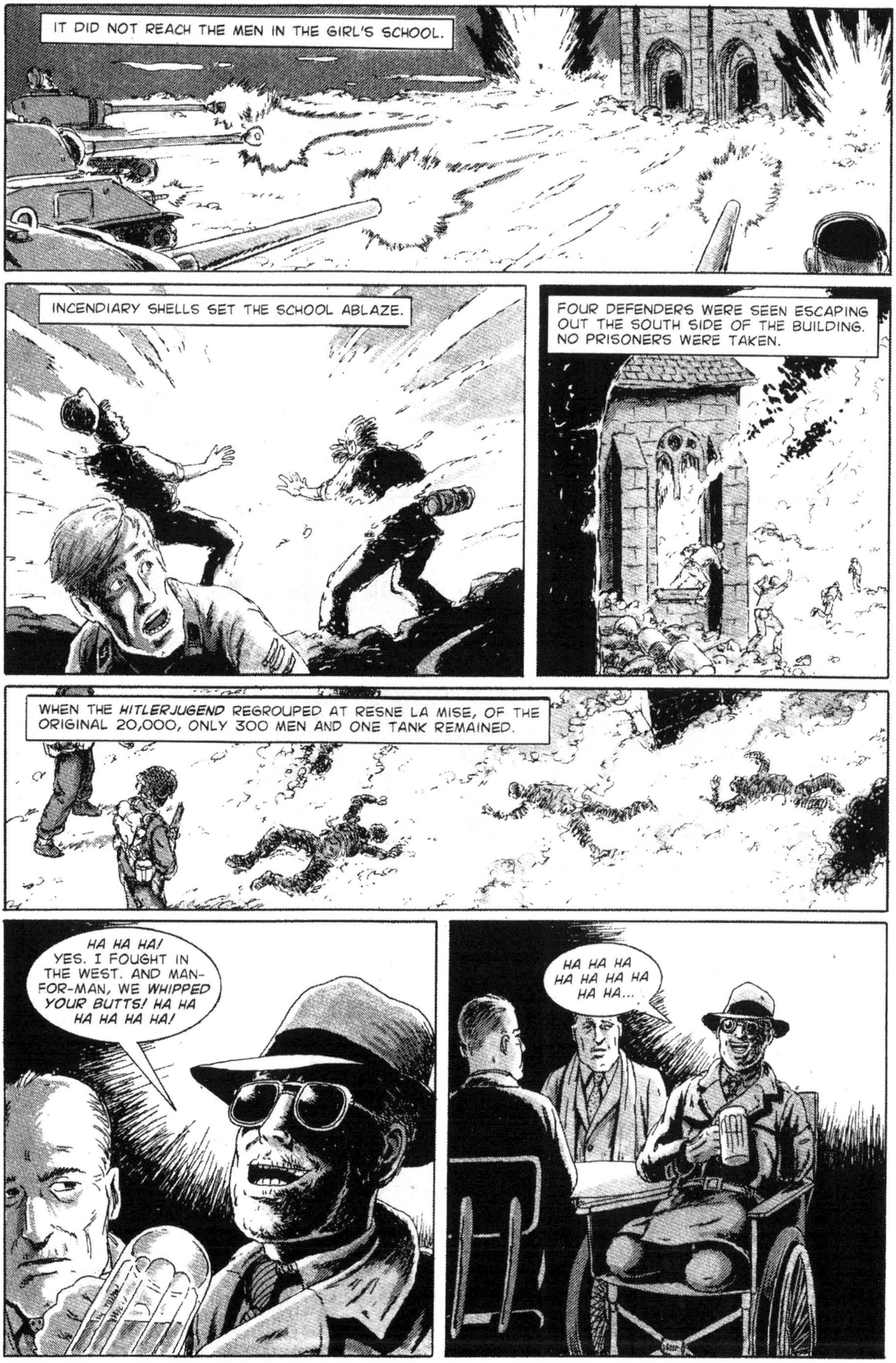

IT DID NOT REACH THE MEN IN THE GIRL'S SCHOOL.
INCENDIARY SHELLS SET THE SCHOOL ABLAZE.
FOUR DEFENDERS WERE SEEN ESCAPING OUT THE SOUTH SIDE OF THE BUILDING. NO PRISONERS WERE TAKEN.
WHEN THE *HITLERJUGEND* REGROUPED AT RESNE LA MISE, OF THE ORIGINAL 20,000, ONLY 300 MEN AND ONE TANK REMAINED.
HA HA HA! YES. I FOUGHT IN THE WEST. AND MAN-FOR-MAN, WE *WHIPPED YOUR BUTTS!* HA HA HA HA HA HA!
HA HA HA HA HA HA HA HA HA...

WITCHES' CALDRON

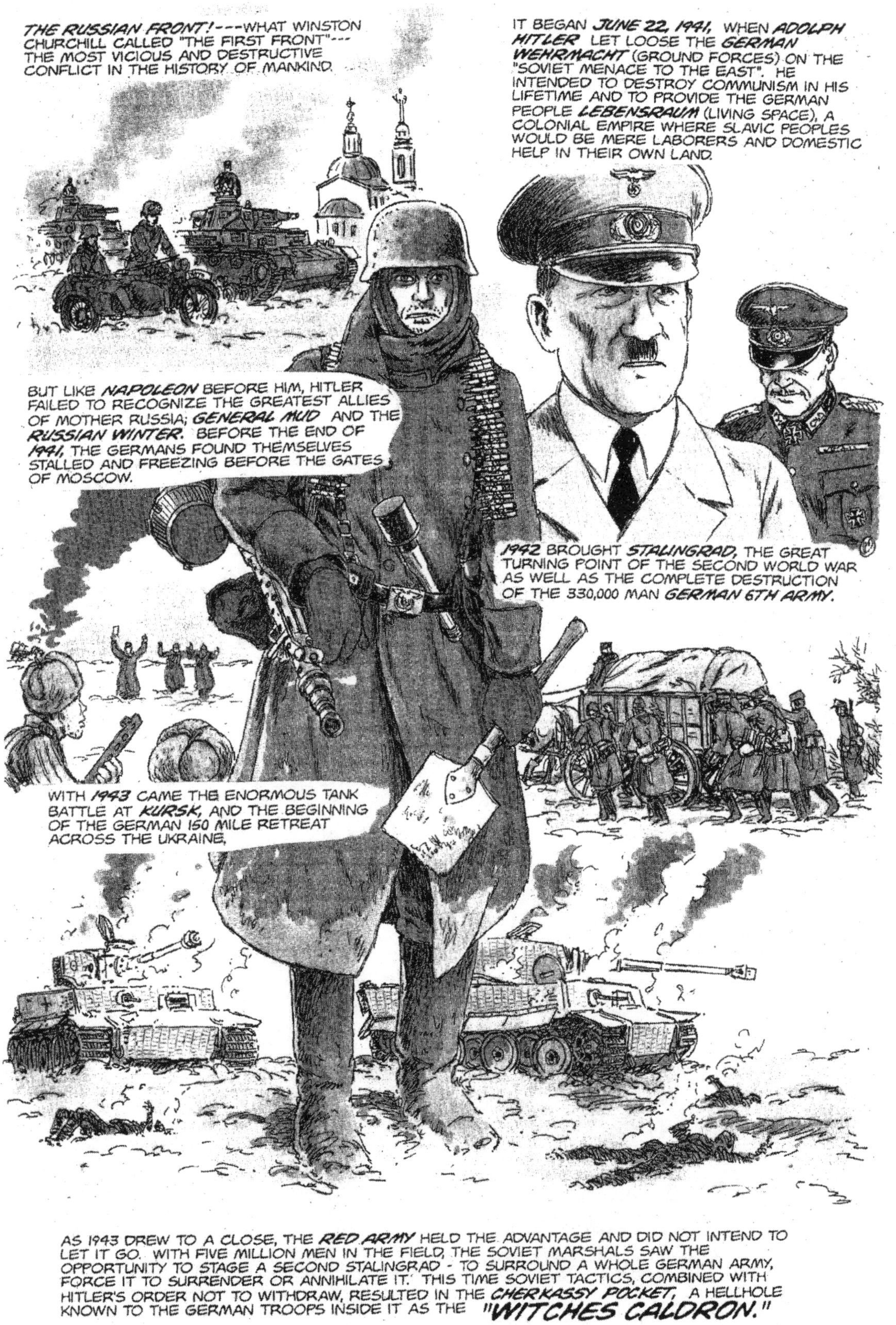
THE RUSSIAN FRONT!---WHAT WINSTON CHURCHILL CALLED "THE FIRST FRONT"---THE MOST VICIOUS AND DESTRUCTIVE CONFLICT IN THE HISTORY OF MANKIND.
IT BEGAN JUNE 22, 1941, WHEN ADOLPH HITLER LET LOOSE THE GERMAN WEHRMACHT (GROUND FORCES) ON THE "SOVIET MENACE TO THE EAST". HE INTENDED TO DESTROY COMMUNISM IN HIS LIFETIME AND TO PROVIDE THE GERMAN PEOPLE LEBENSRAUM (LIVING SPACE), A COLONIAL EMPIRE WHERE SLAVIC PEOPLES WOULD BE MERE LABORERS AND DOMESTIC HELP IN THEIR OWN LAND.
BUT LIKE NAPOLEON BEFORE HIM, HITLER FAILED TO RECOGNIZE THE GREATEST ALLIES OF MOTHER RUSSIA; GENERAL MUD AND THE RUSSIAN WINTER. BEFORE THE END OF 1941, THE GERMANS FOUND THEMSELVES STALLED AND FREEZING BEFORE THE GATES OF MOSCOW.
1942 BROUGHT STALINGRAD, THE GREAT TURNING POINT OF THE SECOND WORLD WAR AS WELL AS THE COMPLETE DESTRUCTION OF THE 330,000 MAN GERMAN 6TH ARMY.
WITH 1943 CAME THE ENORMOUS TANK BATTLE AT KURSK, AND THE BEGINNING OF THE GERMAN 150 MILE RETREAT ACROSS THE UKRAINE.

AS 1943 DREW TO A CLOSE, THE *RED ARMY* HELD THE ADVANTAGE AND DID NOT INTEND TO LET IT GO. WITH FIVE MILLION MEN IN THE FIELD, THE SOVIET MARSHALS SAW THE OPPORTUNITY TO STAGE A SECOND STALINGRAD - TO SURROUND A WHOLE GERMAN ARMY, FORCE IT TO SURRENDER OR ANNIHILATE IT. THIS TIME SOVIET TACTICS, COMBINED WITH HITLER'S ORDER NOT TO WITHDRAW, RESULTED IN THE *CHERKASSY POCKET,* A HELLHOLE KNOWN TO THE GERMAN TROOPS INSIDE IT AS THE ***"WITCHES CALDRON."***

WAR IS WAGED BY MEN; NOT BY BEAST, OR BY GODS. IT IS A PECULIARLY HUMAN ACTIVITY. TO CALL IT A CRIME AGAINST MANKIND IS TO MISS AT LEAST HALF ITS SIGNIFICANCE; IT IS ALSO THE PUNISHMENT OF A CRIME.

FREDERICK MANNING
THE MIDDLE PARTS OF FORTUNE

WITCHES' CALDRON

THE BATTLE OF THE CHERKASSY POCKET

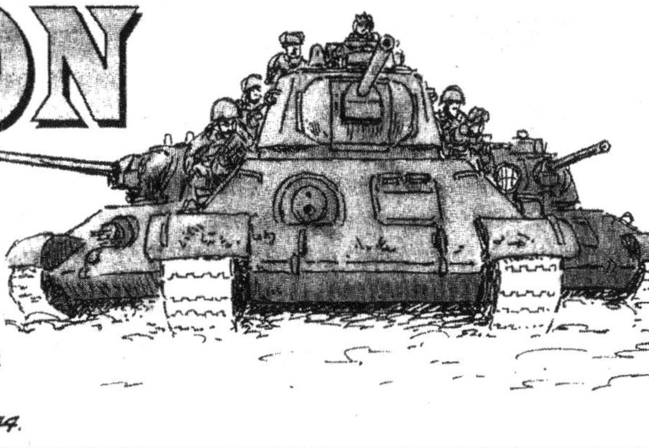

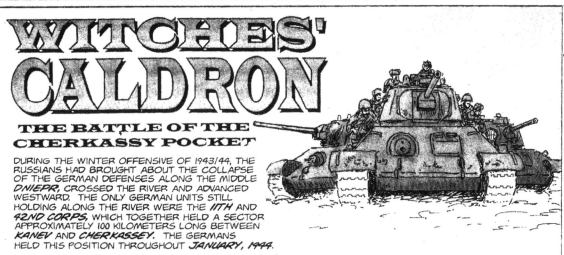

DURING THE WINTER OFFENSIVE OF 1943/44, THE RUSSIANS HAD BROUGHT ABOUT THE COLLAPSE OF THE GERMAN DEFENSES ALONG THE MIDDLE *DNIEPR,* CROSSED THE RIVER AND ADVANCED WESTWARD. THE ONLY GERMAN UNITS STILL HOLDING ALONG THE RIVER WERE THE *11TH* AND *42ND CORPS,* WHICH TOGETHER HELD A SECTOR APPROXIMATELY 100 KILOMETERS LONG BETWEEN *KANEV* AND *CHERKASSEY.* THE GERMANS HELD THIS POSITION THROUGHOUT *JANUARY, 1944.*

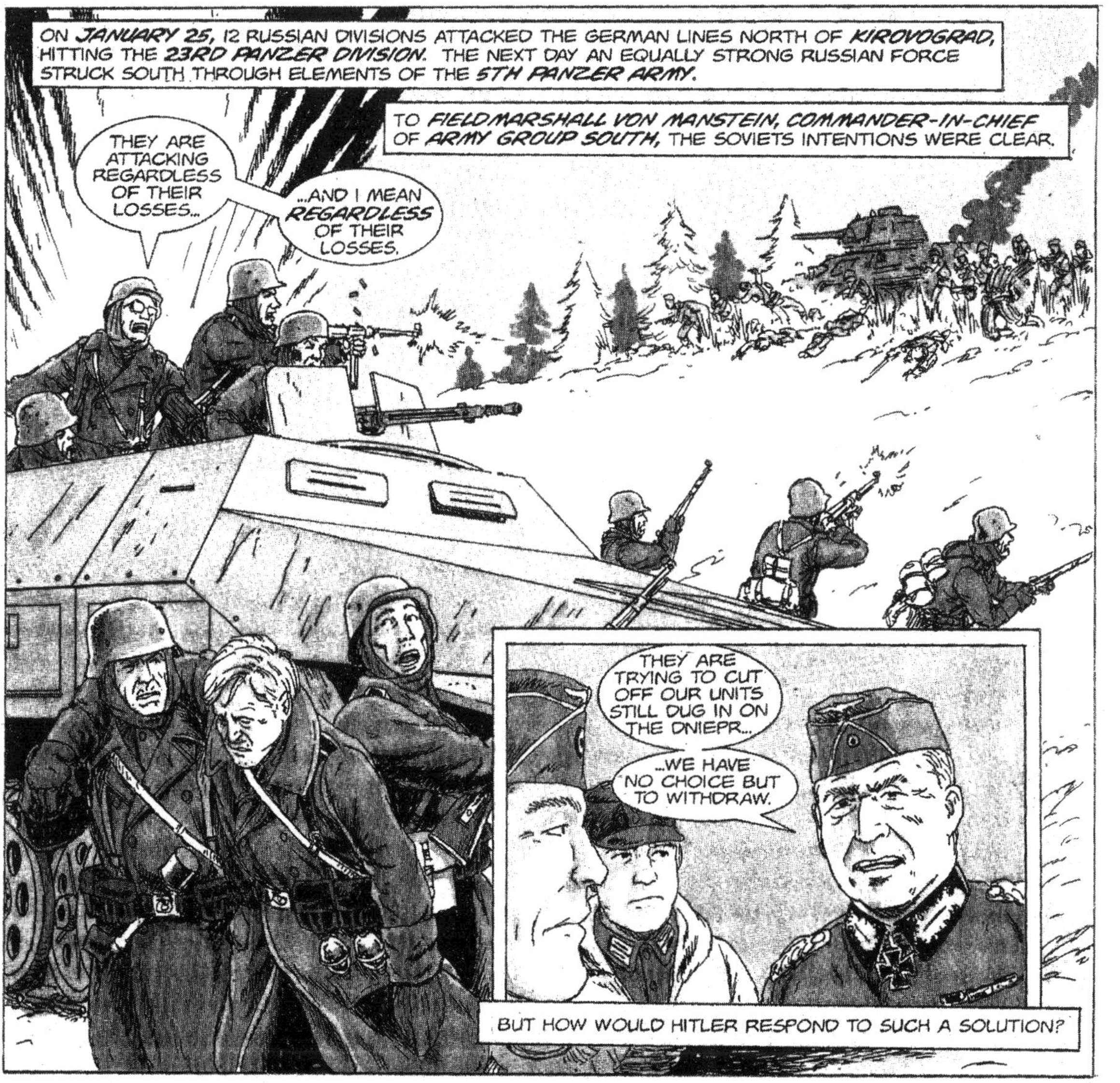
ON *JANUARY 25,* 12 RUSSIAN DIVISIONS ATTACKED THE GERMAN LINES NORTH OF *KIROVOGRAD,* HITTING THE *23RD PANZER DIVISION.* THE NEXT DAY AN EQUALLY STRONG RUSSIAN FORCE STRUCK SOUTH THROUGH ELEMENTS OF THE *5TH PANZER ARMY.*
TO *FIELDMARSHALL VON MANSTEIN, COMMANDER-IN-CHIEF* OF *ARMY GROUP SOUTH,* THE SOVIETS INTENTIONS WERE CLEAR.
THEY ARE ATTACKING REGARDLESS OF THEIR LOSSES...
...AND I MEAN *REGARDLESS* OF THEIR LOSSES.
THEY ARE TRYING TO CUT OFF OUR UNITS STILL DUG IN ON THE DNIEPR...
...WE HAVE NO CHOICE BUT TO WITHDRAW.
BUT HOW WOULD HITLER RESPOND TO SUCH A SOLUTION?

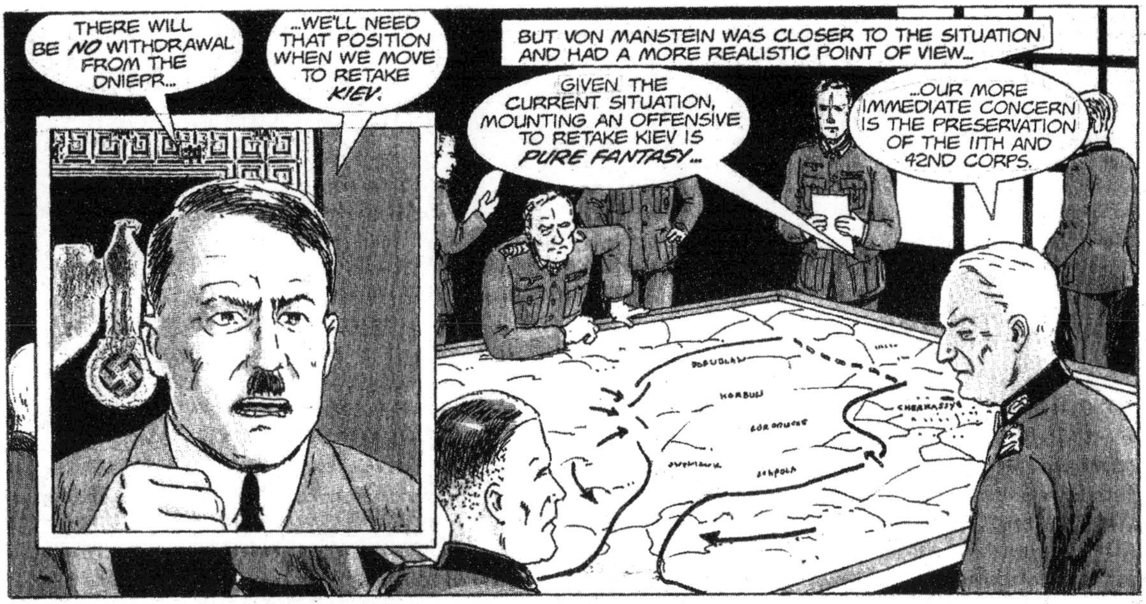
THERE WILL BE *NO* WITHDRAWAL FROM THE DNIEPR...
...WE'LL NEED THAT POSITION WHEN WE MOVE TO RETAKE *KIEV.*
BUT VON MANSTEIN WAS CLOSER TO THE SITUATION AND HAD A MORE REALISTIC POINT OF VIEW...
GIVEN THE CURRENT SITUATION, MOUNTING AN OFFENSIVE TO RETAKE KIEV IS *PURE FANTASY*...
...OUR MORE IMMEDIATE CONCERN IS THE PRESERVATION OF THE 11TH AND 42ND CORPS.

ON ***JANUARY 28,*** THE TWO SOVIET SPEARHEADS MET, TRAPPING ***56,000 GERMAN TROOPS.***

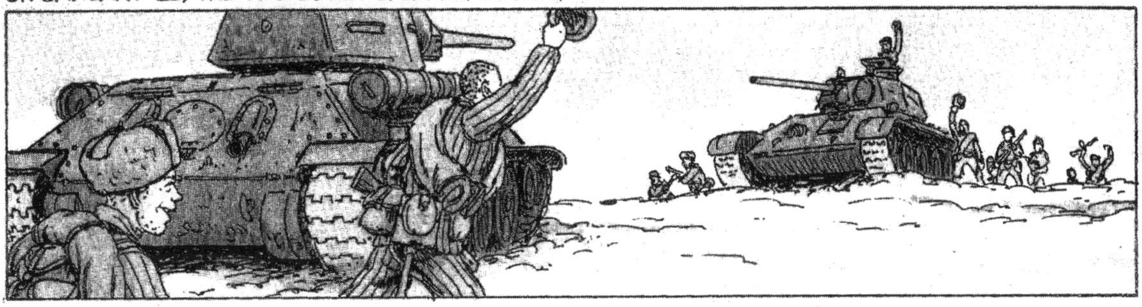

WITHIN THE POCKET, POSITIONED ALONG THE DNIEPR ITSELF, WERE 2000 MEN OF THE FRENCH SPEAKING ***"WALLONIA" ASSAULT BRIGADE,*** PART OF THE ***5TH SS "VIKING" DIVISION.*** THESE MEN WERE ALL VOLUNTEERS FROM SOUTHERN BELGIUM, WHO HAD JOINED THE GERMAN ARMY TO FIGHT COMMUNISM.

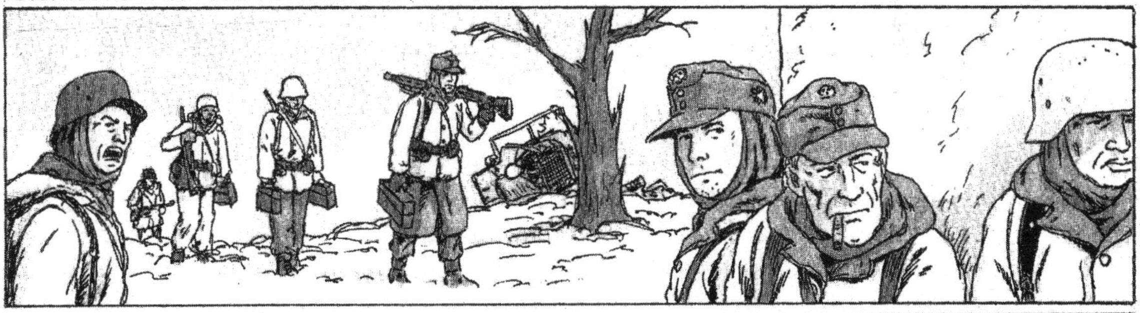

37 YEAR OLD ***LEON DEGRELLE.*** INTELLIGENT, WELL-EDUCATED, AND A SUCCESSFUL NEWSPAPER EDITOR, LEON WAS CLOSELY AFFILIATED WITH THE CONSERVATIVE CATHOLIC YOUTH MOVEMENT, ***CHRISTUS REX.*** A LIFELONG OPPONENT OF COMMUNISM, DEGRELLE WAS IMPRISONED IN ***1940*** BY MARXIST ELEMENTS IN HIS OWN GOVERNMENT. HIS WIFE, BROTHER AND PARENTS HAD ALL DIED AT THE HANDS OF HIS ENEMIES, AND HIS 8 CHILDREN WERE NOW IN ORPHANAGES. WHEN GERMAN INVADED RUSSIA IN 1941, LEON JOINED THE GERMAN ARMY AS A PRIVATE AND QUICKLY ROSE TO THE RANK OF ASSISTANT COMMANDER OF THE WALLOONS.

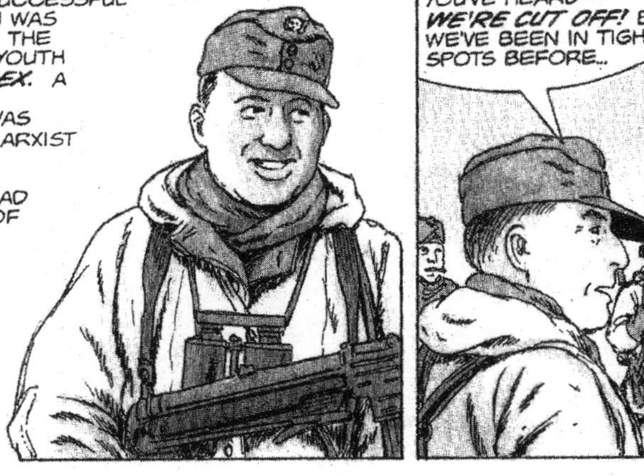

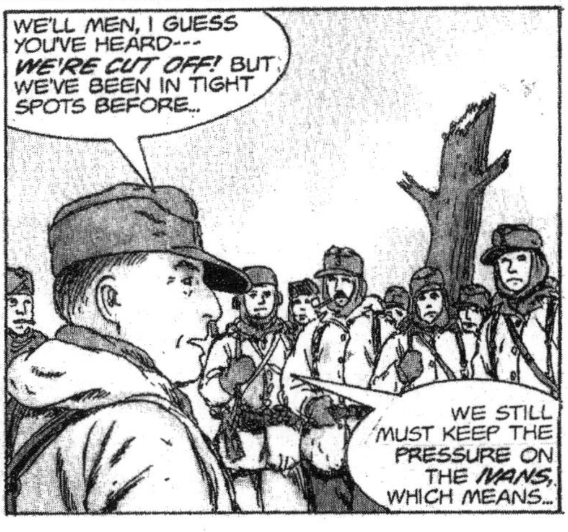
WE'LL MEN, I GUESS YOU'VE HEARD--- ***WE'RE CUT OFF!*** BUT WE'VE BEEN IN TIGHT SPOTS BEFORE...
WE STILL MUST KEEP THE PRESSURE ON THE ***IVANS,*** WHICH MEANS...

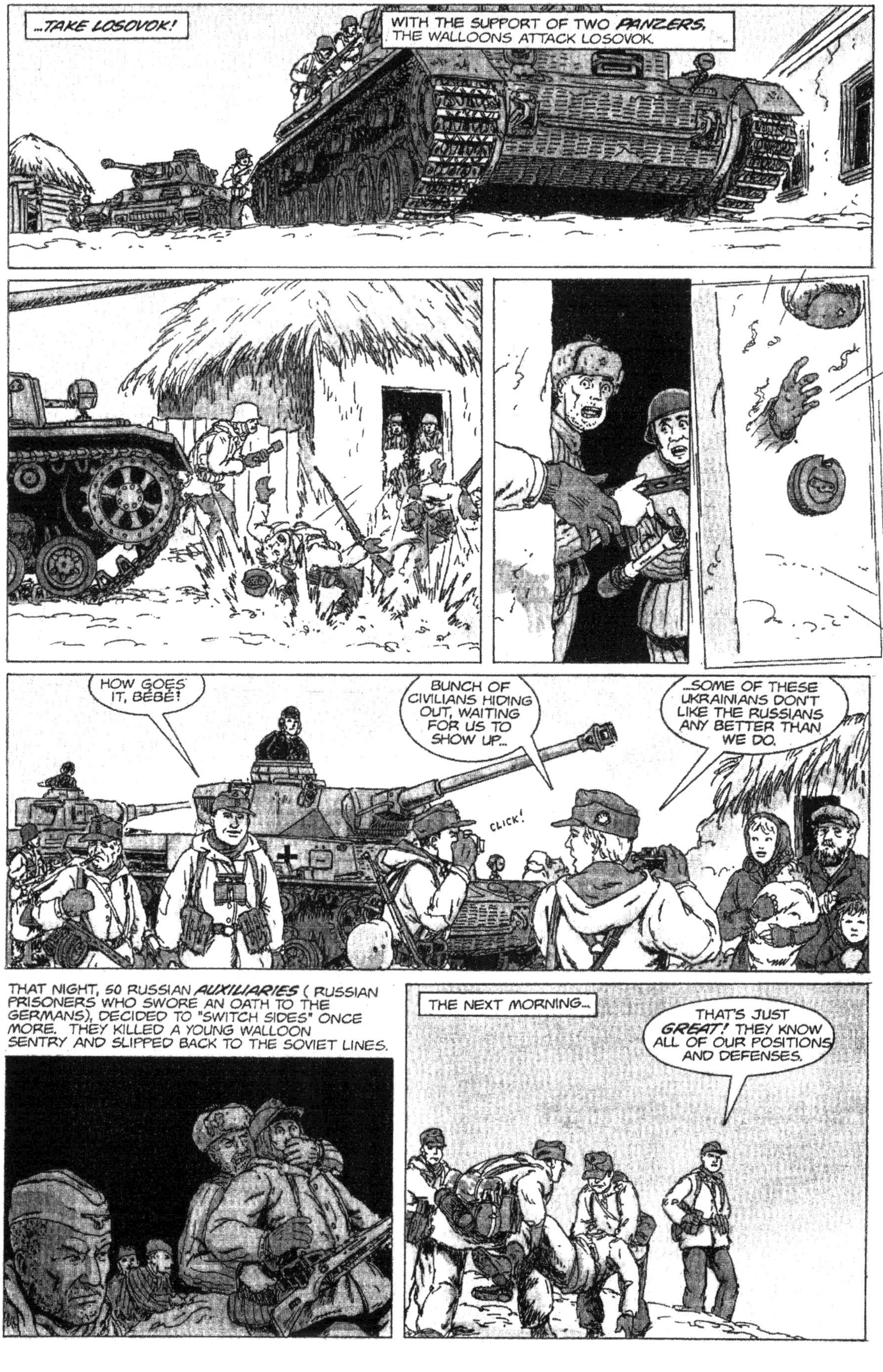
...TAKE LOSOVOK!
WITH THE SUPPORT OF TWO PANZERS, THE WALLOONS ATTACK LOSOVOK.
HOW GOES IT, BEBÉ!
BUNCH OF CIVILIANS HIDING OUT, WAITING FOR US TO SHOW UP...
CLICK!
...SOME OF THESE UKRAINIANS DON'T LIKE THE RUSSIANS ANY BETTER THAN WE DO.
THAT NIGHT, 50 RUSSIAN AUXILIARIES (RUSSIAN PRISONERS WHO SWORE AN OATH TO THE GERMANS), DECIDED TO "SWITCH SIDES" ONCE MORE. THEY KILLED A YOUNG WALLOON SENTRY AND SLIPPED BACK TO THE SOVIET LINES.
THE NEXT MORNING...
THAT'S JUST GREAT! THEY KNOW ALL OF OUR POSITIONS AND DEFENSES.

AS THE RUSSIANS POURED IN MORE TROOPS TO WIDEN AND STRENGTHEN THE GAP BETWEEN THE TRAPPED FORCES AND THEIR MAIN LINES, THE GERMANS READIED A RELIEF FORCE. THIS FORCE CONSISTED OF THE *1ST, 16TH* AND *17TH PANZER DIVISIONS* AND THE *SS LEIBSTANDARTE ADOLF HITLER DIVISION*. THE SPEARHEAD OF THIS FORCE WAS *HEAVY PANZER REGIMENT BÄKE*, LED BY DAREDEVIL TANK VETERAN *LIEUTENANT COLONEL DR. FRANZ BÄKE*. HIS UNIT CONSISTED OF 47 *PANTHER* AND 34 *TIGER* TANKS.

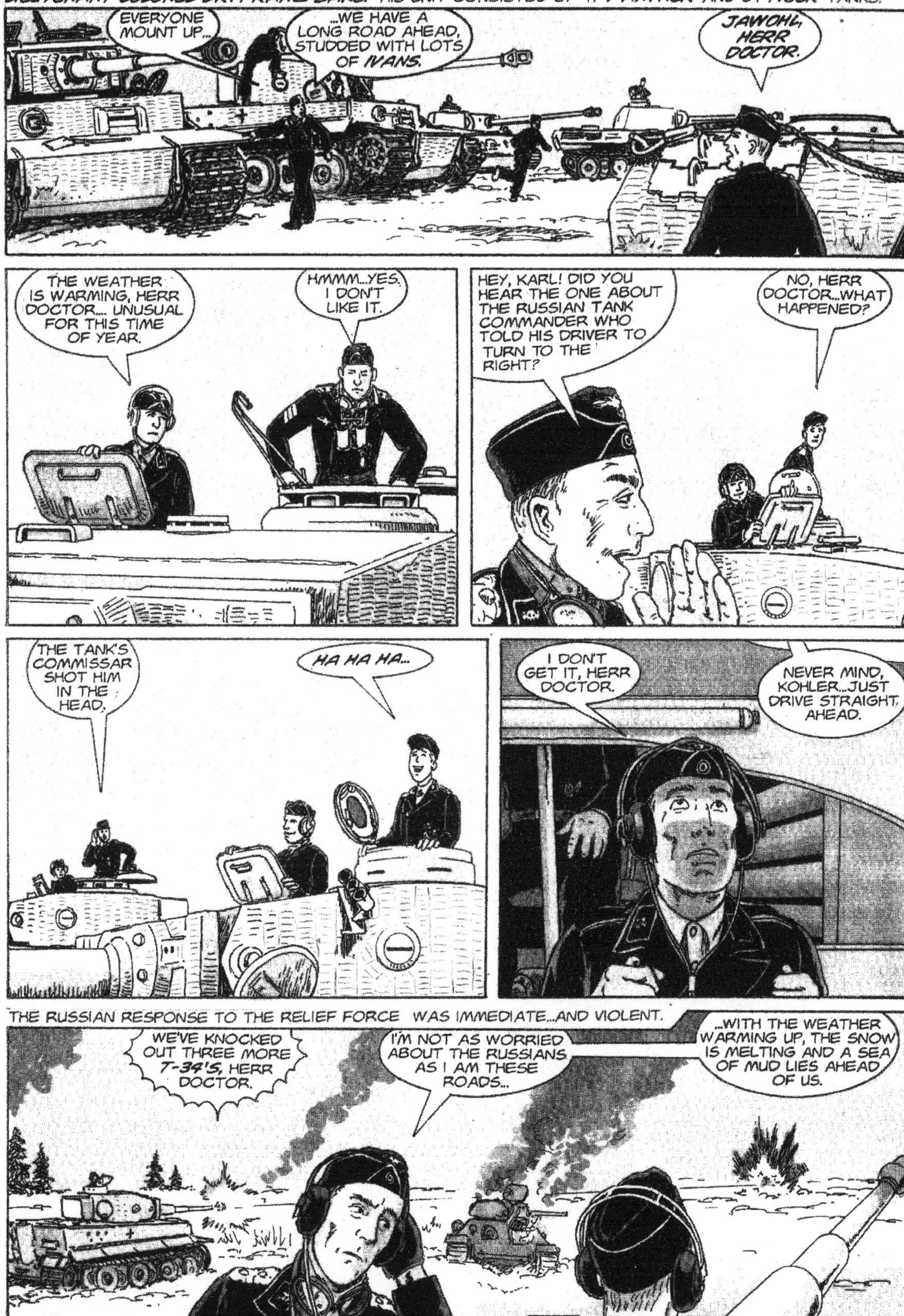

EVERYONE MOUNT UP...
...WE HAVE A LONG ROAD AHEAD, STUDDED WITH LOTS OF IVANS.
JAWOHL, HERR DOCTOR.
THE WEATHER IS WARMING, HERR DOCTOR.... UNUSUAL FOR THIS TIME OF YEAR.
HMMM...YES. I DON'T LIKE IT.
HEY, KARL! DID YOU HEAR THE ONE ABOUT THE RUSSIAN TANK COMMANDER WHO TOLD HIS DRIVER TO TURN TO THE RIGHT?
NO, HERR DOCTOR...WHAT HAPPENED?
THE TANK'S COMMISSAR SHOT HIM IN THE HEAD.
HA HA HA...
I DON'T GET IT, HERR DOCTOR.
NEVER MIND, KOHLER...JUST DRIVE STRAIGHT AHEAD.
THE RUSSIAN RESPONSE TO THE RELIEF FORCE WAS IMMEDIATE...AND VIOLENT.
WE'VE KNOCKED OUT THREE MORE T-34'S, HERR DOCTOR.
I'M NOT AS WORRIED ABOUT THE RUSSIANS AS I AM THESE ROADS...
...WITH THE WEATHER WARMING UP, THE SNOW IS MELTING AND A SEA OF MUD LIES AHEAD OF US.

MEANWHILE, THE SOVIET FORCES BEGAN BUILDING A MULTI LAYERED DEFENSIVE BELT AROUND THE POCKET.

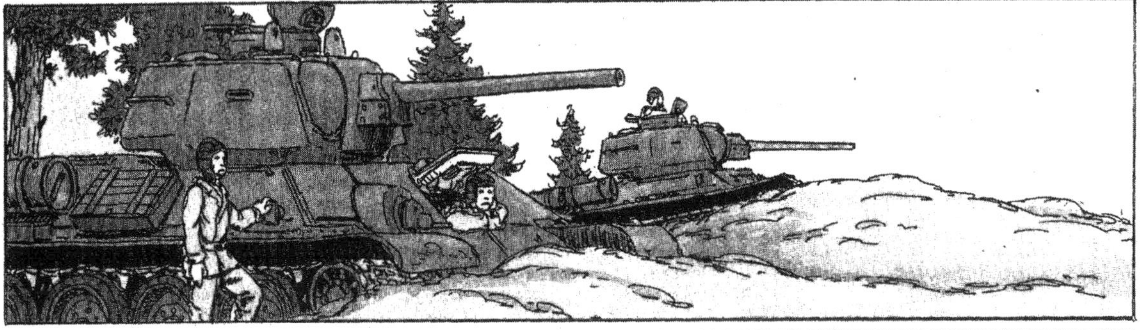

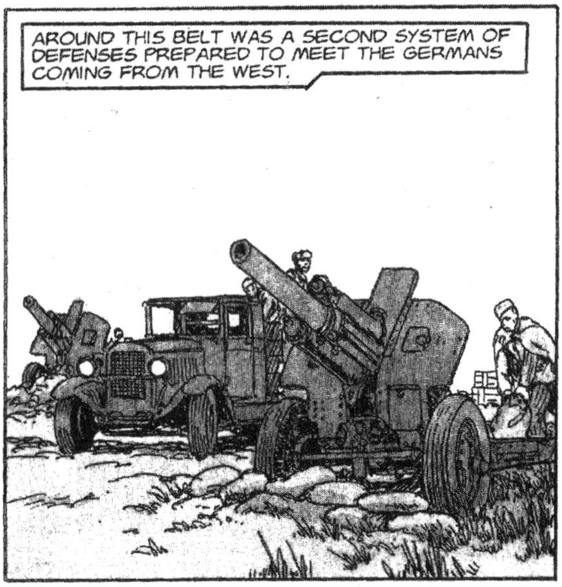
AROUND THIS BELT WAS A SECOND SYSTEM OF DEFENSES PREPARED TO MEET THE GERMANS COMING FROM THE WEST.

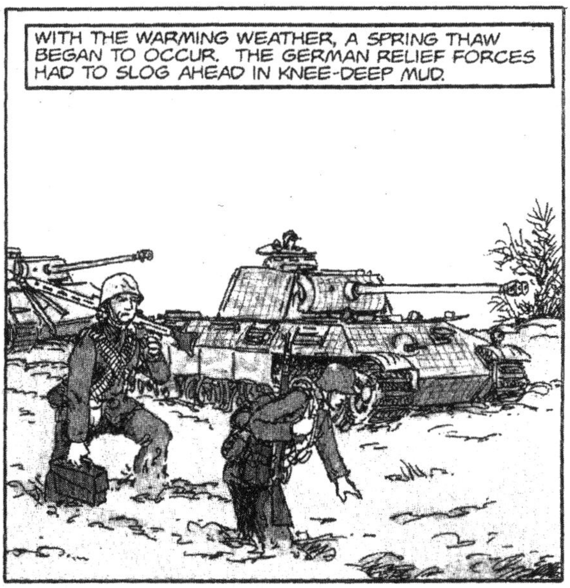
WITH THE WARMING WEATHER, A SPRING THAW BEGAN TO OCCUR. THE GERMAN RELIEF FORCES HAD TO SLOG AHEAD IN KNEE-DEEP MUD.

THE MUD CAUSED THE TANKS TO WORK TWICE AS HARD AND TO BURN TWICE AS MUCH FUEL. THE HIGH FUEL CONSUMPTION SOON BROUGHT THE GERMAN ADVANCE TO A HALT.

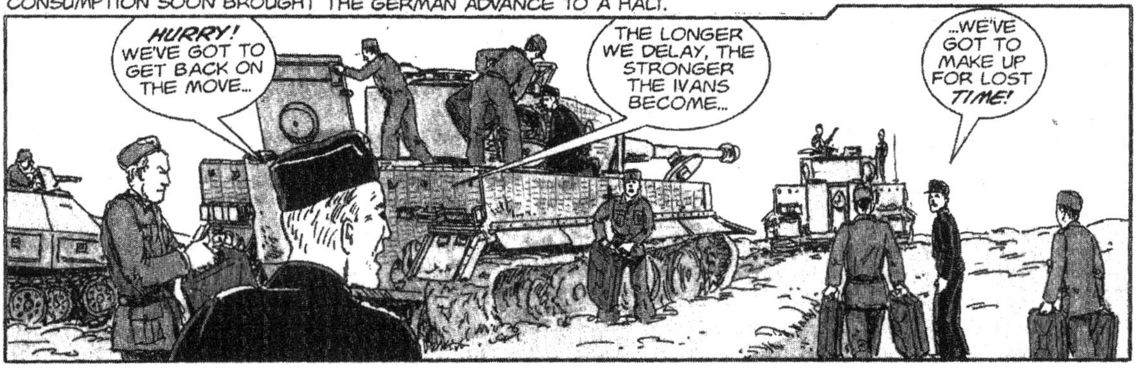
HURRY! WE'VE GOT TO GET BACK ON THE MOVE...
THE LONGER WE DELAY, THE STRONGER THE IVANS BECOME...
...WE'VE GOT TO MAKE UP FOR LOST TIME!

TIME! VON MANSTEIN KNEW THAT IT WAS NOT ON HIS SIDE.

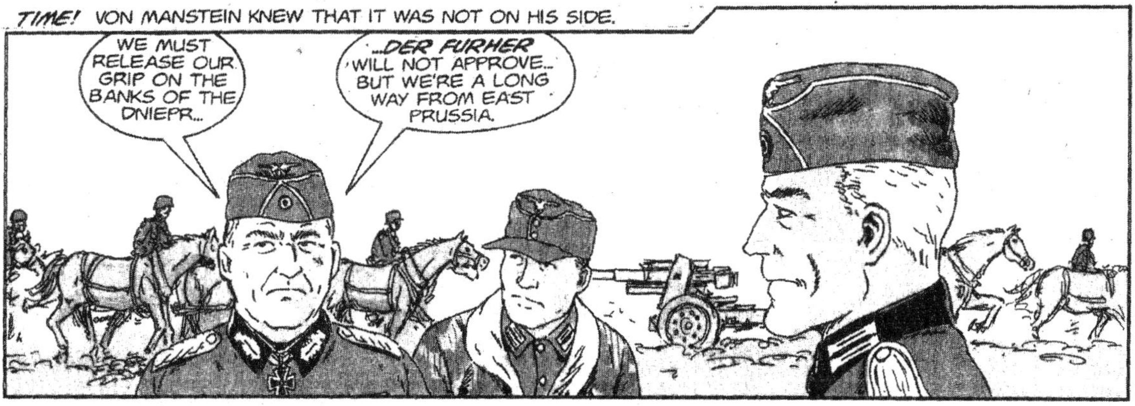
WE MUST RELEASE OUR GRIP ON THE BANKS OF THE DNIEPR...
...DER FURHER WILL NOT APPROVE... BUT WE'RE A LONG WAY FROM EAST PRUSSIA.

HAVE YOU EVER NOTICED THE EYES OF THESE UKRAINIAN GIRLS?

...THEY'RE SO *BIG!*

THIS MUD WOULD BE BETTER FOR US IF WE WERE STAYING...

OUI!! IF WE HAD TO MOVE IN A HURRY, I'D RATHER HAVE IT *FROZEN.*

CLICK!

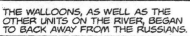

THE WALLOONS, AS WELL AS THE OTHER UNITS ON THE RIVER, BEGAN TO BACK AWAY FROM THE RUSSIANS.

WE SHOULD RUN THOSE CIVILIANS BACK TO WHERE THEY CAME FROM...

THEY'LL JUST SLOW US DOWN.

MANY OF THE UKRAINIANS DON'T LOOK AT US AS *ENEMIES,* OR AT THE RUSSIANS AS *LIBERATORS...*

...THEY WOULD MOVE WEST NO MATTER WHAT WE'D DO.

LOOK! A JABO!

A FIGHTER-BOMBER! *DISPERSE!*

TRAPPED WITHIN THE POCKET, SUPPLIED BY THE SINGLE AIRFIELD AT *KORSUN*, WERE THE FOLLOWING UNITS; THE *57TH INFANTRY DIVISION,* MADE UP OF RESERVIST WHOM HAD DISTINGUISHED THEMSELVES IN POLAND AND FRANCE. THE BAVARIANS AND RHINELANDERS OF THE *72ND DIVISION,* WHICH HAD HELPED CONQUER SEVASTOPOL. THE *88TH DIVISION,* WHICH HAD SUFFERED HEAVY CASUALTIES AT KIEV A FEW MONTHS EARLIER, AND THE *5TH SS "VIKING" PANZER DIVISION,* WHICH HAD MANY SCANDINAVIANS, DUTCH AND FLEMISH VOLUNTEERS.

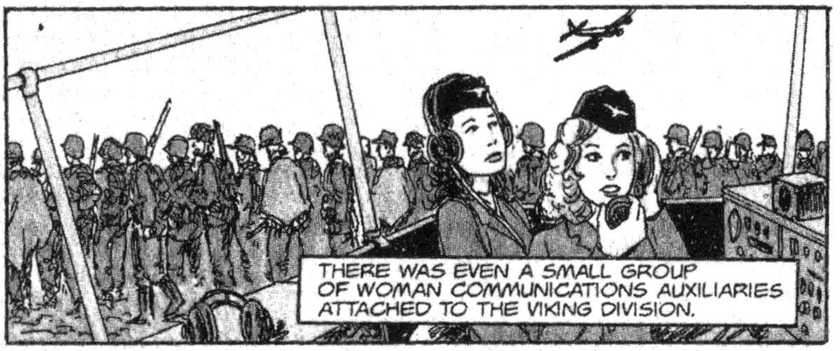
THERE WAS EVEN A SMALL GROUP OF WOMAN COMMUNICATIONS AUXILIARIES ATTACHED TO THE VIKING DIVISION.

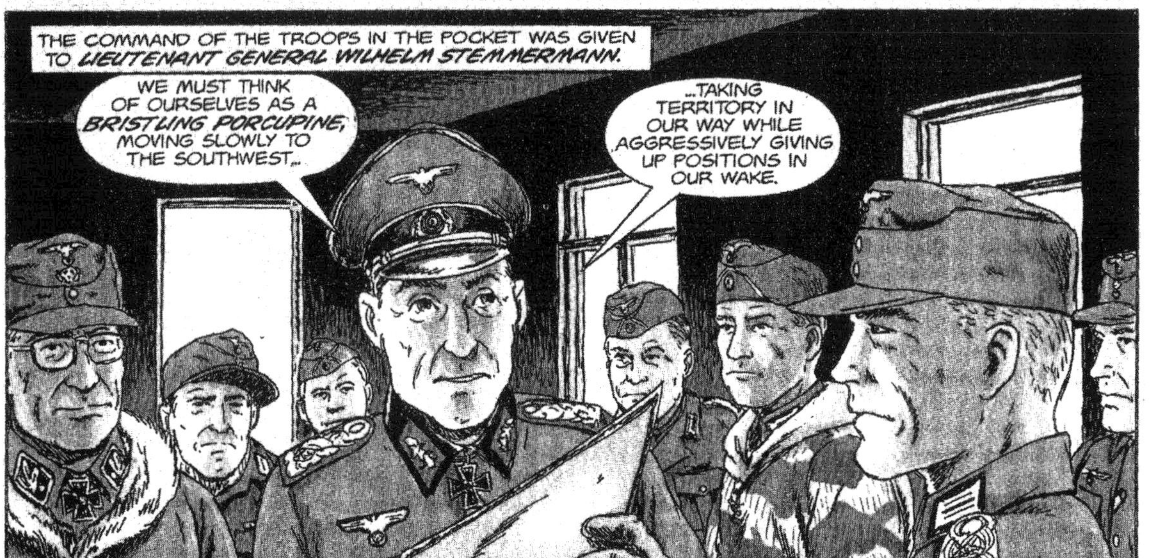
THE COMMAND OF THE TROOPS IN THE POCKET WAS GIVEN TO *LIEUTENANT GENERAL WILHELM STEMMERMANN.*
WE MUST THINK OF OURSELVES AS A *BRISTLING PORCUPINE,* MOVING SLOWLY TO THE SOUTHWEST...
...TAKING TERRITORY IN OUR WAY WHILE AGGRESSIVELY GIVING UP POSITIONS IN OUR WAKE.

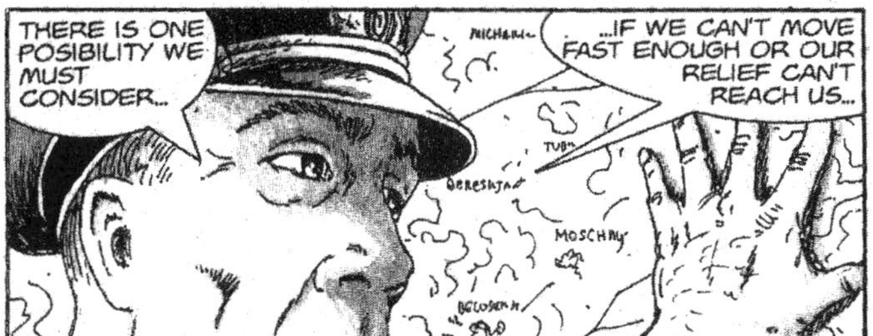
THERE IS ONE POSIBILITY WE MUST CONSIDER...
...IF WE CAN'T MOVE FAST ENOUGH OR OUR RELIEF CAN'T REACH US...
...WE MUST CONSIDER SURRENDER.

LIEUTENANT GENERAL HERBERT GILLE, COMMANDER OF THE "VIKING" DIVISION...

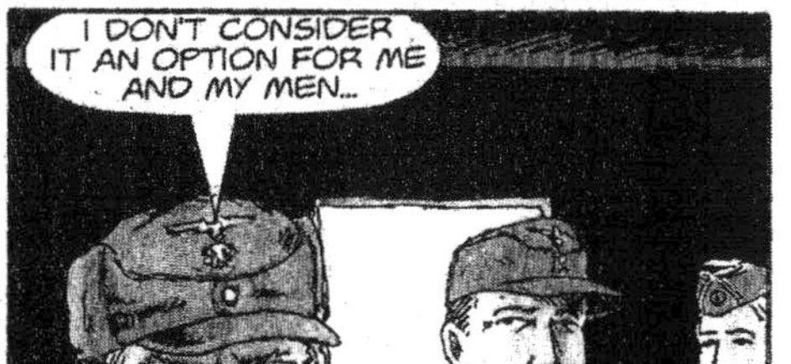
I DON'T CONSIDER IT AN OPTION FOR ME AND MY MEN...
...I'D RATHER DIE HERE THAN WHILE BEING MARCHED TO A LICE-INFESTED CAMP IN CENTRAL ASIA.

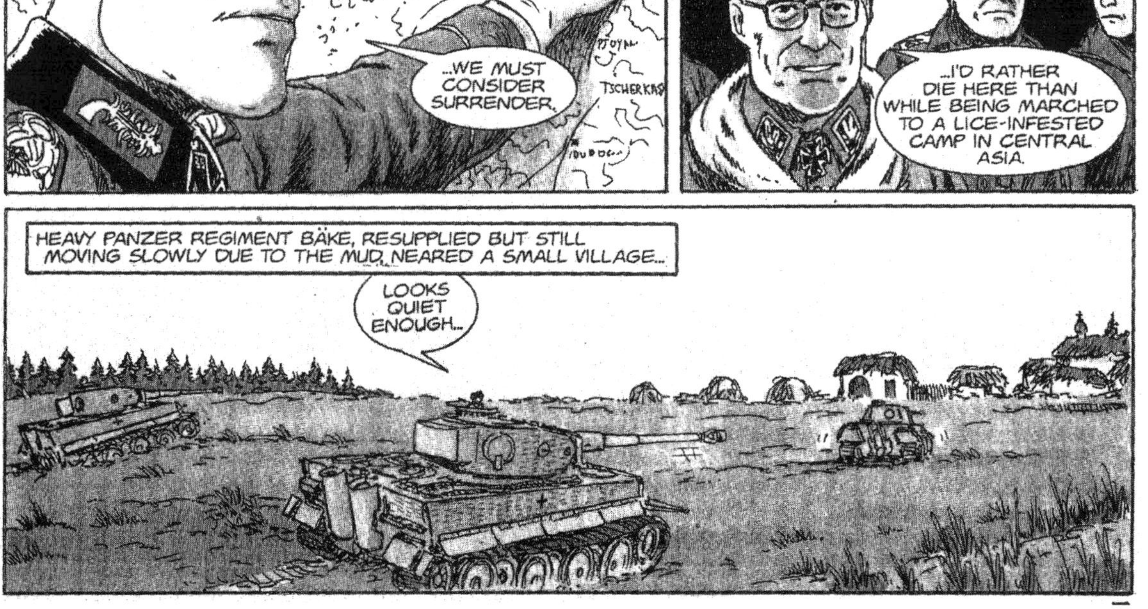
HEAVY PANZER REGIMENT BÄKE, RESUPPLIED BUT STILL MOVING SLOWLY DUE TO THE MUD, NEARED A SMALL VILLAGE...
LOOKS QUIET ENOUGH...

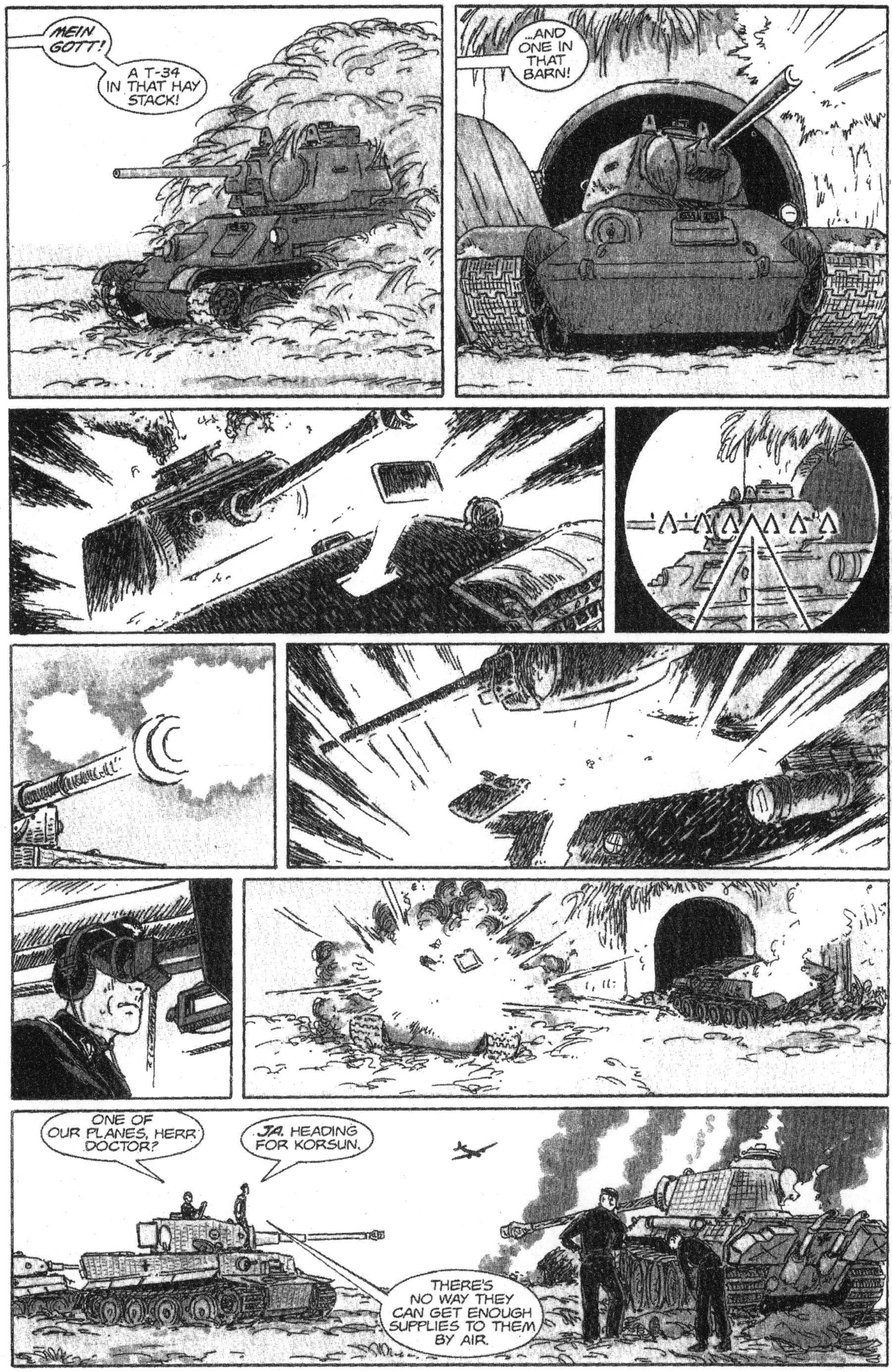
MEIN GOTT!
A T-34 IN THAT HAY STACK!
...AND ONE IN THAT BARN!
ONE OF OUR PLANES, HERR DOCTOR?
JA. HEADING FOR KORSUN.
THERE'S NO WAY THEY CAN GET ENOUGH SUPPLIES TO THEM BY AIR.

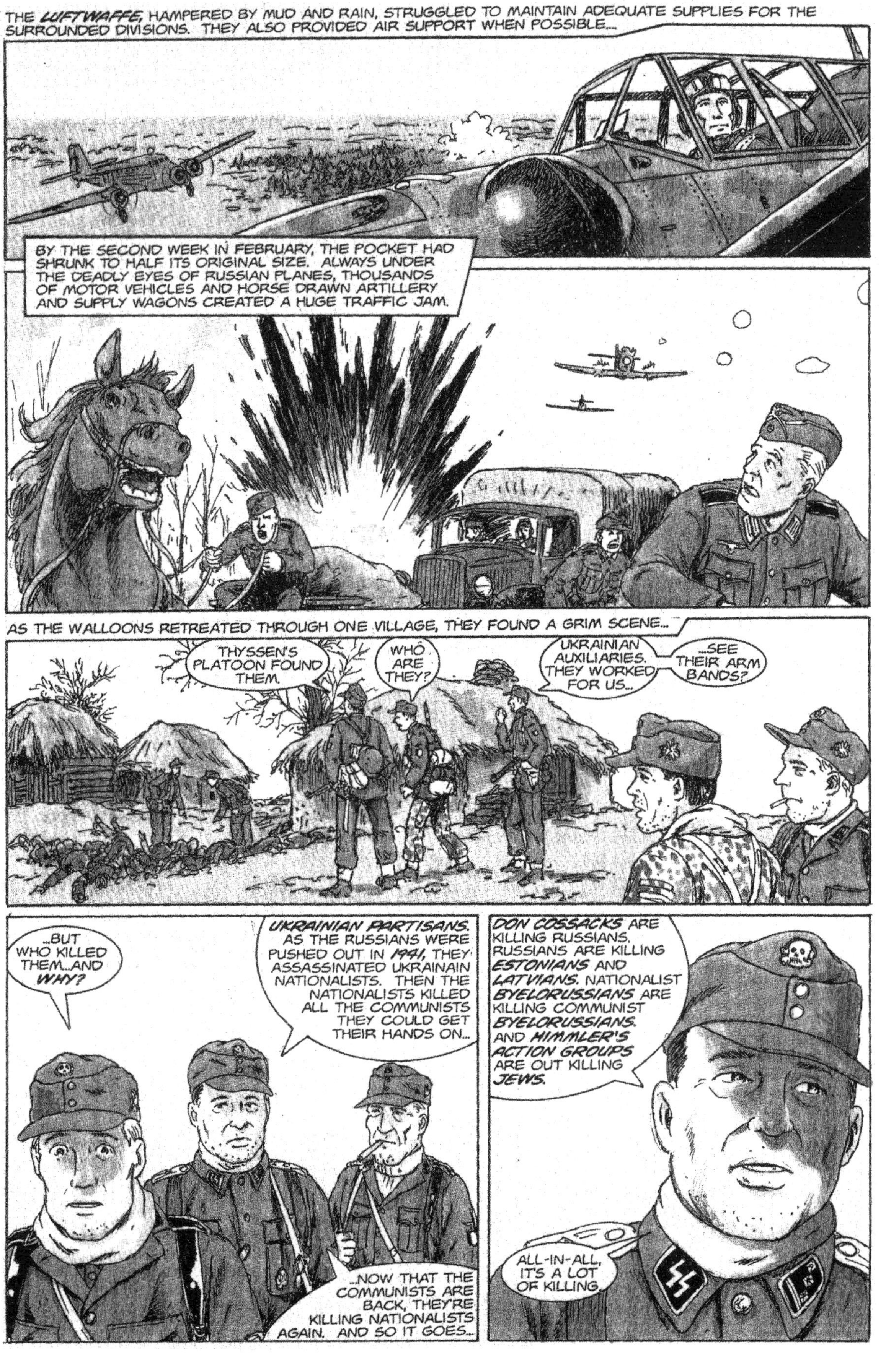
THE LUFTWAFFE, HAMPERED BY MUD AND RAIN, STRUGGLED TO MAINTAIN ADEQUATE SUPPLIES FOR THE SURROUNDED DIVISIONS. THEY ALSO PROVIDED AIR SUPPORT WHEN POSSIBLE...
BY THE SECOND WEEK IN FEBRUARY, THE POCKET HAD SHRUNK TO HALF ITS ORIGINAL SIZE. ALWAYS UNDER THE DEADLY EYES OF RUSSIAN PLANES, THOUSANDS OF MOTOR VEHICLES AND HORSE DRAWN ARTILLERY AND SUPPLY WAGONS CREATED A HUGE TRAFFIC JAM.
AS THE WALLOONS RETREATED THROUGH ONE VILLAGE, THEY FOUND A GRIM SCENE...
THYSSEN'S PLATOON FOUND THEM.
WHO ARE THEY?
UKRAINIAN AUXILIARIES. THEY WORKED FOR US...
...SEE THEIR ARM BANDS?
...BUT WHO KILLED THEM...AND WHY?
UKRAINIAN PARTISANS. AS THE RUSSIANS WERE PUSHED OUT IN 1941, THEY ASSASSINATED UKRAINAIN NATIONALISTS. THEN THE NATIONALISTS KILLED ALL THE COMMUNISTS THEY COULD GET THEIR HANDS ON...
...NOW THAT THE COMMUNISTS ARE BACK, THEY'RE KILLING NATIONALISTS AGAIN. AND SO IT GOES...
DON COSSACKS ARE KILLING RUSSIANS. RUSSIANS ARE KILLING ESTONIANS AND LATVIANS. NATIONALIST BYELORUSSIANS ARE KILLING COMMUNIST BYELORUSSIANS. AND HIMMLER'S ACTION GROUPS ARE OUT KILLING JEWS.
ALL-IN-ALL, IT'S A LOT OF KILLING.

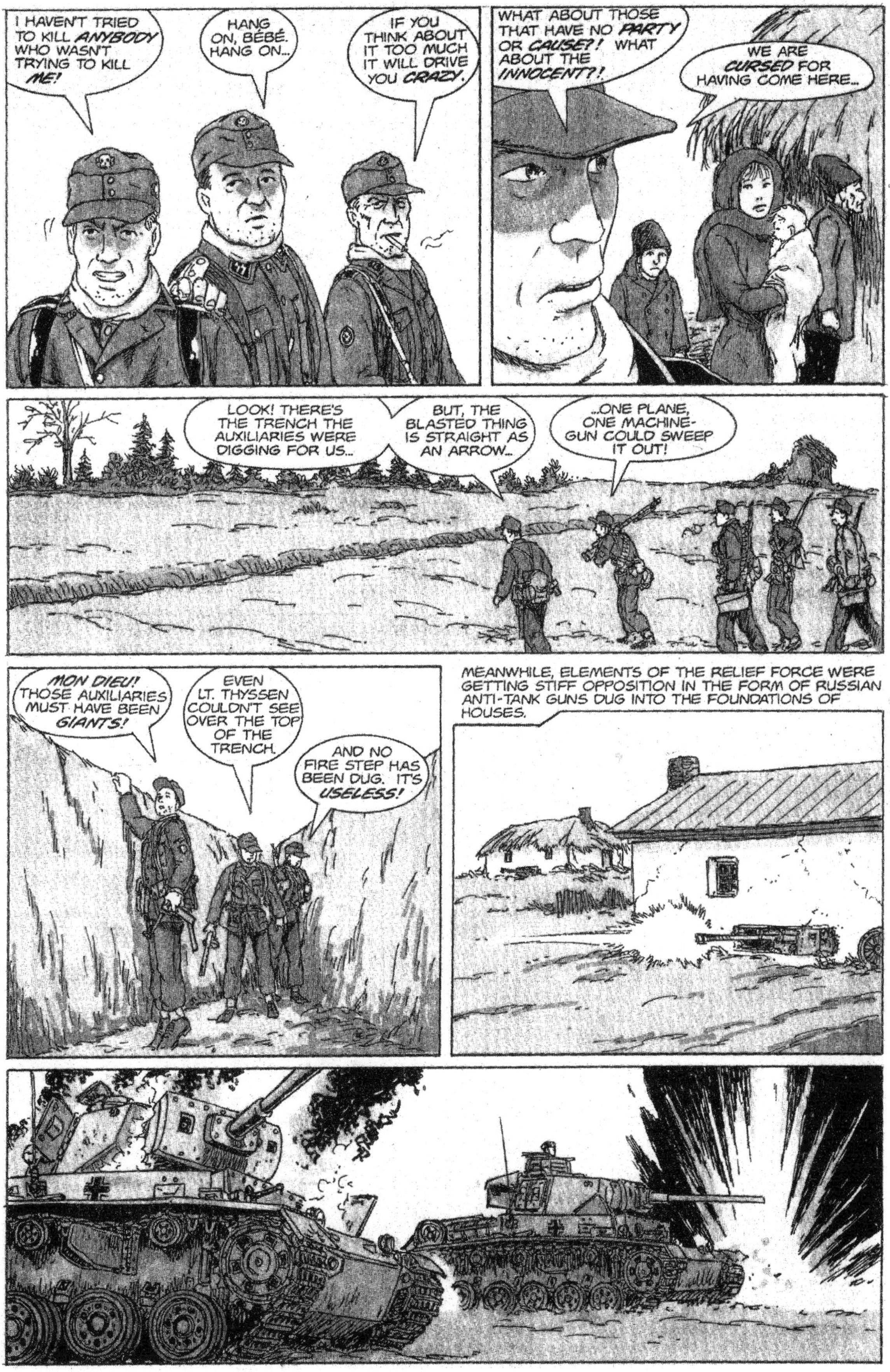
I HAVEN'T TRIED TO KILL ANYBODY WHO WASN'T TRYING TO KILL ME!
HANG ON, BÉBÉ. HANG ON...
IF YOU THINK ABOUT IT TOO MUCH IT WILL DRIVE YOU CRAZY.
WHAT ABOUT THOSE THAT HAVE NO PARTY OR CAUSE?! WHAT ABOUT THE INNOCENT?!
WE ARE CURSED FOR HAVING COME HERE...
LOOK! THERE'S THE TRENCH THE AUXILIARIES WERE DIGGING FOR US...
BUT, THE BLASTED THING IS STRAIGHT AS AN ARROW...
...ONE PLANE, ONE MACHINE-GUN COULD SWEEP IT OUT!
MON DIEU! THOSE AUXILIARIES MUST HAVE BEEN GIANTS!
EVEN LT. THYSSEN COULDN'T SEE OVER THE TOP OF THE TRENCH.
AND NO FIRE STEP HAS BEEN DUG. IT'S USELESS!
MEANWHILE, ELEMENTS OF THE RELIEF FORCE WERE GETTING STIFF OPPOSITION IN THE FORM OF RUSSIAN ANTI-TANK GUNS DUG INTO THE FOUNDATIONS OF HOUSES.

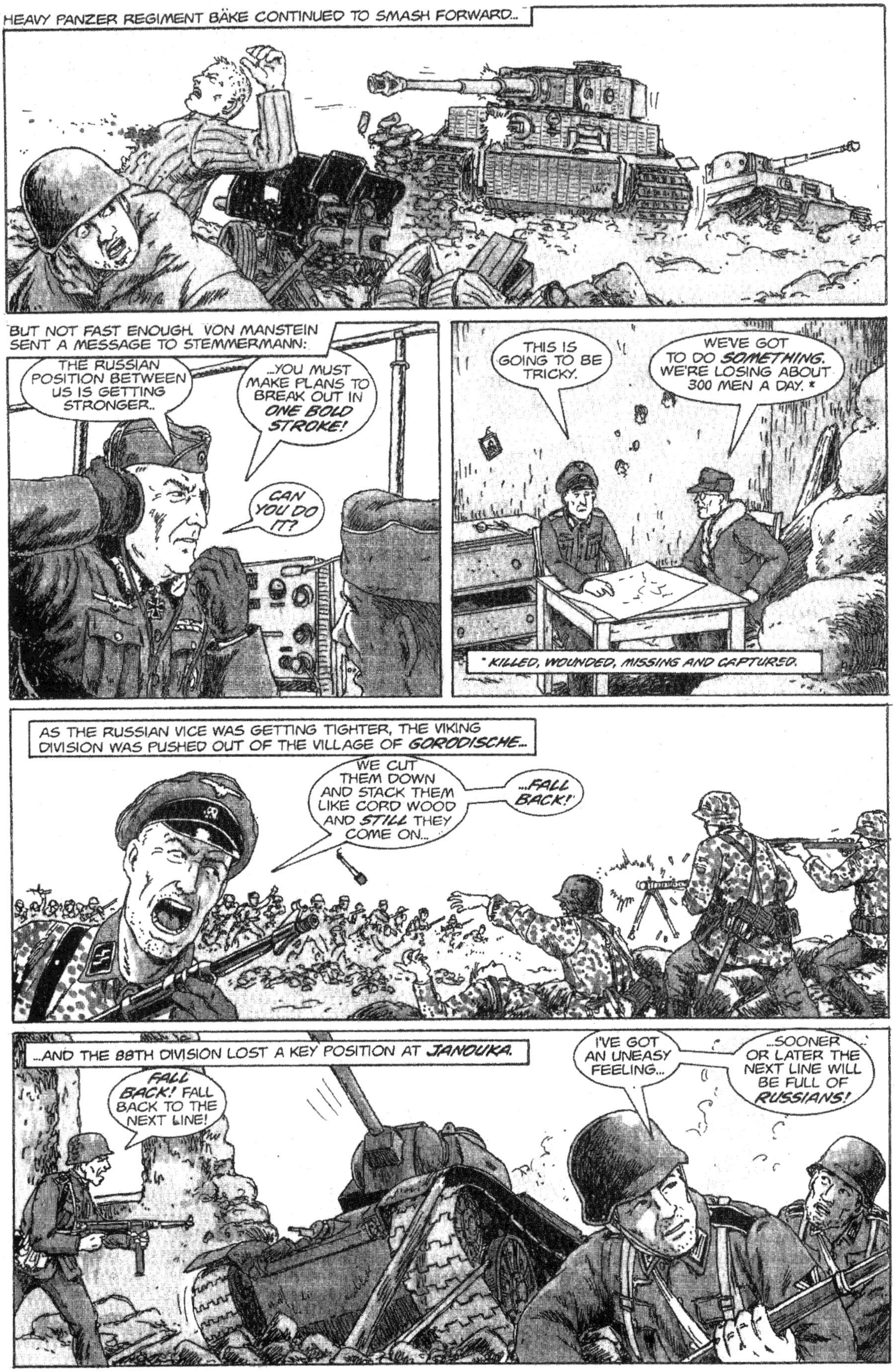
HEAVY PANZER REGIMENT BÄKE CONTINUED TO SMASH FORWARD...
BUT NOT FAST ENOUGH. VON MANSTEIN SENT A MESSAGE TO STEMMERMANN:
THE RUSSIAN POSITION BETWEEN US IS GETTING STRONGER..
...YOU MUST MAKE PLANS TO BREAK OUT IN ONE BOLD STROKE!
CAN YOU DO IT?
THIS IS GOING TO BE TRICKY.
WE'VE GOT TO DO SOMETHING. WE'RE LOSING ABOUT 300 MEN A DAY. *
* KILLED, WOUNDED, MISSING AND CAPTURED.
AS THE RUSSIAN VICE WAS GETTING TIGHTER, THE VIKING DIVISION WAS PUSHED OUT OF THE VILLAGE OF GORODISCHE...
WE CUT THEM DOWN AND STACK THEM LIKE CORD WOOD AND STILL THEY COME ON...
...FALL BACK!
...AND THE 88TH DIVISION LOST A KEY POSITION AT JANOUKA.
FALL BACK! FALL BACK TO THE NEXT LINE!
I'VE GOT AN UNEASY FEELING...
...SOONER OR LATER THE NEXT LINE WILL BE FULL OF RUSSIANS!

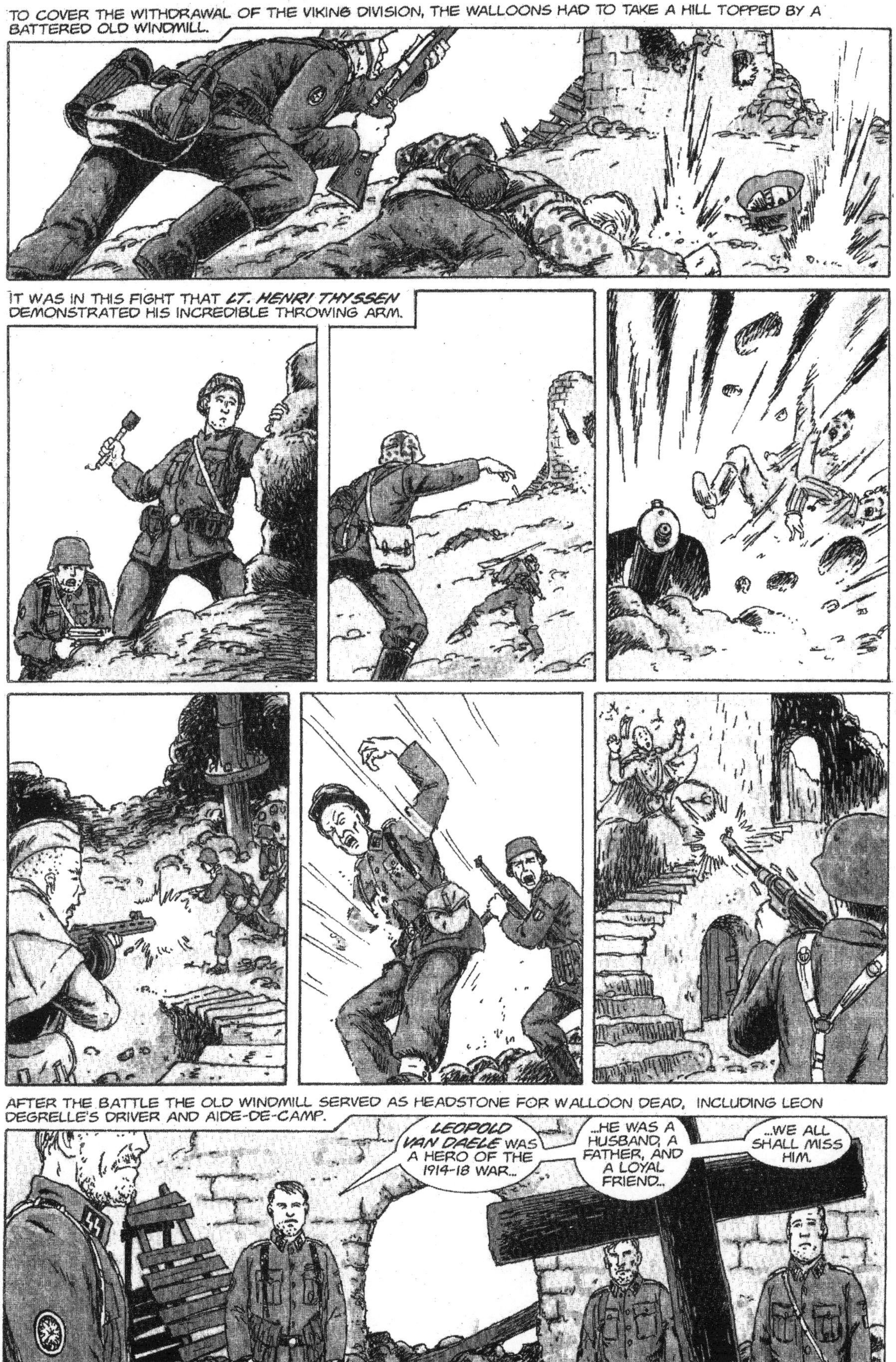
TO COVER THE WITHDRAWAL OF THE VIKING DIVISION, THE WALLOONS HAD TO TAKE A HILL TOPPED BY A BATTERED OLD WINDMILL.
IT WAS IN THIS FIGHT THAT LT. HENRI THYSSEN DEMONSTRATED HIS INCREDIBLE THROWING ARM.
AFTER THE BATTLE THE OLD WINDMILL SERVED AS HEADSTONE FOR WALLOON DEAD, INCLUDING LEON DEGRELLE'S DRIVER AND AIDE-DE-CAMP.
LEOPOLD VAN DAELE WAS A HERO OF THE 1914-18 WAR...
...HE WAS A HUSBAND, A FATHER, AND A LOYAL FRIEND..
...WE ALL SHALL MISS HIM.

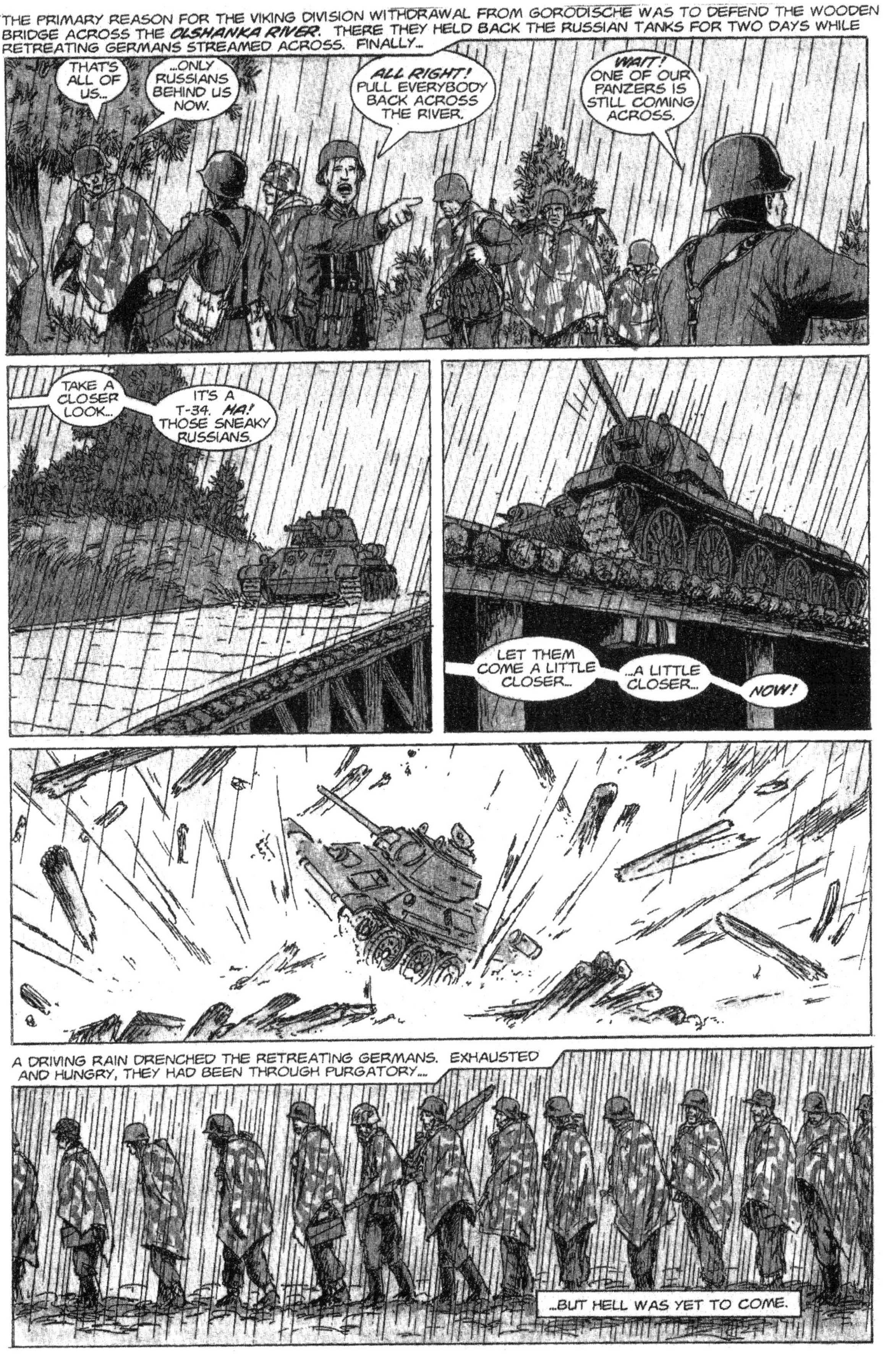
THE PRIMARY REASON FOR THE VIKING DIVISION WITHDRAWAL FROM GORODISCHE WAS TO DEFEND THE WOODEN BRIDGE ACROSS THE OLSHANKA RIVER. THERE THEY HELD BACK THE RUSSIAN TANKS FOR TWO DAYS WHILE RETREATING GERMANS STREAMED ACROSS. FINALLY...
THAT'S ALL OF US...
...ONLY RUSSIANS BEHIND US NOW.
ALL RIGHT! PULL EVERYBODY BACK ACROSS THE RIVER.
WAIT! ONE OF OUR PANZERS IS STILL COMING ACROSS.
TAKE A CLOSER LOOK...
IT'S A T-34. HA! THOSE SNEAKY RUSSIANS.
LET THEM COME A LITTLE CLOSER...
...A LITTLE CLOSER...
NOW!
A DRIVING RAIN DRENCHED THE RETREATING GERMANS. EXHAUSTED AND HUNGRY, THEY HAD BEEN THROUGH PURGATORY...
...BUT HELL WAS YET TO COME.

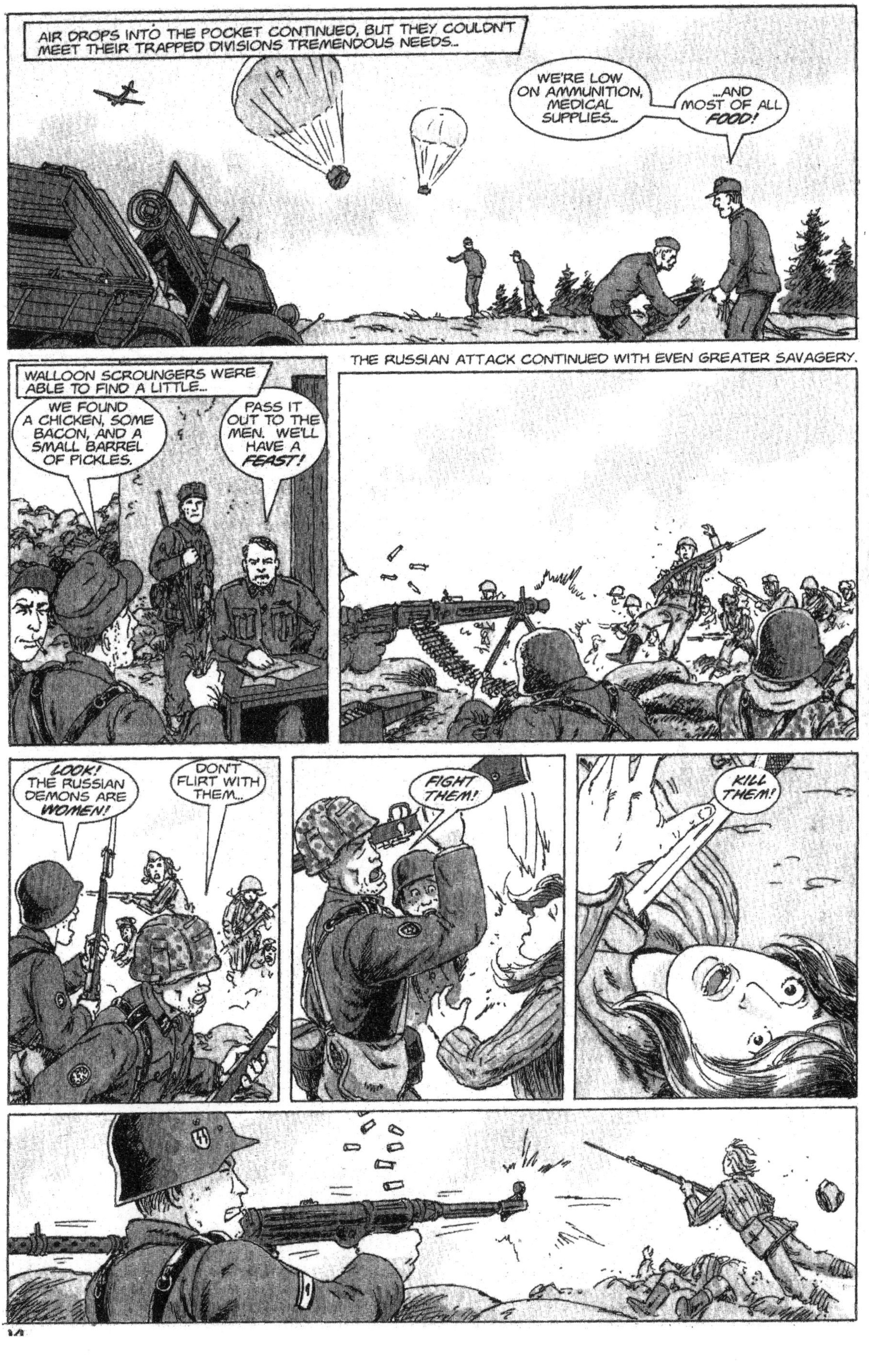
AIR DROPS INTO THE POCKET CONTINUED, BUT THEY COULDN'T MEET THEIR TRAPPED DIVISIONS TREMENDOUS NEEDS...
WE'RE LOW ON AMMUNITION, MEDICAL SUPPLIES...
...AND MOST OF ALL FOOD!
WALLOON SCROUNGERS WERE ABLE TO FIND A LITTLE...
WE FOUND A CHICKEN, SOME BACON, AND A SMALL BARREL OF PICKLES.
PASS IT OUT TO THE MEN. WE'LL HAVE A FEAST!
THE RUSSIAN ATTACK CONTINUED WITH EVEN GREATER SAVAGERY.
LOOK! THE RUSSIAN DEMONS ARE WOMEN!
DON'T FLIRT WITH THEM...
FIGHT THEM!
KILL THEM!

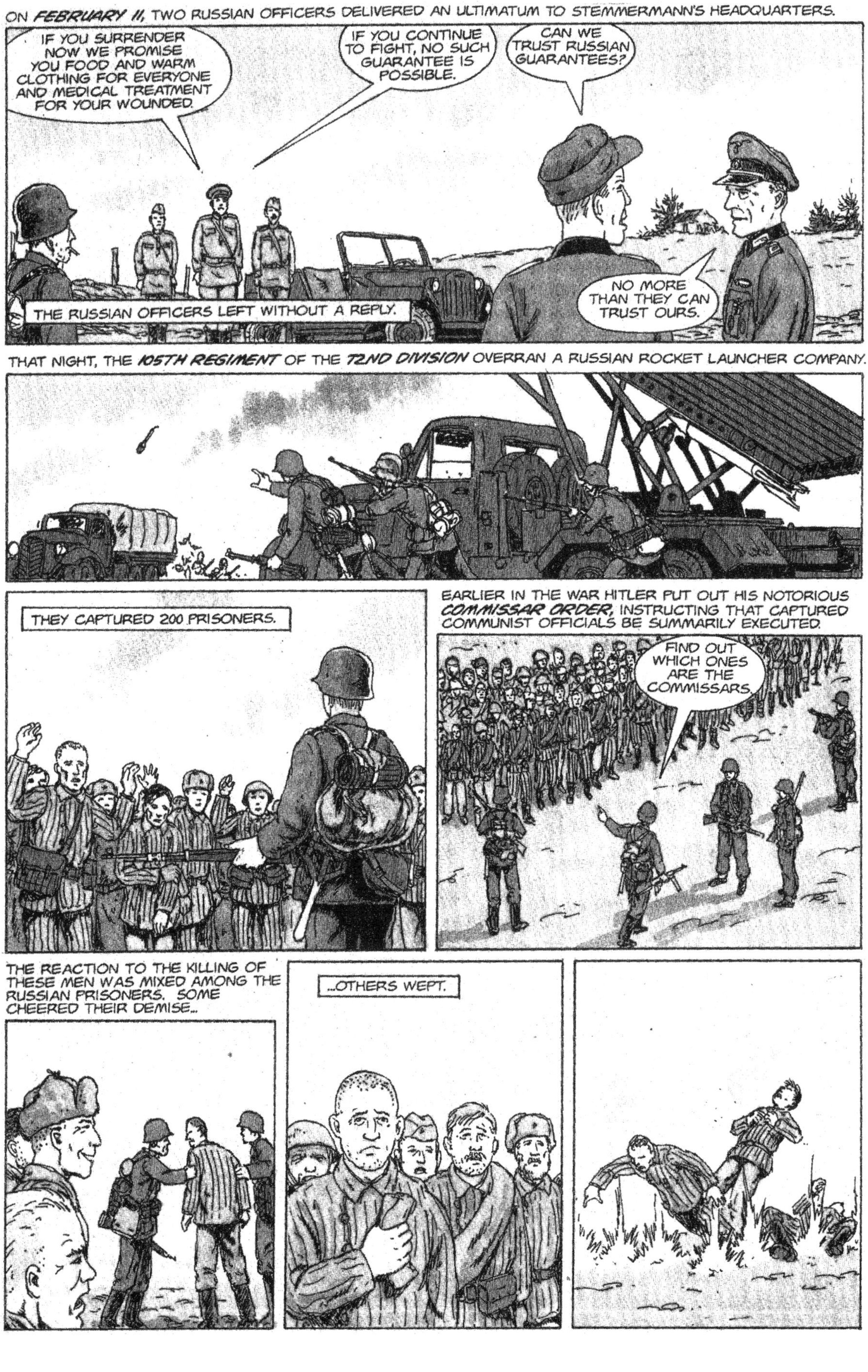
ON FEBRUARY 11, TWO RUSSIAN OFFICERS DELIVERED AN ULTIMATUM TO STEMMERMANN'S HEADQUARTERS.
IF YOU SURRENDER NOW WE PROMISE YOU FOOD AND WARM CLOTHING FOR EVERYONE AND MEDICAL TREATMENT FOR YOUR WOUNDED.
IF YOU CONTINUE TO FIGHT, NO SUCH GUARANTEE IS POSSIBLE.
CAN WE TRUST RUSSIAN GUARANTEES?
NO MORE THAN THEY CAN TRUST OURS.
THE RUSSIAN OFFICERS LEFT WITHOUT A REPLY.
THAT NIGHT, THE 105TH REGIMENT OF THE 72ND DIVISION OVERRAN A RUSSIAN ROCKET LAUNCHER COMPANY.
THEY CAPTURED 200 PRISONERS.
EARLIER IN THE WAR HITLER PUT OUT HIS NOTORIOUS COMMISSAR ORDER, INSTRUCTING THAT CAPTURED COMMUNIST OFFICIALS BE SUMMARILY EXECUTED.
FIND OUT WHICH ONES ARE THE COMMISSARS.
THE REACTION TO THE KILLING OF THESE MEN WAS MIXED AMONG THE RUSSIAN PRISONERS. SOME CHEERED THEIR DEMISE...
...OTHERS WEPT.

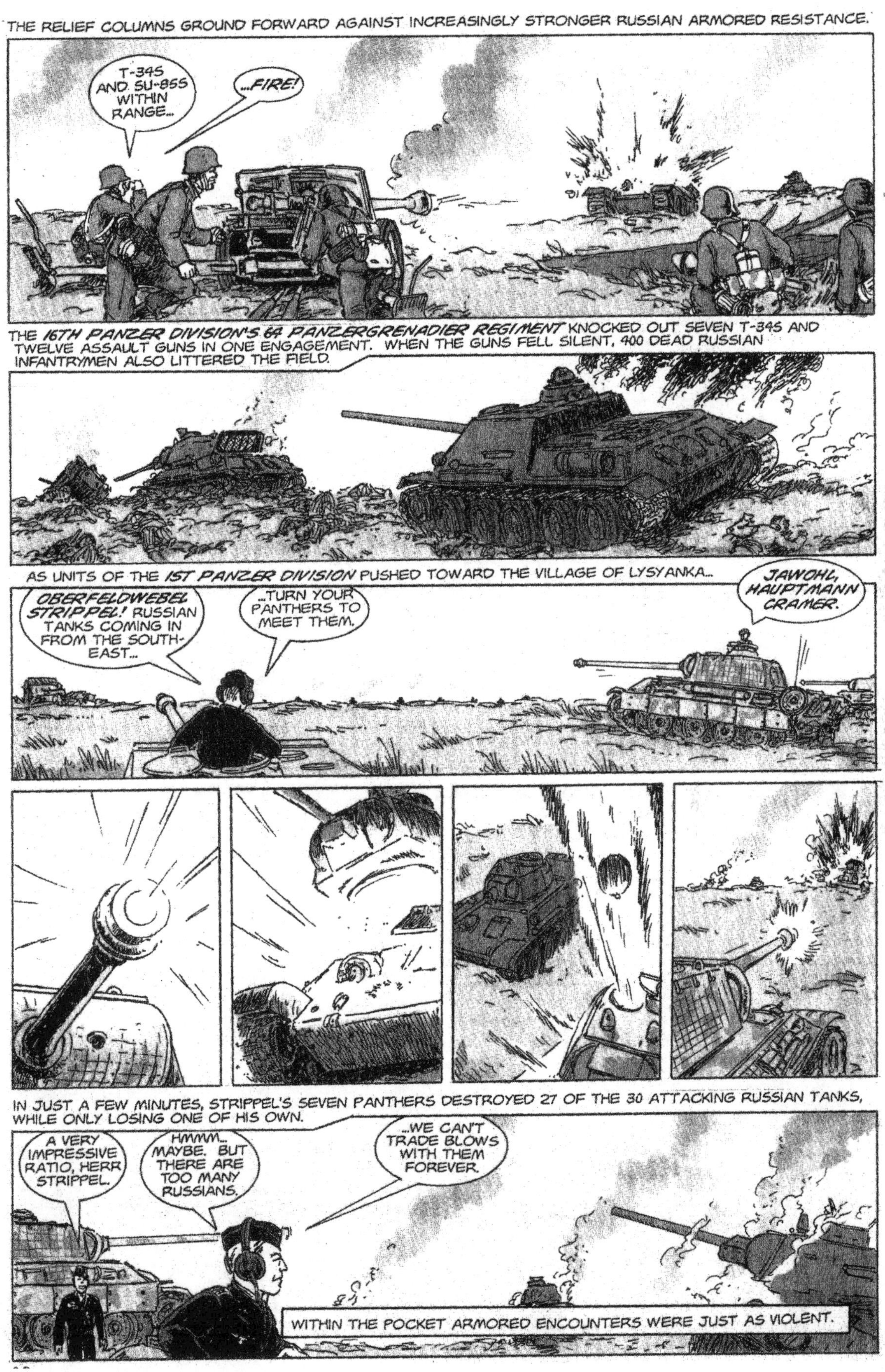
THE RELIEF COLUMNS GROUND FORWARD AGAINST INCREASINGLY STRONGER RUSSIAN ARMORED RESISTANCE.
T-34S AND SU-85S WITHIN RANGE...
...FIRE!
THE 16TH PANZER DIVISION'S 64 PANZERGRENADIER REGIMENT KNOCKED OUT SEVEN T-34S AND TWELVE ASSAULT GUNS IN ONE ENGAGEMENT. WHEN THE GUNS FELL SILENT, 400 DEAD RUSSIAN INFANTRYMEN ALSO LITTERED THE FIELD.
AS UNITS OF THE 1ST PANZER DIVISION PUSHED TOWARD THE VILLAGE OF LYSYANKA...
OBERFELDWEBEL STRIPPEL! RUSSIAN TANKS COMING IN FROM THE SOUTH-EAST...
...TURN YOUR PANTHERS TO MEET THEM.
JAWOHL, HAUPTMANN CRAMER.
IN JUST A FEW MINUTES, STRIPPEL'S SEVEN PANTHERS DESTROYED 27 OF THE 30 ATTACKING RUSSIAN TANKS, WHILE ONLY LOSING ONE OF HIS OWN.
A VERY IMPRESSIVE RATIO, HERR STRIPPEL.
HMMM... MAYBE. BUT THERE ARE TOO MANY RUSSIANS.
...WE CAN'T TRADE BLOWS WITH THEM FOREVER.
WITHIN THE POCKET ARMORED ENCOUNTERS WERE JUST AS VIOLENT.

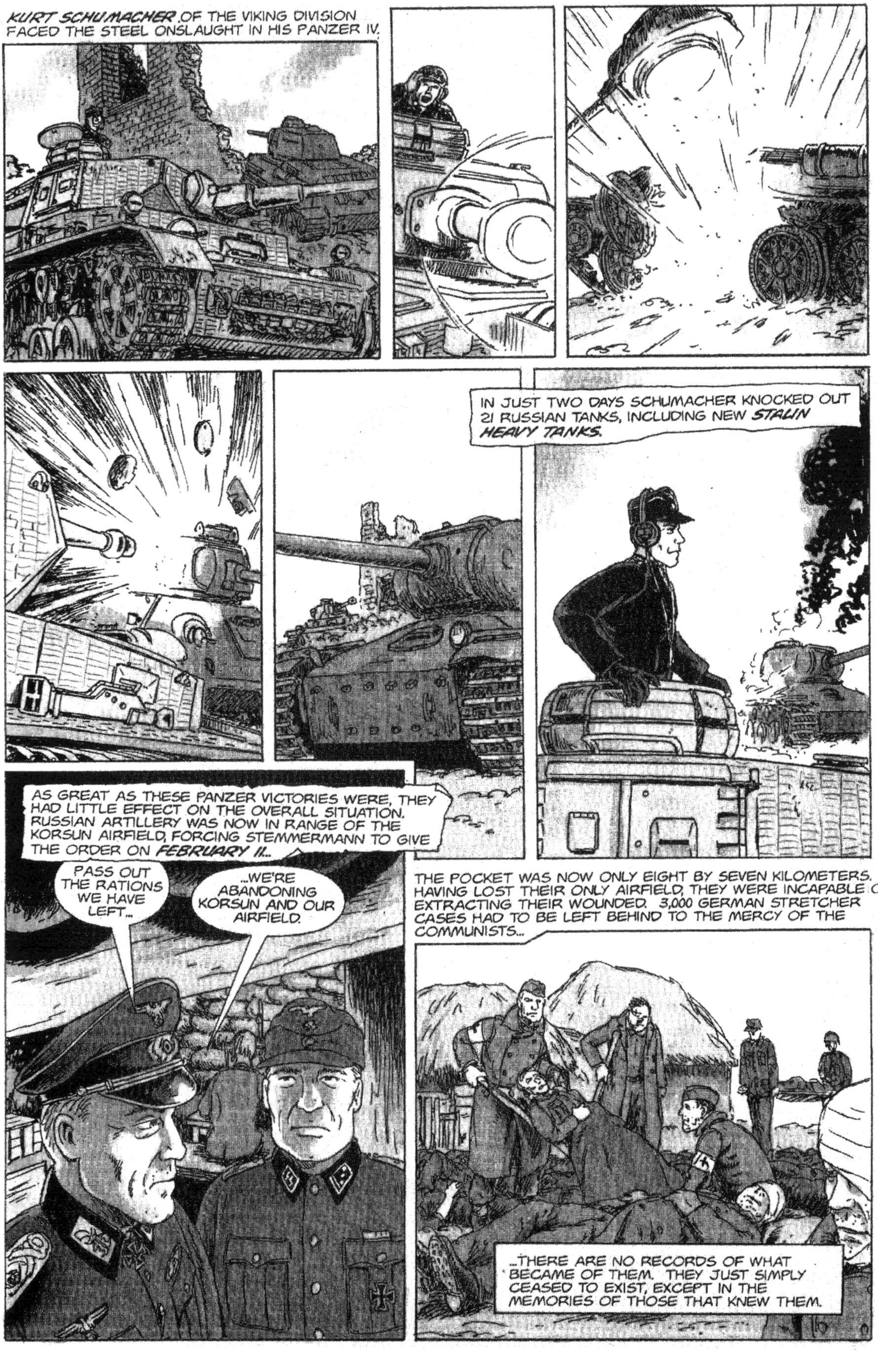
KURT SCHUMACHER OF THE VIKING DIVISION FACED THE STEEL ONSLAUGHT IN HIS PANZER IV.
IN JUST TWO DAYS SCHUMACHER KNOCKED OUT 21 RUSSIAN TANKS, INCLUDING NEW STALIN HEAVY TANKS.
AS GREAT AS THESE PANZER VICTORIES WERE, THEY HAD LITTLE EFFECT ON THE OVERALL SITUATION. RUSSIAN ARTILLERY WAS NOW IN RANGE OF THE KORSUN AIRFIELD, FORCING STEMMERMANN TO GIVE THE ORDER ON FEBRUARY 11...
PASS OUT THE RATIONS WE HAVE LEFT...
...WE'RE ABANDONING KORSUN AND OUR AIRFIELD.
THE POCKET WAS NOW ONLY EIGHT BY SEVEN KILOMETERS. HAVING LOST THEIR ONLY AIRFIELD, THEY WERE INCAPABLE OF EXTRACTING THEIR WOUNDED. 3,000 GERMAN STRETCHER CASES HAD TO BE LEFT BEHIND TO THE MERCY OF THE COMMUNISTS...
...THERE ARE NO RECORDS OF WHAT BECAME OF THEM. THEY JUST SIMPLY CEASED TO EXIST, EXCEPT IN THE MEMORIES OF THOSE THAT KNEW THEM.

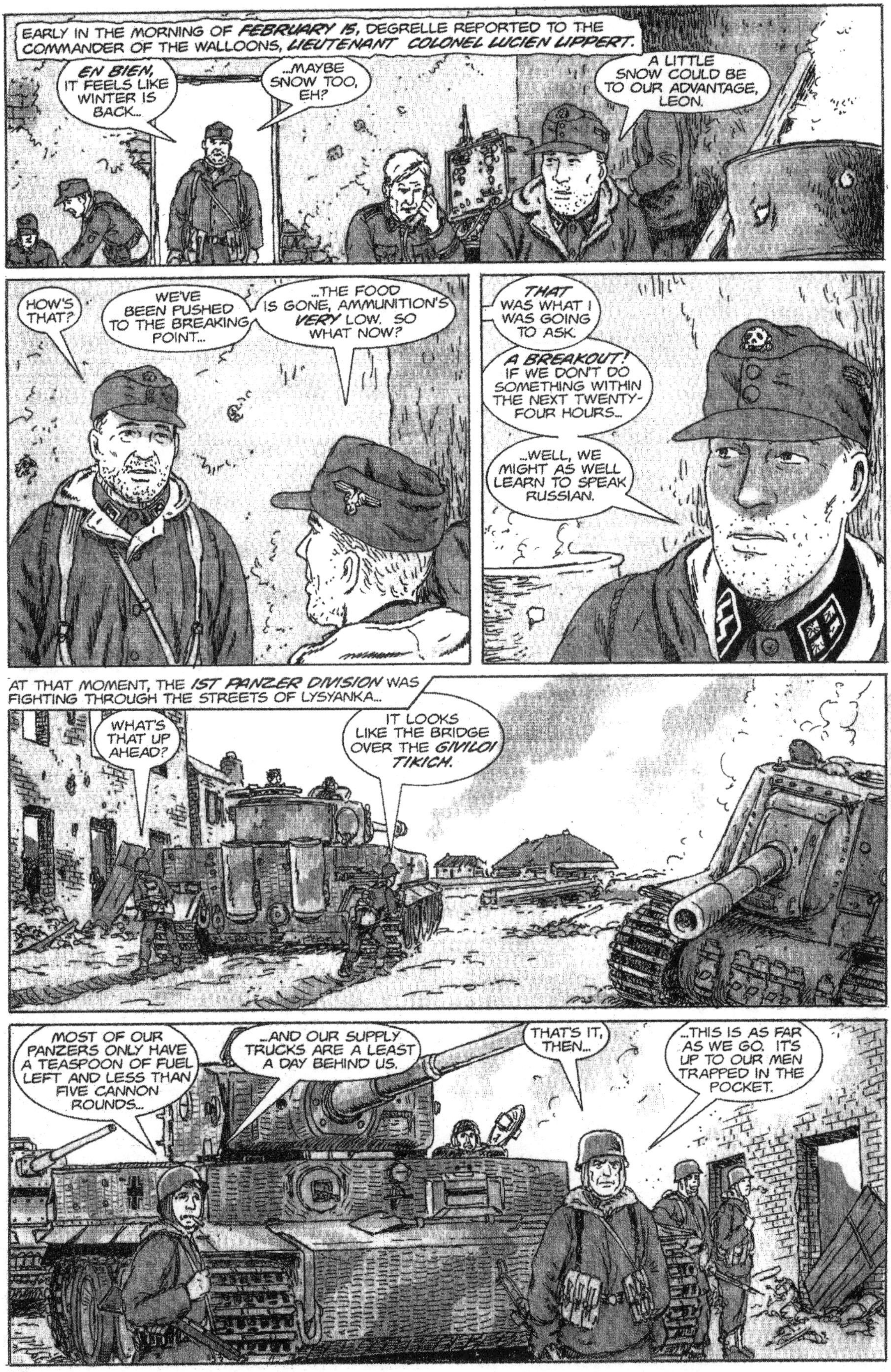
EARLY IN THE MORNING OF FEBRUARY 15, DEGRELLE REPORTED TO THE COMMANDER OF THE WALLOONS, LIEUTENANT COLONEL LUCIEN LIPPERT.
EN BIEN, IT FEELS LIKE WINTER IS BACK...
...MAYBE SNOW TOO, EH?
A LITTLE SNOW COULD BE TO OUR ADVANTAGE, LEON.
HOW'S THAT?
WE'VE BEEN PUSHED TO THE BREAKING POINT...
...THE FOOD IS GONE, AMMUNITION'S VERY LOW. SO WHAT NOW?
THAT WAS WHAT I WAS GOING TO ASK.
A BREAKOUT! IF WE DON'T DO SOMETHING WITHIN THE NEXT TWENTY-FOUR HOURS...
...WELL, WE MIGHT AS WELL LEARN TO SPEAK RUSSIAN.
AT THAT MOMENT, THE 1ST PANZER DIVISION WAS FIGHTING THROUGH THE STREETS OF LYSYANKA...
WHAT'S THAT UP AHEAD?
IT LOOKS LIKE THE BRIDGE OVER THE GIVILOI TIKICH.
MOST OF OUR PANZERS ONLY HAVE A TEASPOON OF FUEL LEFT AND LESS THAN FIVE CANNON ROUNDS...
...AND OUR SUPPLY TRUCKS ARE A LEAST A DAY BEHIND US.
THAT'S IT, THEN...
...THIS IS AS FAR AS WE GO. IT'S UP TO OUR MEN TRAPPED IN THE POCKET.

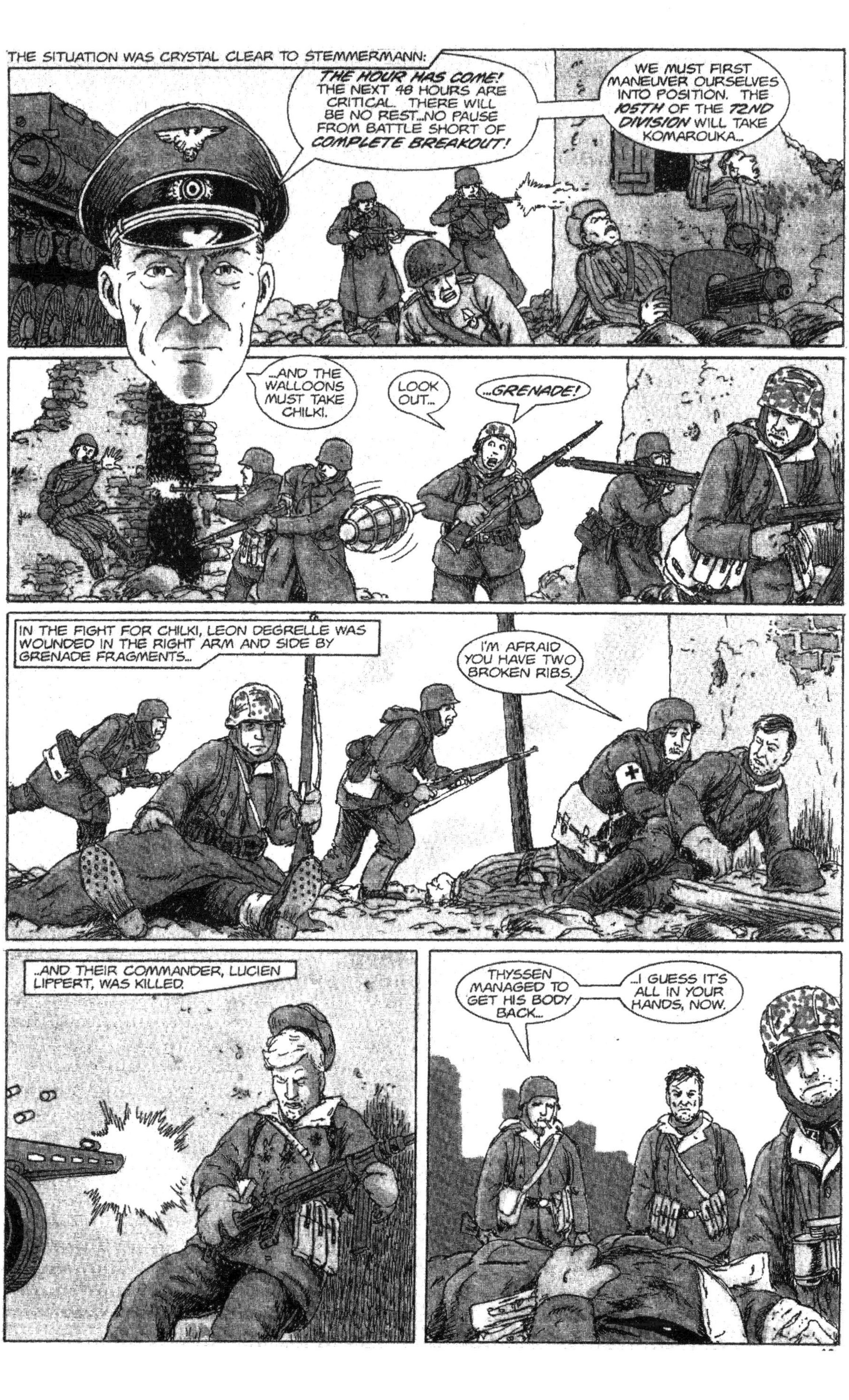
THE SITUATION WAS CRYSTAL CLEAR TO STEMMERMANN:
THE HOUR HAS COME! THE NEXT 48 HOURS ARE CRITICAL. THERE WILL BE NO REST...NO PAUSE FROM BATTLE SHORT OF COMPLETE BREAKOUT!
WE MUST FIRST MANEUVER OURSELVES INTO POSITION. THE 105TH OF THE 72ND DIVISION WILL TAKE KOMAROUKA...
...AND THE WALLOONS MUST TAKE CHILKI.
LOOK OUT...
...GRENADE!
IN THE FIGHT FOR CHILKI, LEON DEGRELLE WAS WOUNDED IN THE RIGHT ARM AND SIDE BY GRENADE FRAGMENTS...
I'M AFRAID YOU HAVE TWO BROKEN RIBS.
...AND THEIR COMMANDER, LUCIEN LIPPERT, WAS KILLED.
THYSSEN MANAGED TO GET HIS BODY BACK...
...I GUESS IT'S ALL IN YOUR HANDS, NOW.

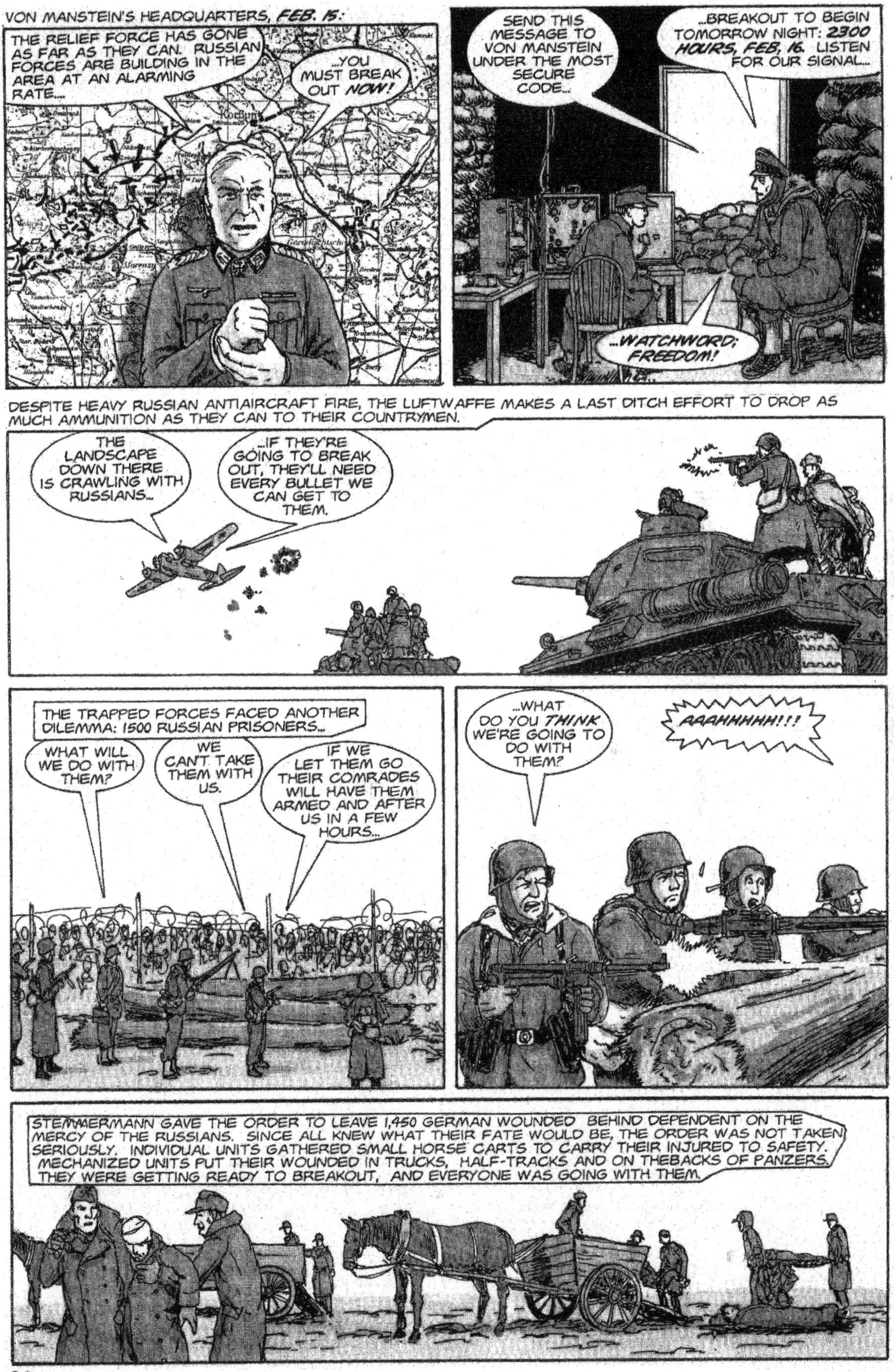
VON MANSTEIN'S HEADQUARTERS, FEB. 15:
THE RELIEF FORCE HAS GONE AS FAR AS THEY CAN. RUSSIAN FORCES ARE BUILDING IN THE AREA AT AN ALARMING RATE...
...YOU MUST BREAK OUT NOW!
SEND THIS MESSAGE TO VON MANSTEIN UNDER THE MOST SECURE CODE...
...BREAKOUT TO BEGIN TOMORROW NIGHT: 2300 HOURS, FEB. 16. LISTEN FOR OUR SIGNAL...
...WATCHWORD: FREEDOM!
DESPITE HEAVY RUSSIAN ANTIAIRCRAFT FIRE, THE LUFTWAFFE MAKES A LAST DITCH EFFORT TO DROP AS MUCH AMMUNITION AS THEY CAN TO THEIR COUNTRYMEN.
THE LANDSCAPE DOWN THERE IS CRAWLING WITH RUSSIANS...
...IF THEY'RE GOING TO BREAK OUT, THEY'LL NEED EVERY BULLET WE CAN GET TO THEM.
THE TRAPPED FORCES FACED ANOTHER DILEMMA: 1500 RUSSIAN PRISONERS...
WHAT WILL WE DO WITH THEM?
WE CAN'T TAKE THEM WITH US.
IF WE LET THEM GO THEIR COMRADES WILL HAVE THEM ARMED AND AFTER US IN A FEW HOURS...
...WHAT DO YOU THINK WE'RE GOING TO DO WITH THEM?
AAAHHHHH!!!
STEMMERMANN GAVE THE ORDER TO LEAVE 1,450 GERMAN WOUNDED BEHIND DEPENDENT ON THE MERCY OF THE RUSSIANS. SINCE ALL KNEW WHAT THEIR FATE WOULD BE, THE ORDER WAS NOT TAKEN SERIOUSLY. INDIVIDUAL UNITS GATHERED SMALL HORSE CARTS TO CARRY THEIR INJURED TO SAFETY. MECHANIZED UNITS PUT THEIR WOUNDED IN TRUCKS, HALF-TRACKS AND ON THEBACKS OF PANZERS. THEY WERE GETTING READY TO BREAKOUT, AND EVERYONE WAS GOING WITH THEM.

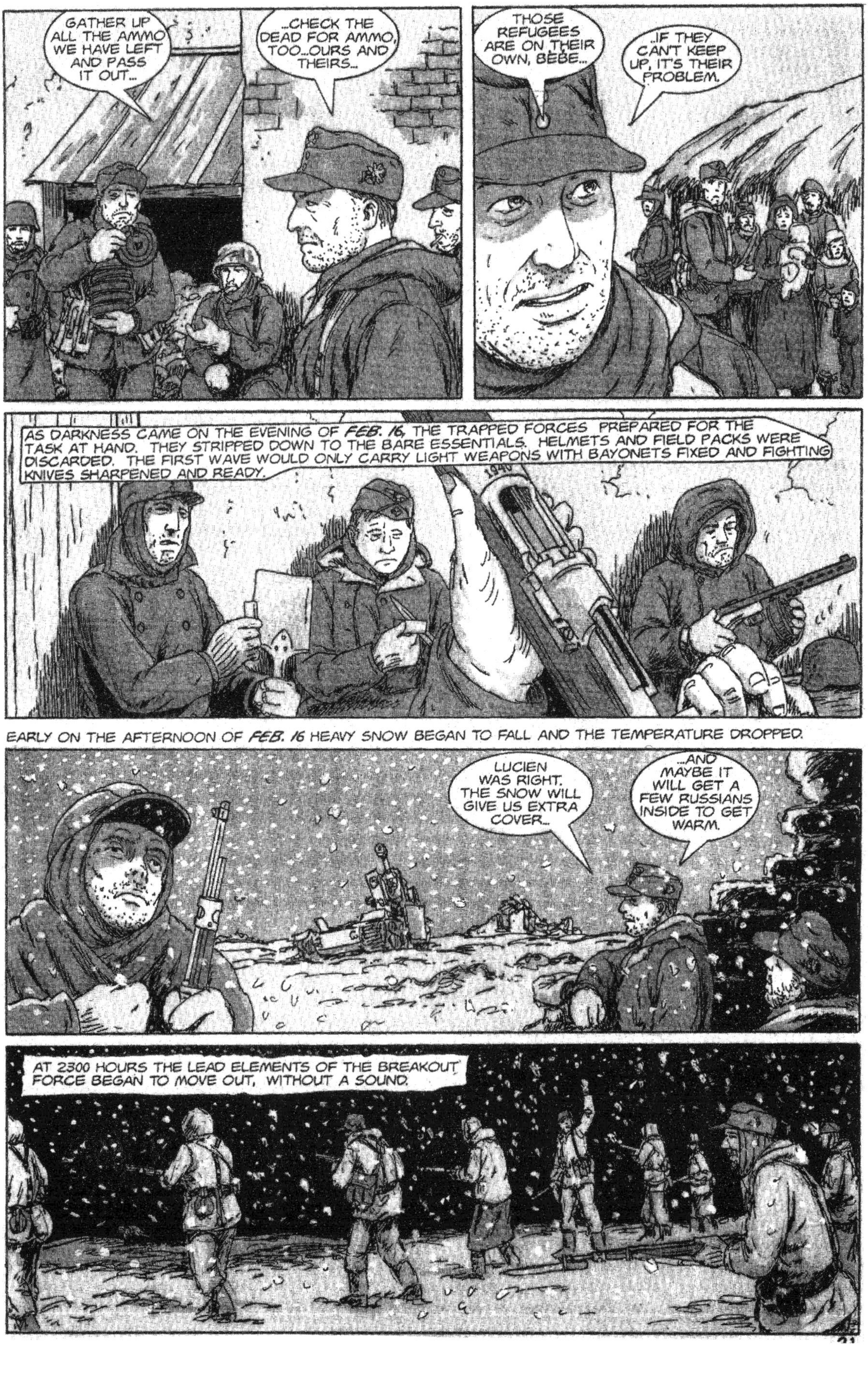
GATHER UP ALL THE AMMO WE HAVE LEFT AND PASS IT OUT...
...CHECK THE DEAD FOR AMMO, TOO...OURS AND THEIRS...
THOSE REFUGEES ARE ON THEIR OWN, BEBE...
..IF THEY CAN'T KEEP UP, IT'S THEIR PROBLEM.
AS DARKNESS CAME ON THE EVENING OF FEB. 16, THE TRAPPED FORCES PREPARED FOR THE TASK AT HAND. THEY STRIPPED DOWN TO THE BARE ESSENTIALS. HELMETS AND FIELD PACKS WERE DISCARDED. THE FIRST WAVE WOULD ONLY CARRY LIGHT WEAPONS WITH BAYONETS FIXED AND FIGHTING KNIVES SHARPENED AND READY.
EARLY ON THE AFTERNOON OF FEB. 16 HEAVY SNOW BEGAN TO FALL AND THE TEMPERATURE DROPPED.
LUCIEN WAS RIGHT. THE SNOW WILL GIVE US EXTRA COVER...
...AND MAYBE IT WILL GET A FEW RUSSIANS INSIDE TO GET WARM.
AT 2300 HOURS THE LEAD ELEMENTS OF THE BREAKOUT FORCE BEGAN TO MOVE OUT, WITHOUT A SOUND.

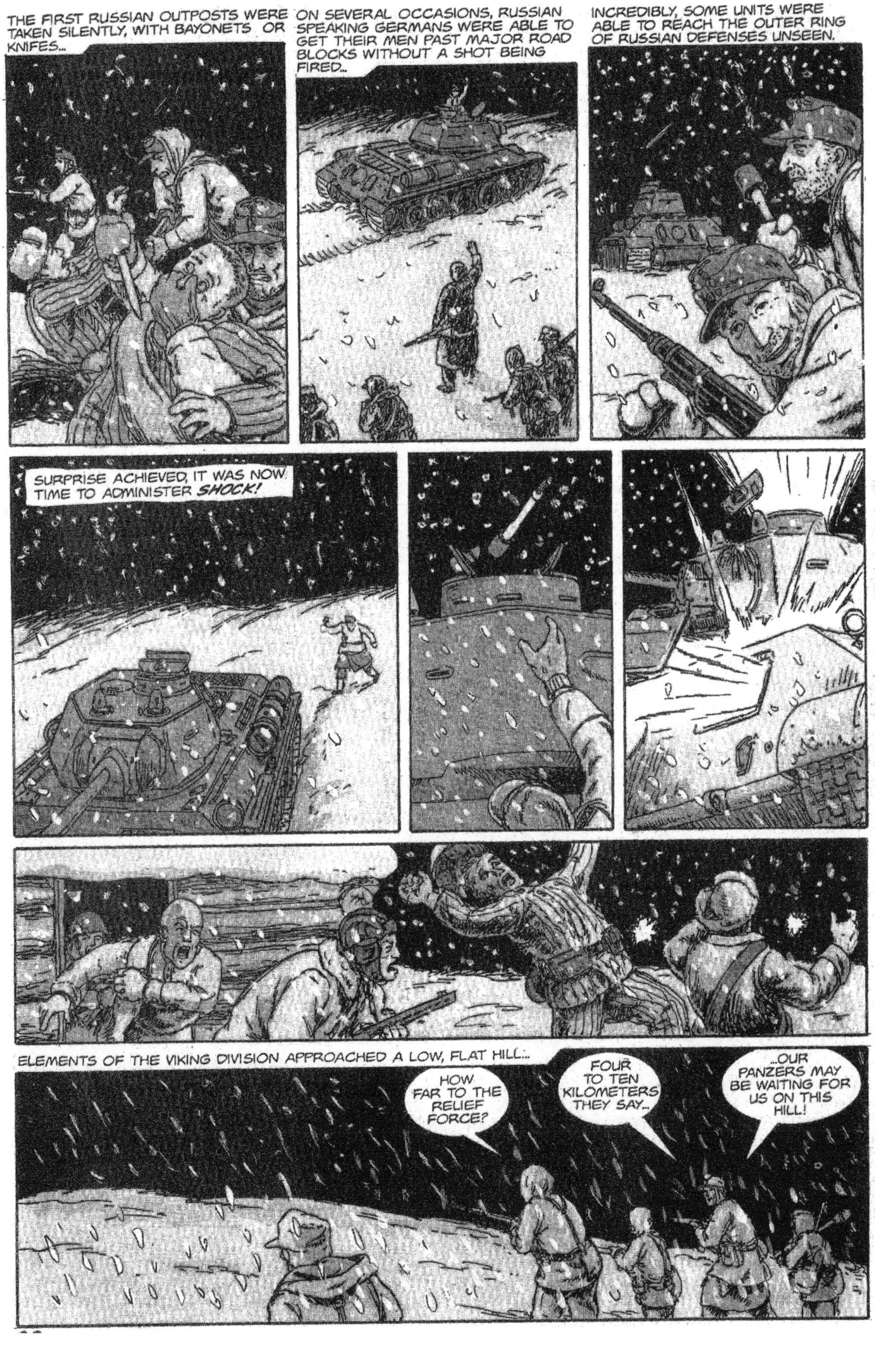
THE FIRST RUSSIAN OUTPOSTS WERE TAKEN SILENTLY, WITH BAYONETS OR KNIFES...
ON SEVERAL OCCASIONS, RUSSIAN SPEAKING GERMANS WERE ABLE TO GET THEIR MEN PAST MAJOR ROAD BLOCKS WITHOUT A SHOT BEING FIRED...
INCREDIBLY, SOME UNITS WERE ABLE TO REACH THE OUTER RING OF RUSSIAN DEFENSES UNSEEN.
SURPRISE ACHIEVED, IT WAS NOW TIME TO ADMINISTER SHOCK!
ELEMENTS OF THE VIKING DIVISION APPROACHED A LOW, FLAT HILL...
HOW FAR TO THE RELIEF FORCE?
FOUR TO TEN KILOMETERS THEY SAY...
...OUR PANZERS MAY BE WAITING FOR US ON THIS HILL!

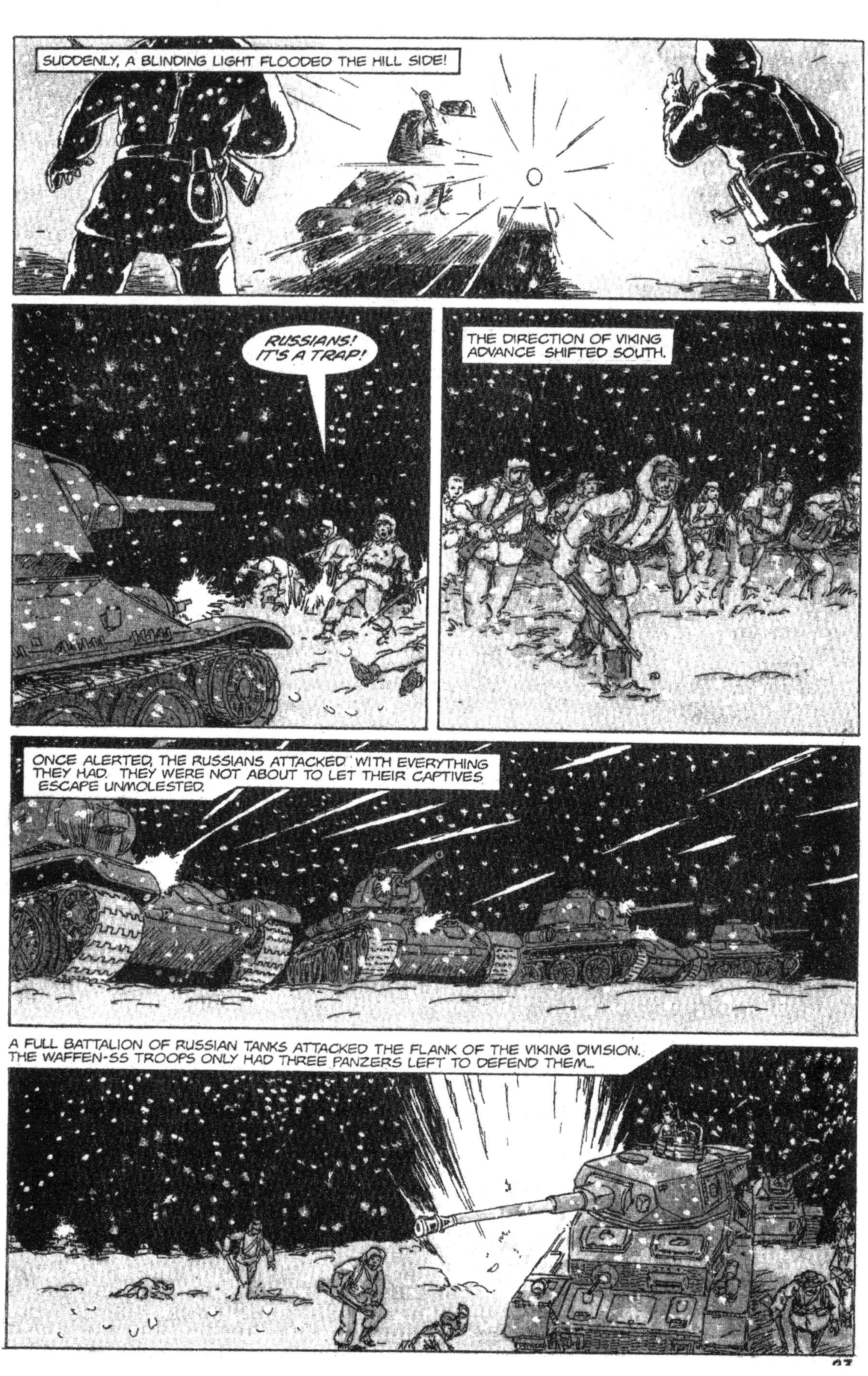
SUDDENLY, A BLINDING LIGHT FLOODED THE HILL SIDE!
RUSSIANS! IT'S A TRAP!
THE DIRECTION OF VIKING ADVANCE SHIFTED SOUTH.
ONCE ALERTED, THE RUSSIANS ATTACKED WITH EVERYTHING THEY HAD. THEY WERE NOT ABOUT TO LET THEIR CAPTIVES ESCAPE UNMOLESTED.
A FULL BATTALION OF RUSSIAN TANKS ATTACKED THE FLANK OF THE VIKING DIVISION. THE WAFFEN-SS TROOPS ONLY HAD THREE PANZERS LEFT TO DEFEND THEM...

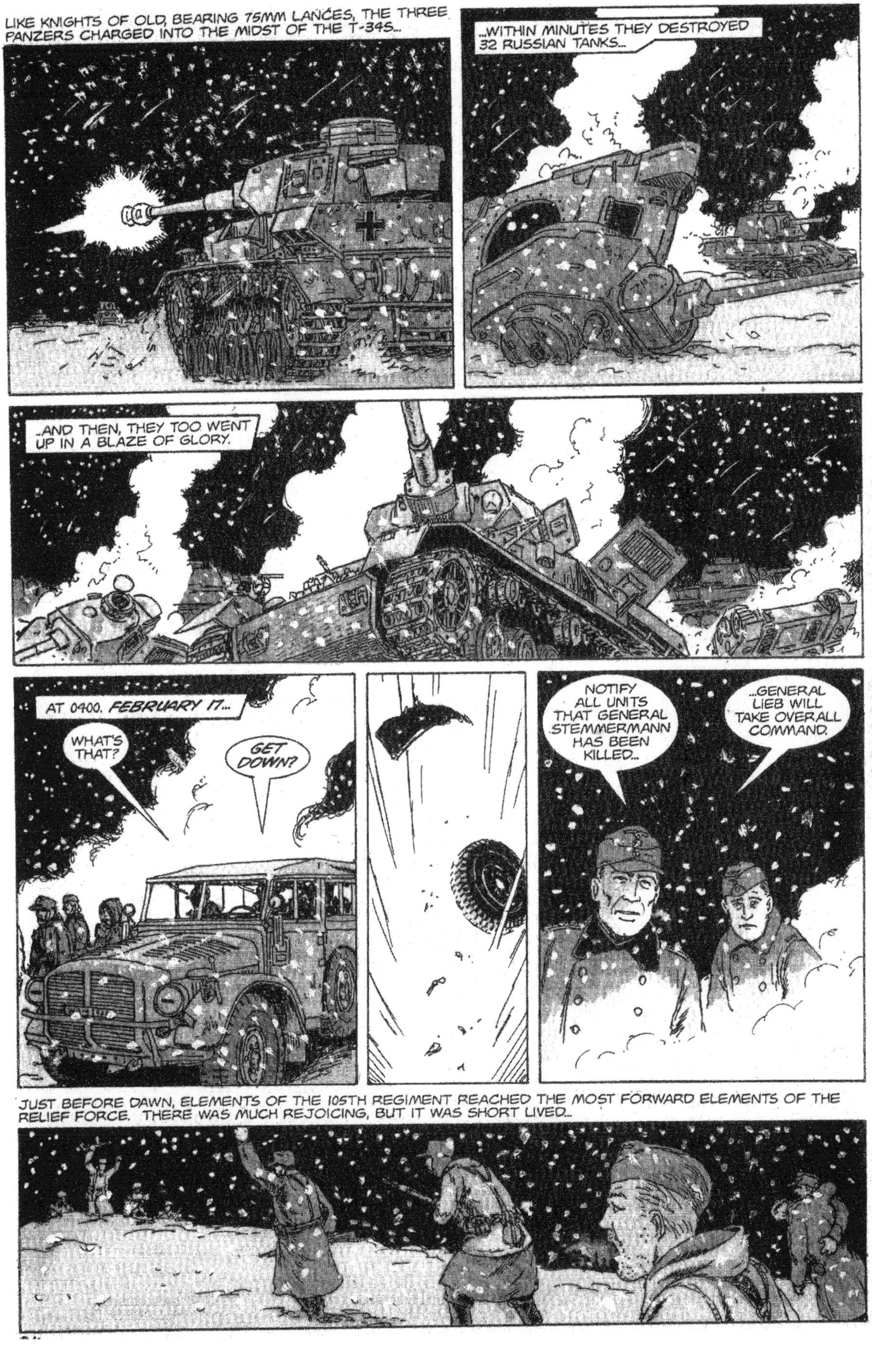

LIKE KNIGHTS OF OLD, BEARING 75MM LANCES, THE THREE PANZERS CHARGED INTO THE MIDST OF THE T-34S...
...WITHIN MINUTES THEY DESTROYED 32 RUSSIAN TANKS...
...AND THEN, THEY TOO WENT UP IN A BLAZE OF GLORY.
AT 0400, FEBRUARY 17...
WHAT'S THAT?
GET DOWN?
NOTIFY ALL UNITS THAT GENERAL STEMMERMANN HAS BEEN KILLED...
...GENERAL LIEB WILL TAKE OVERALL COMMAND.
JUST BEFORE DAWN, ELEMENTS OF THE 105TH REGIMENT REACHED THE MOST FORWARD ELEMENTS OF THE RELIEF FORCE. THERE WAS MUCH REJOICING, BUT IT WAS SHORT LIVED...

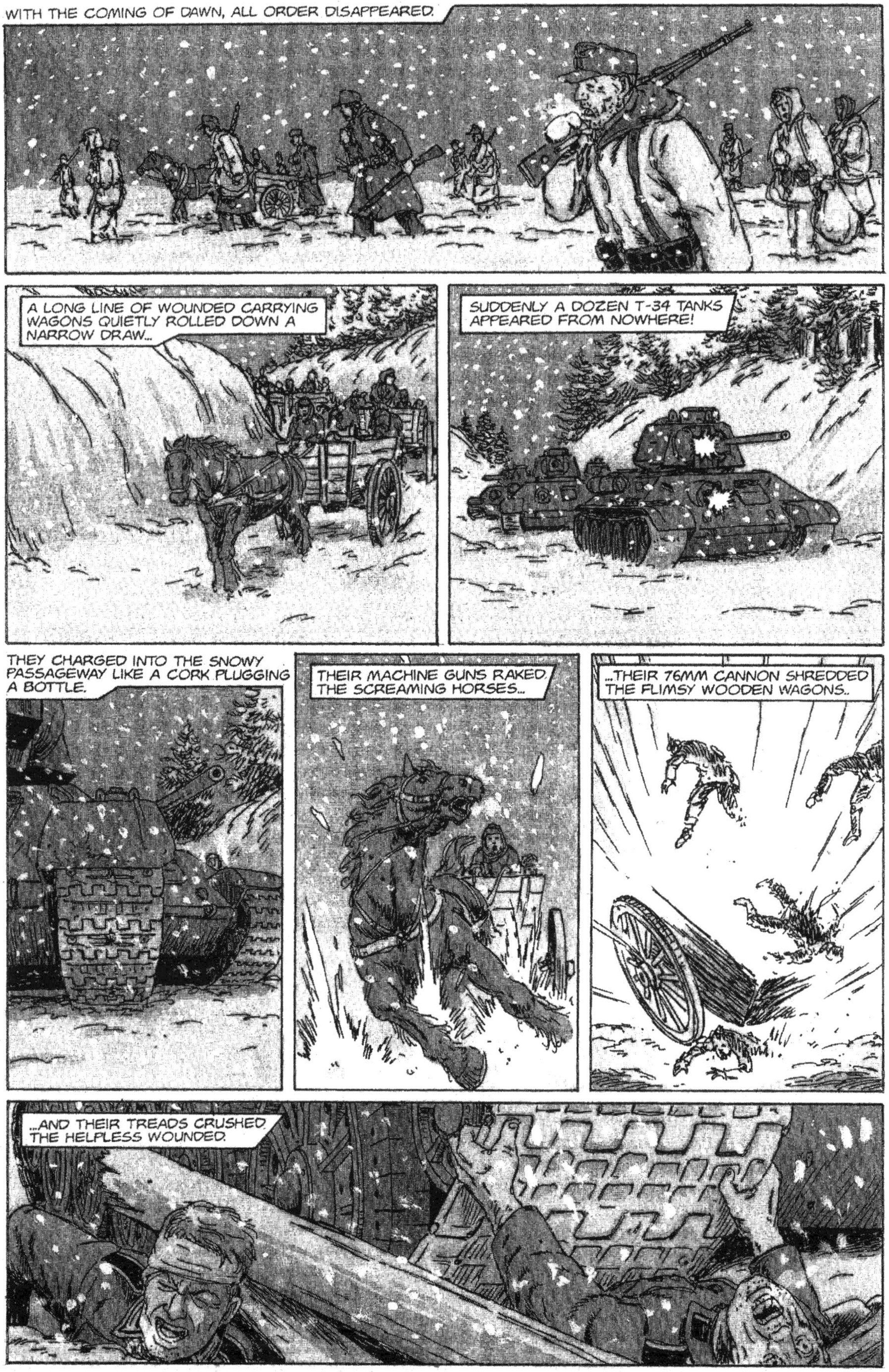
WITH THE COMING OF DAWN, ALL ORDER DISAPPEARED.
A LONG LINE OF WOUNDED CARRYING WAGONS QUIETLY ROLLED DOWN A NARROW DRAW...
SUDDENLY A DOZEN T-34 TANKS APPEARED FROM NOWHERE!
THEY CHARGED INTO THE SNOWY PASSAGEWAY LIKE A CORK PLUGGING A BOTTLE.
THEIR MACHINE GUNS RAKED THE SCREAMING HORSES...
...THEIR 76MM CANNON SHREDDED THE FLIMSY WOODEN WAGONS...
...AND THEIR TREADS CRUSHED THE HELPLESS WOUNDED.

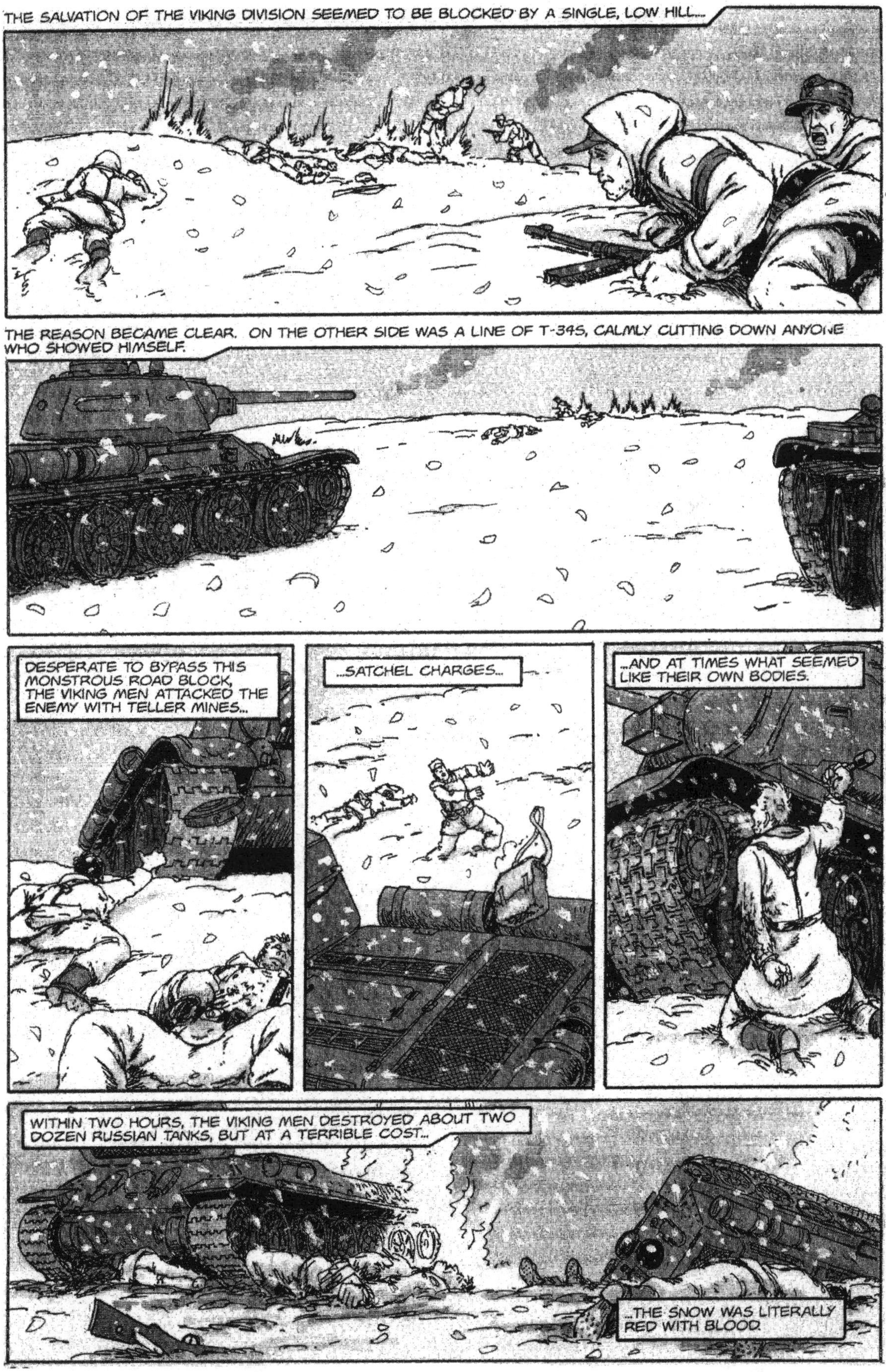
THE SALVATION OF THE VIKING DIVISION SEEMED TO BE BLOCKED BY A SINGLE, LOW HILL...
THE REASON BECAME CLEAR. ON THE OTHER SIDE WAS A LINE OF T-34S, CALMLY CUTTING DOWN ANYONE WHO SHOWED HIMSELF.
DESPERATE TO BYPASS THIS MONSTROUS ROAD BLOCK, THE VIKING MEN ATTACKED THE ENEMY WITH TELLER MINES...
...SATCHEL CHARGES...
...AND AT TIMES WHAT SEEMED LIKE THEIR OWN BODIES.
WITHIN TWO HOURS, THE VIKING MEN DESTROYED ABOUT TWO DOZEN RUSSIAN TANKS, BUT AT A TERRIBLE COST...
...THE SNOW WAS LITERALLY RED WITH BLOOD.

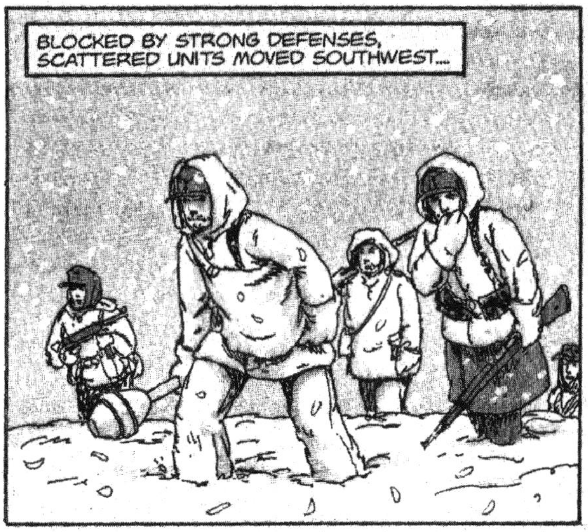
BLOCKED BY STRONG DEFENSES, SCATTERED UNITS MOVED SOUTHWEST...

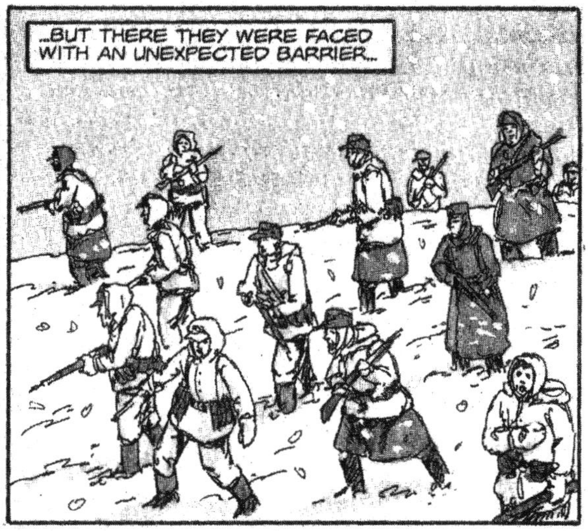
...BUT THERE THEY WERE FACED WITH AN UNEXPECTED BARRIER...

...THE GNILOY TIKICH RIVER! ONLY TWENTY FEET WIDE, BUT TEN FEET DEEP AND VERY SWIFT.

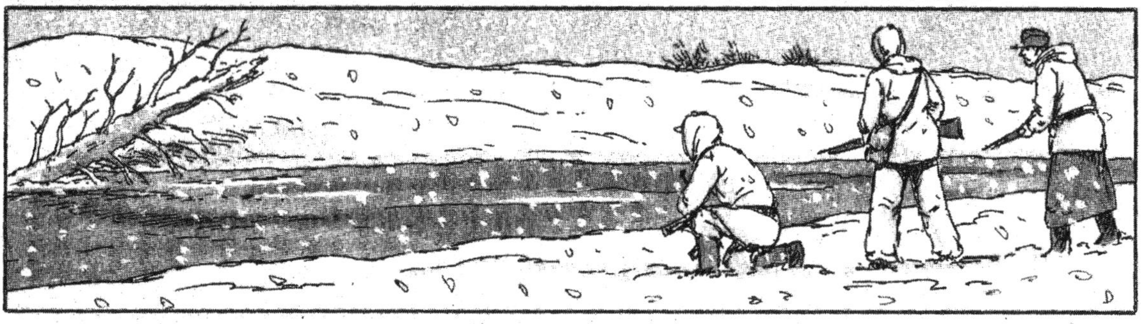

A 17TON HALF TRACK WAS DRIVEN INTO THE RIVER IN AN ATTEMPT TO MAKE AN IMPROVISED BRIDGE, BUT THE CURRENT WAS SO SWIFT IT WASHED THE VEHICLE AWAY. A GROUP OF MEN TRIED TO RIG A ROPE AND HARNESS... WITH LITTLE SUCCESS.

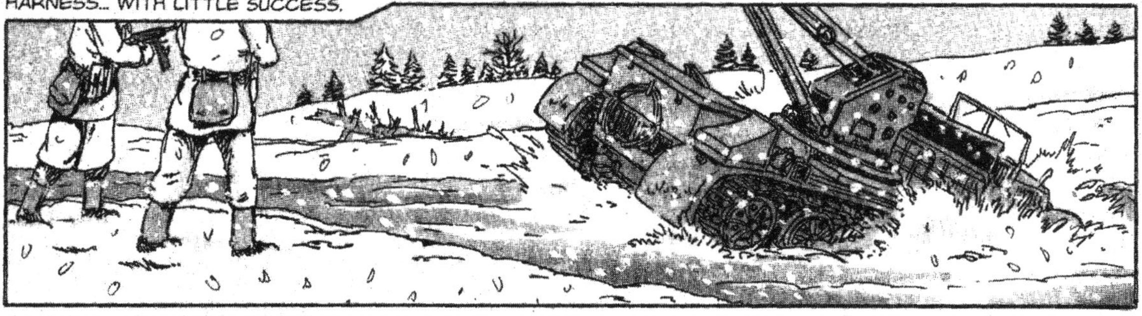

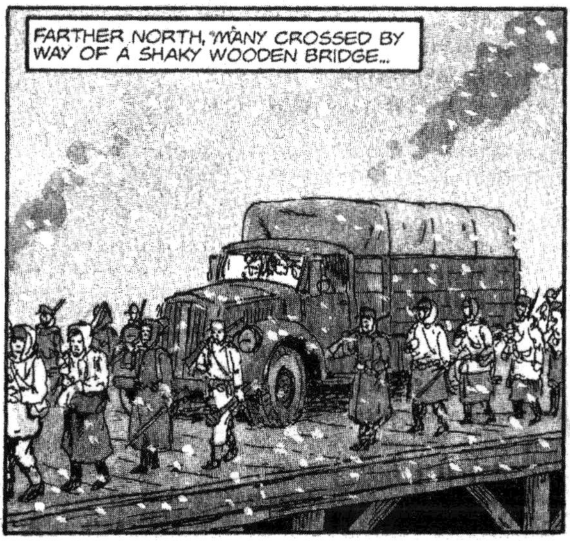
FARTHER NORTH, MANY CROSSED BY WAY OF A SHAKY WOODEN BRIDGE...

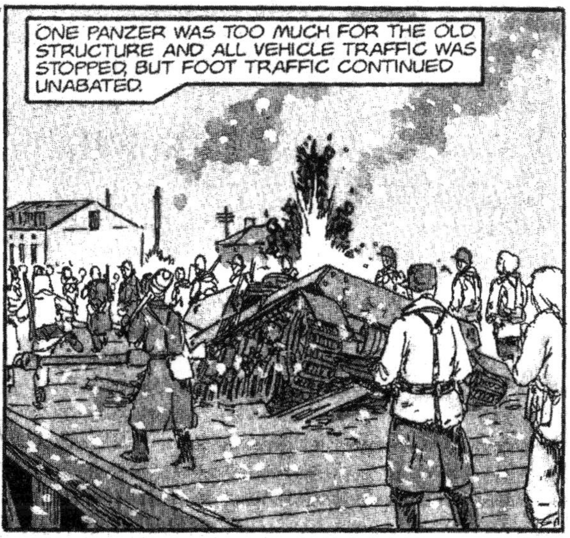
ONE PANZER WAS TOO MUCH FOR THE OLD STRUCTURE AND ALL VEHICLE TRAFFIC WAS STOPPED, BUT FOOT TRAFFIC CONTINUED UNABATED.

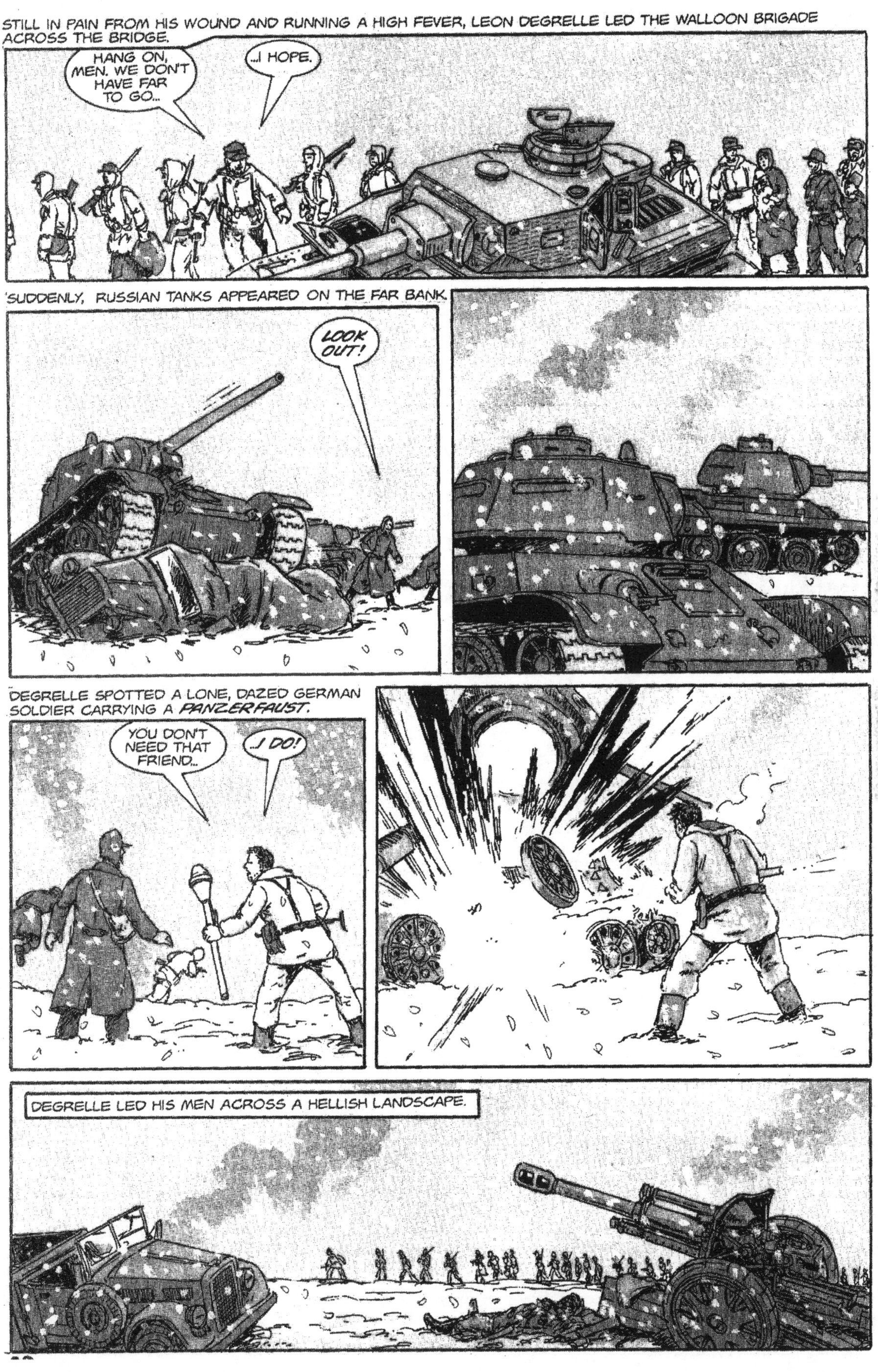
STILL IN PAIN FROM HIS WOUND AND RUNNING A HIGH FEVER, LEON DEGRELLE LED THE WALLOON BRIGADE ACROSS THE BRIDGE.
HANG ON, MEN. WE DON'T HAVE FAR TO GO...
...I HOPE.
SUDDENLY, RUSSIAN TANKS APPEARED ON THE FAR BANK.
LOOK OUT!
DEGRELLE SPOTTED A LONE, DAZED GERMAN SOLDIER CARRYING A PANZERFAUST.
YOU DON'T NEED THAT FRIEND...
...I DO!
DEGRELLE LED HIS MEN ACROSS A HELLISH LANDSCAPE.

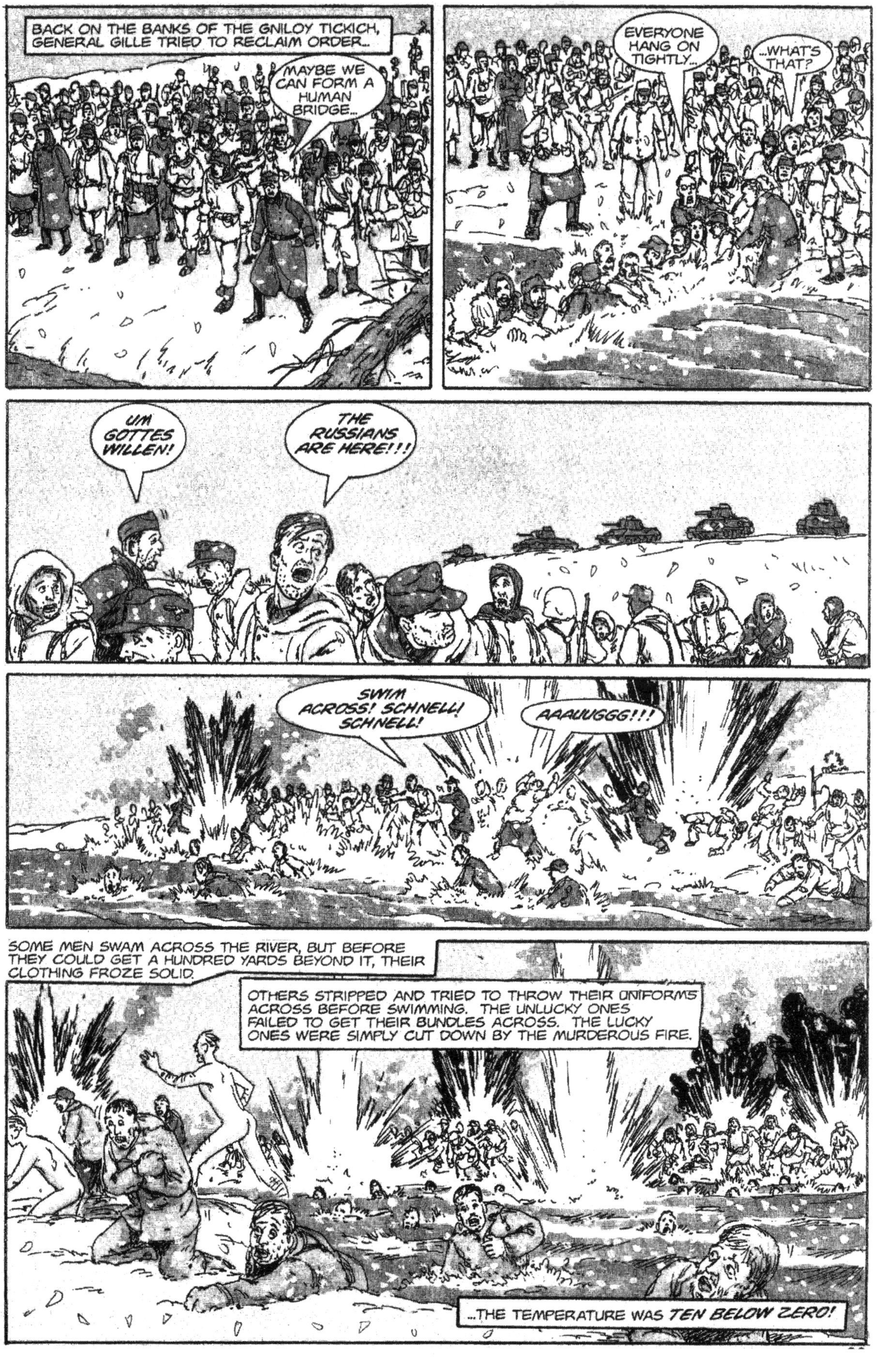
BACK ON THE BANKS OF THE GNILOY TICKICH, GENERAL GILLE TRIED TO RECLAIM ORDER...
MAYBE WE CAN FORM A HUMAN BRIDGE...
EVERYONE HANG ON TIGHTLY...
...WHAT'S THAT?
UM GOTTES WILLEN!
THE RUSSIANS ARE HERE!!!
SWIM ACROSS! SCHNELL! SCHNELL!
AAAUUGGG!!!
SOME MEN SWAM ACROSS THE RIVER, BUT BEFORE THEY COULD GET A HUNDRED YARDS BEYOND IT, THEIR CLOTHING FROZE SOLID.
OTHERS STRIPPED AND TRIED TO THROW THEIR UNIFORMS ACROSS BEFORE SWIMMING. THE UNLUCKY ONES FAILED TO GET THEIR BUNDLES ACROSS. THE LUCKY ONES WERE SIMPLY CUT DOWN BY THE MURDEROUS FIRE.
...THE TEMPERATURE WAS TEN BELOW ZERO!

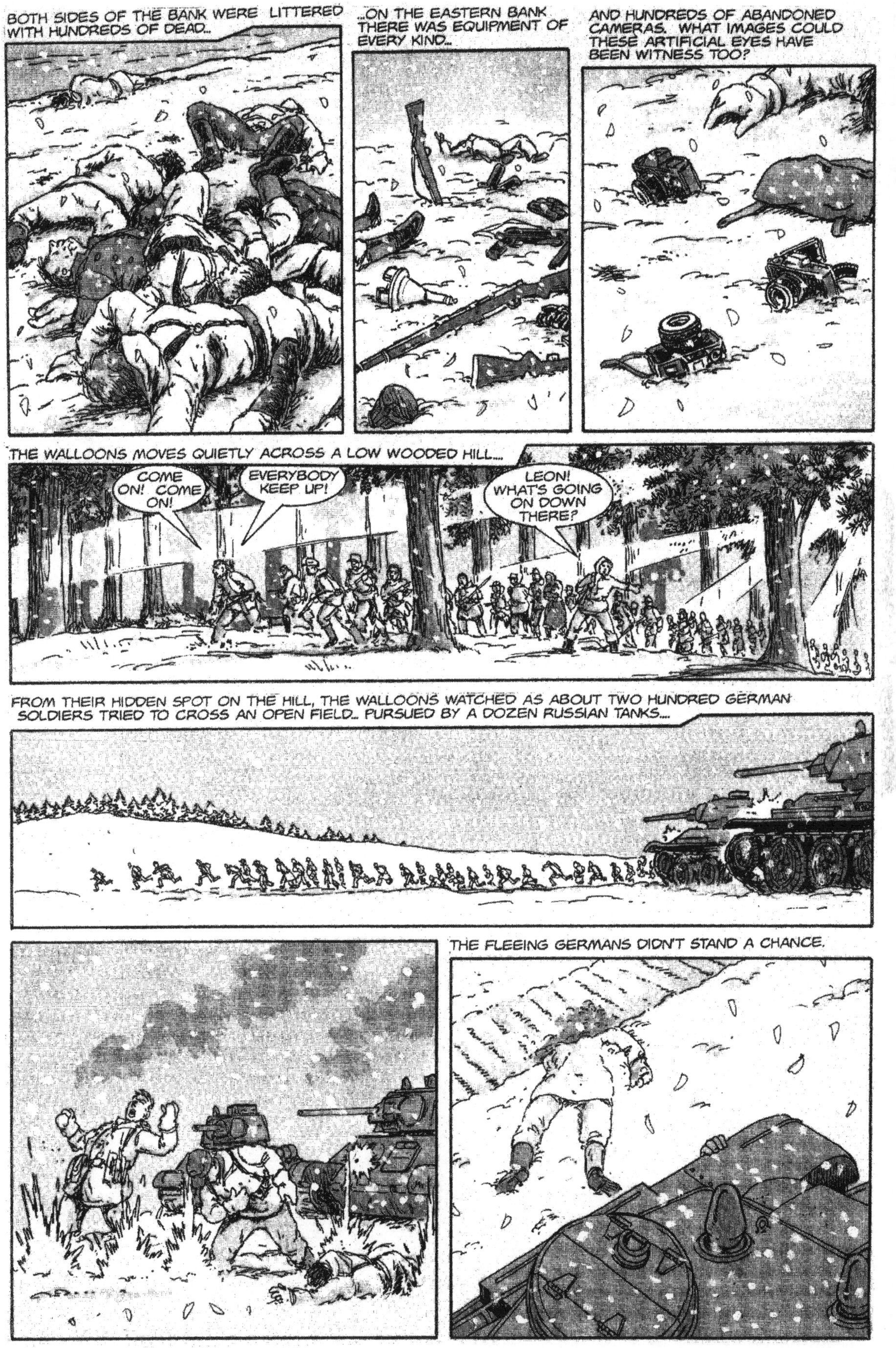
BOTH SIDES OF THE BANK WERE LITTERED WITH HUNDREDS OF DEAD..
..ON THE EASTERN BANK THERE WAS EQUIPMENT OF EVERY KIND..
AND HUNDREDS OF ABANDONED CAMERAS. WHAT IMAGES COULD THESE ARTIFICIAL EYES HAVE BEEN WITNESS TOO?
THE WALLOONS MOVES QUIETLY ACROSS A LOW WOODED HILL....
COME ON! COME ON!
EVERYBODY KEEP UP!
LEON! WHAT'S GOING ON DOWN THERE?
FROM THEIR HIDDEN SPOT ON THE HILL, THE WALLOONS WATCHED AS ABOUT TWO HUNDRED GERMAN SOLDIERS TRIED TO CROSS AN OPEN FIELD.. PURSUED BY A DOZEN RUSSIAN TANKS....
THE FLEEING GERMANS DIDN'T STAND A CHANCE.

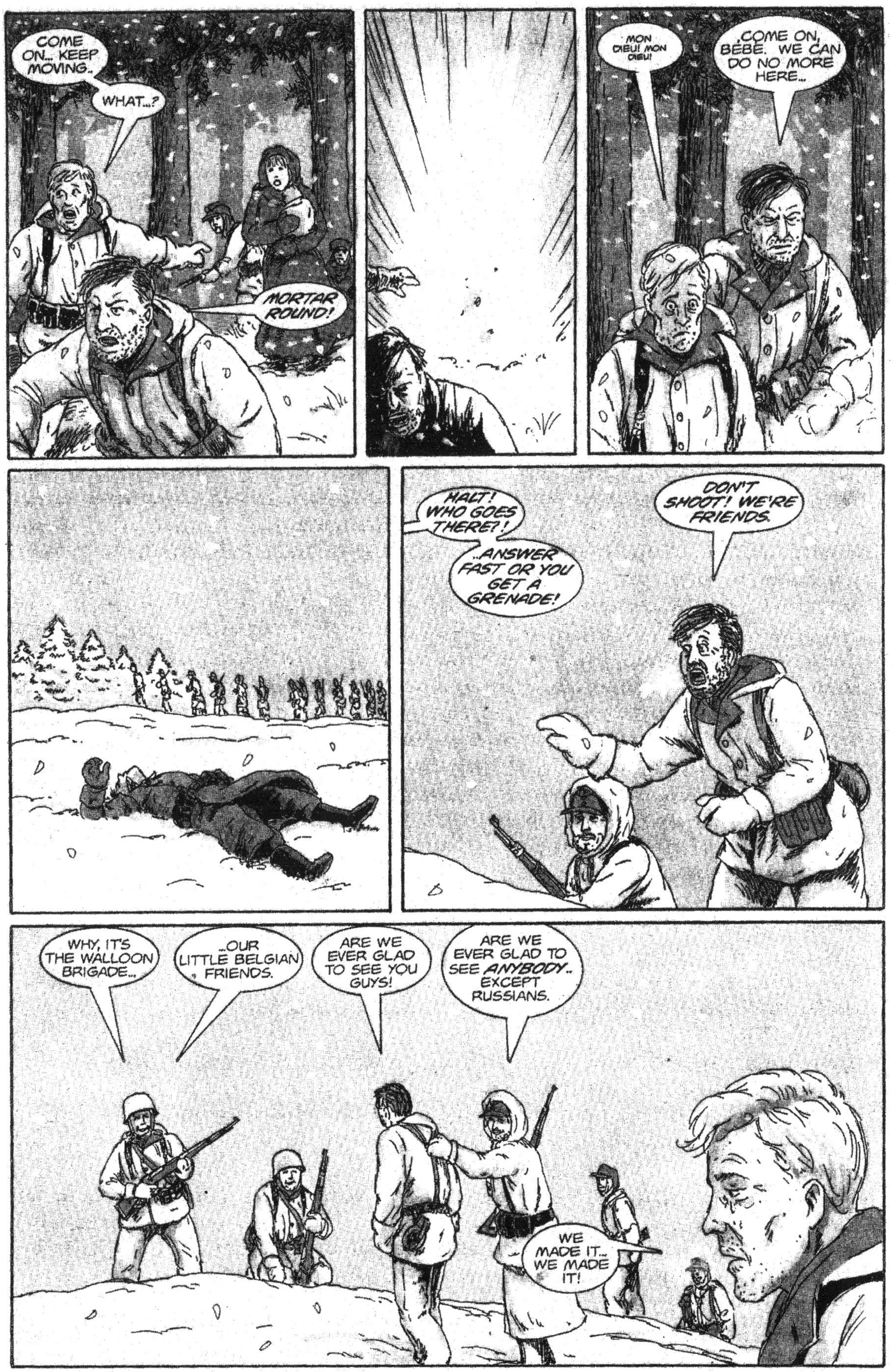
COME ON... KEEP MOVING..
WHAT...?
MORTAR ROUND!
MON DIEU! MON DIEU!
..COME ON, BEBE. WE CAN DO NO MORE HERE...
HALT! WHO GOES THERE?!
..ANSWER FAST OR YOU GET A GRENADE!
DON'T SHOOT! WE'RE FRIENDS.
WHY, IT'S THE WALLOON BRIGADE...
..OUR LITTLE BELGIAN FRIENDS.
ARE WE EVER GLAD TO SEE YOU GUYS!
ARE WE EVER GLAD TO SEE ANYBODY.. EXCEPT RUSSIANS.
WE MADE IT... WE MADE IT!

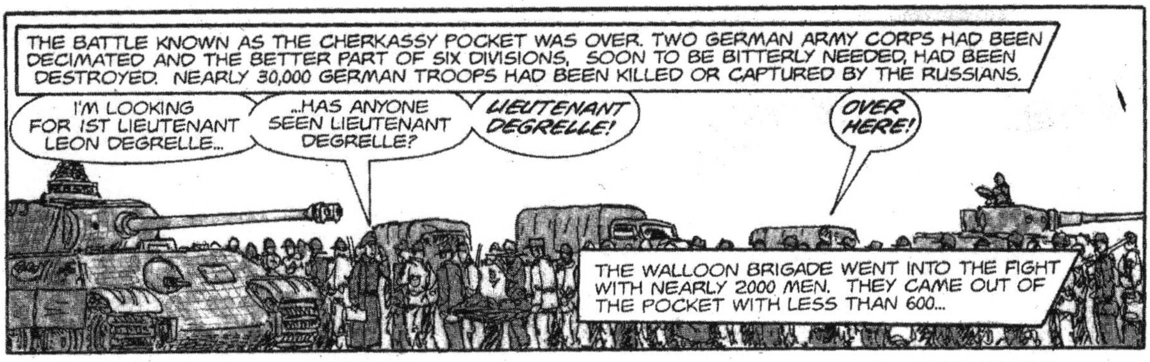
THE BATTLE KNOWN AS THE CHERKASSY POCKET WAS OVER. TWO GERMAN ARMY CORPS HAD BEEN DECIMATED AND THE BETTER PART OF SIX DIVISIONS, SOON TO BE BITTERLY NEEDED, HAD BEEN DESTROYED. NEARLY 30,000 GERMAN TROOPS HAD BEEN KILLED OR CAPTURED BY THE RUSSIANS.
I'M LOOKING FOR 1ST LIEUTENANT LEON DEGRELLE...
...HAS ANYONE SEEN LIEUTENANT DEGRELLE?
LIEUTENANT DEGRELLE!
OVER HERE!
THE WALLOON BRIGADE WENT INTO THE FIGHT WITH NEARLY 2000 MEN. THEY CAME OUT OF THE POCKET WITH LESS THAN 600...

BUT THERE WOULD BE NO REST FOR THESE MEN. THEY WOULD BE THROWN RIGHT BACK INTO BATTLE. WE CAN ONLY WONDER ON HOW MANY SURVIVED THE WAR.

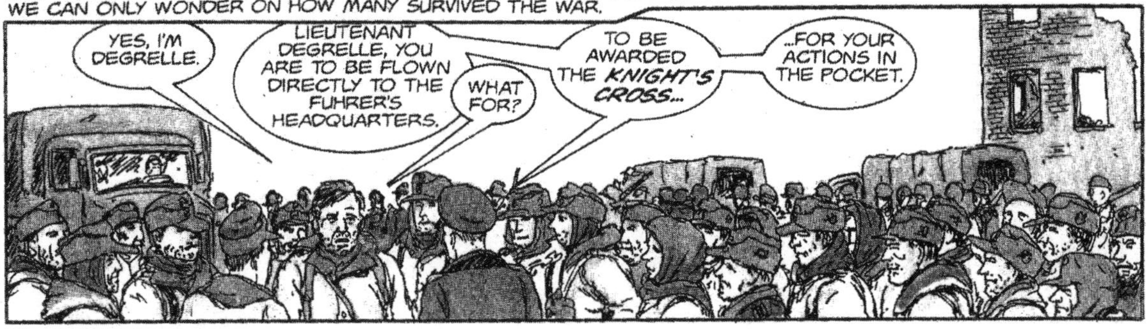
YES, I'M DEGRELLE.
LIEUTENANT DEGRELLE, YOU ARE TO BE FLOWN DIRECTLY TO THE FUHRER'S HEADQUARTERS.
WHAT FOR?
TO BE AWARDED THE KNIGHT'S CROSS...
...FOR YOUR ACTIONS IN THE POCKET.

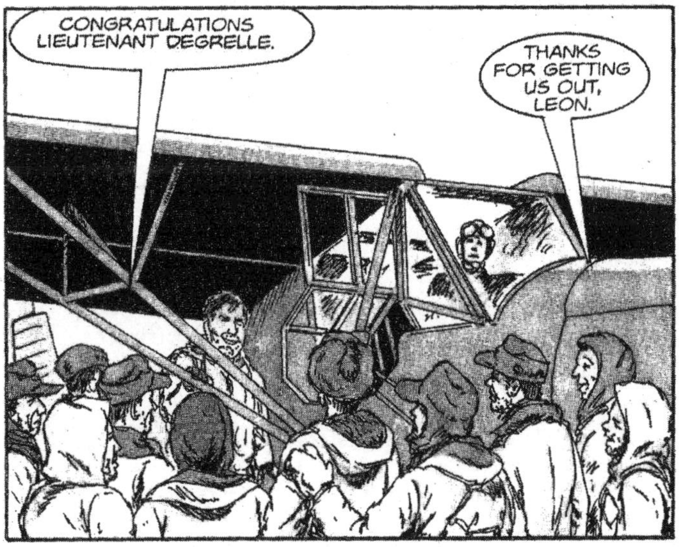
CONGRATULATIONS LIEUTENANT DEGRELLE.
THANKS FOR GETTING US OUT, LEON.

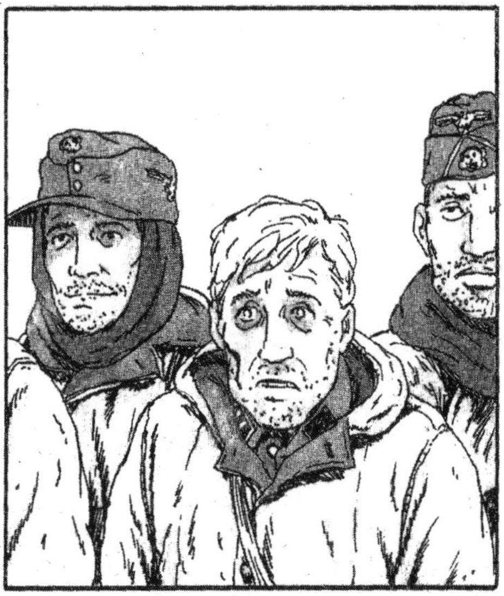

SINCE HE FOUGHT FOR THE NAZIS, LEON DEGRELLE WAS CONSIDERED A CRIMINAL IN HIS OWN COUNTRY...

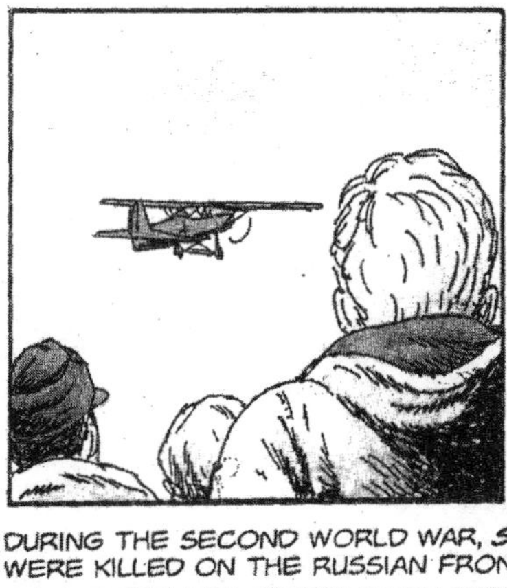

AFTER THE WAR, HE ESCAPED TO SPAIN WITH HIS CHILDREN...

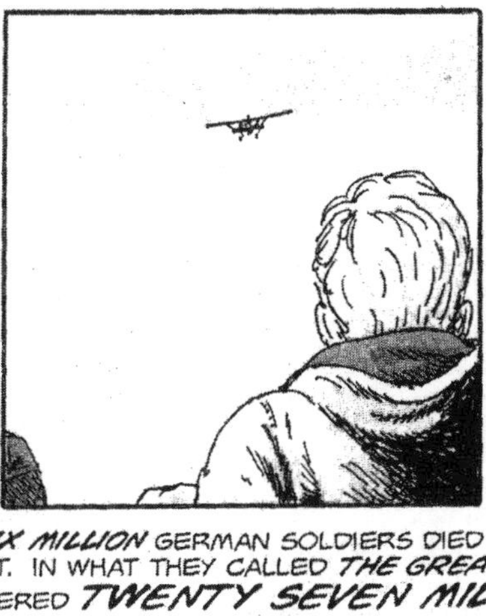

...WHERE HE LIVED THE REST OF HIS LIFE, VISITED OCCASIONALLY BY OLD COMRADES.

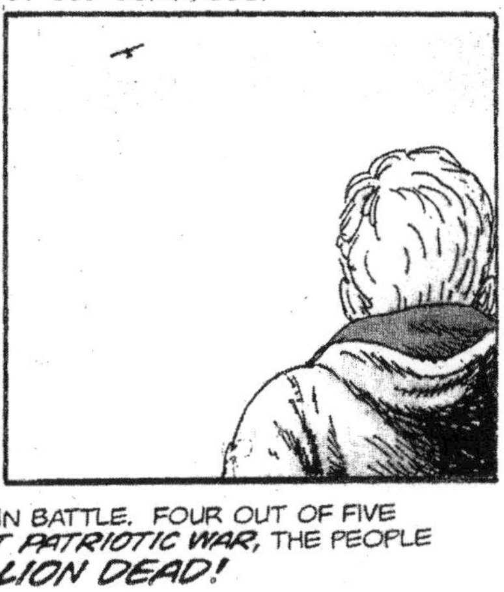

DURING THE SECOND WORLD WAR, ***SIX MILLION*** GERMAN SOLDIERS DIED IN BATTLE. FOUR OUT OF FIVE WERE KILLED ON THE RUSSIAN FRONT. IN WHAT THEY CALLED ***THE GREAT PATRIOTIC WAR,*** THE PEOPLE OF THE FORMER SOVIET UNION SUFFERED ***TWENTY SEVEN MILLION DEAD!***

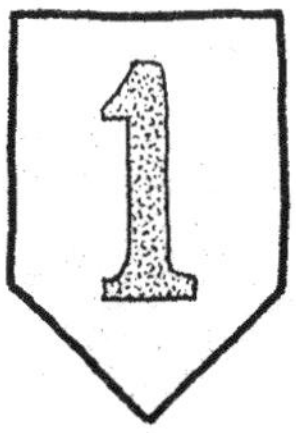

1st: "BIG RED ONE"

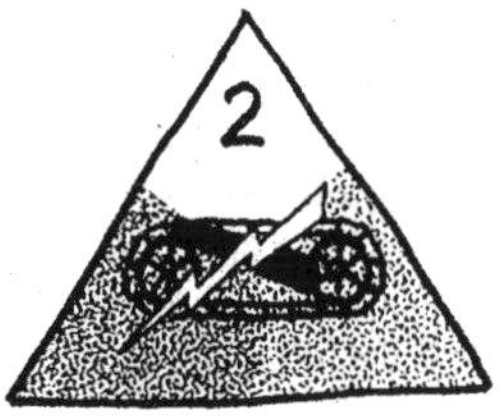
2

2nd ARMORED
"HELL ON WHEELS

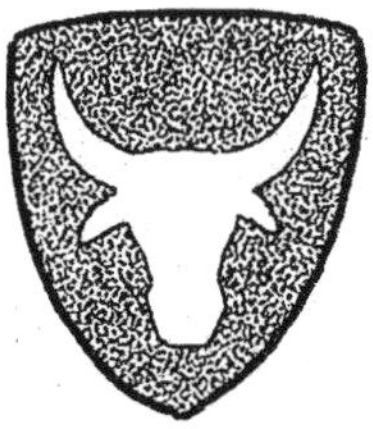

PHILIPPINE DIVISION

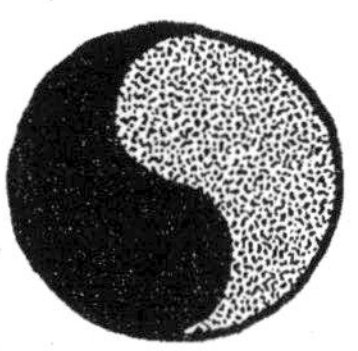

29th: "BLUE AND GRAY"

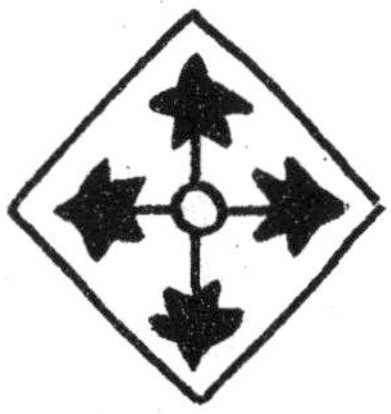

4th: "IVY"

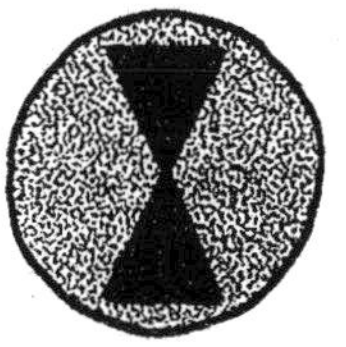

7th: "HOURGLASS

OUTFITS

If you asked an American soldier of World War II what "outfit" he was in, he might answer something like, "The Big Red One", or "Hell on Wheels", or maybe even "The Texas Army". He would be telling you what Division he was in. And no matter what the answer, there would be a long fascinating story behind it.

There were 90 Army Divisions during the war, containing 10,000 to 16,000 men each- one cavalry, one mountain, five airborne, 16 armored and 67 infantry.

Eight of these were regular army divisions, already in existence before the war began and having long histories. In 1940, the National Guard was federalized, forming 19 more divisions. The rest were formed primarily from the draft.

Each division, due to its men, its commanders, and its service, developed its own personality. Some of these divisions, most likely regular or national guard, served long periods in combat from the earliest days of the war, and suffered terrible casualities. A few came in late and were in combat for a relatively short period of time.

Most did their job with a minimum of flare, like a worker that takes it just like another job. But the actions of some should be included in the ranks of legend.

Like the 3rd. Within its ranks were the two most decorated soldiers of the war, plus thirty others that won the Medal of Honor. It suffered more casualities than any U.S. Divison, and on the Anzio beachhead, suffered more casaulties in one day since the Battle of Antietam.

The 32nd from Wisconsin and Michigan, which was the first U.S. Division to fight in the Pacific war, from the swamps of New Guinea, to the Philippines.

The 101st Airborne, which while completely surrounded, held Bastogne during the Battle of the Bulge.

The 2nd, 4th Armored, 1st Cavalry... the list goes on and on. The histories of these World War II Divisions are dying. Dying with the white-haired old men that once wore their colorful shoulder patches. So if you hear one of these old men mention that he was in World War II, ask him what was his "Outfit"? See his face light up...and listen to history.

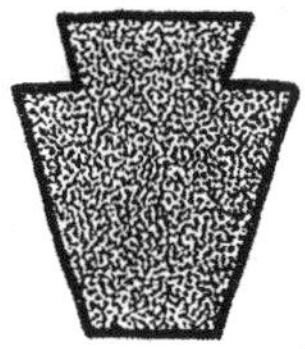

28th: "KEYSTONE"

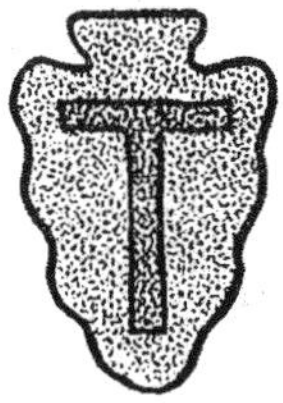

36th: "TEXAS"

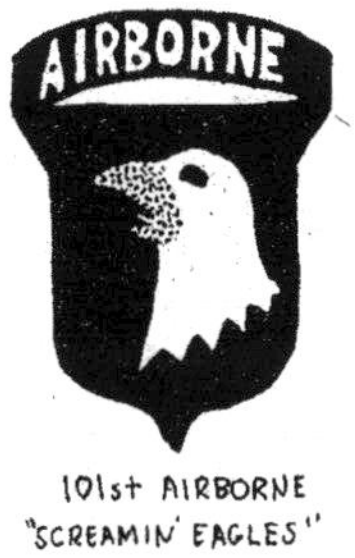
AIRBORNE

101st AIRBORNE
"SCREAMIN' EAGLES"

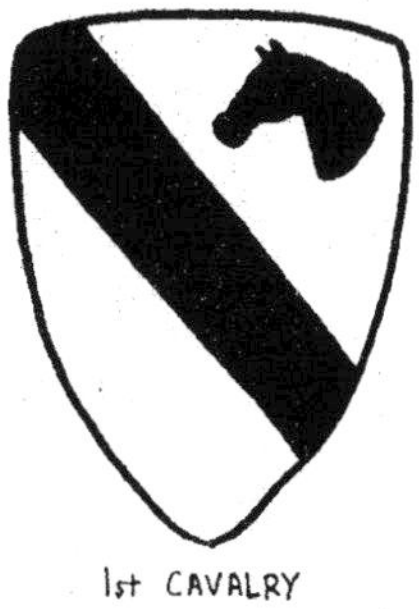

1st CAVALRY
"HELL FOR LEATHER"

ALSO FROM CALIBER

Days of Darkness covers the darkest days of World War II-when the United States went from the tragedy of Pearl Harbor to the triumph at Midway. Covering in detail that attack and devastation of the American Fleet in Hawaii, the evacuation of the Philippines, the horror of Bataan, and the dramatic Battle of Midway which stopped the Japanese juggernaut in the Pacific.

The Battle of Midway!
DAYS of DARKNESS
"...compellingly written and beautifully drawn"

Creator Wayne Vansant, best known for his exacting detail on the popular comic series, The 'Nam, chronicles the participation of the Cahill family as their lives are irrevocably changed forever as the world is plunged in war.

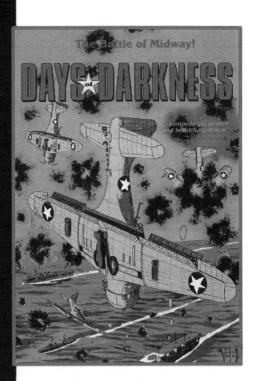

DAYS of DARKNESS

"Heavy on authenticity...compellingly written and beautifully drawn."

---Comic Buyer's Guide

"...conveying to today's fans what life was like-both at war and at home-during this turbulent era."

---Comic Shop News

"Informative and historical, all wrapped up in an entertaining package of fact blended with fiction."

---Joe Pruett, Negative Burn

Wayne Vansant served in the US Navy during the Vietnam War, and graduated from the Atlanta College of Art in 1975. His first published comic work appeared in Marvel Comics' *Savage Tales,* and Wayne was the principle artist for *The 'Nam* for more than fifty issues. He both wrote and illustrated *Days of Darkness* for Apple Comics, telling the story of the early days of the war in the Pacific.

The six issues were later published as a graphic novel by Caliber. As well as doing comic work for Eclipse, Dark Horse, Byron Priess and Caliber, he created a snumber of series of non-fiction, military history comics called the Heritage Collection, which covered the Civil War and World War II.

WWW.CALIBERCOMICS.COM

BATTRON

The adventure of the Legionnaire, Battron, in the tale of "The Trojan Wo[...]
which involves the liberation of a free-booting French ship, the *Martel*, fr[...]
heavily guarded Vichy port. The Allies want the ship destroyed and the Ge[...]
have sent serious firepower to save it.

The key is the beautiful former mistress of the *Martel's* captain, enlisted [...]
hope she can convince him to join the Free French with his ship. But has [...]
them all she knows? Can Battron and his commandos complete their dan[...]
mission under the shadow of the Allied invasion of North Africa?

Written and Illustrated by
WAYNE VANSANT

WAYNE VANSANT was t[...]
artist for The 'Nam (Marve[...]
more than 50 issues and a[...]
his acclaimed *Days of Dark*[...]
(and collected from Calibe[...]
story of the early days of th[...]
cific. One of the most accla[...]
comic artists, Wayne has [...]
trated many comics from M[...]
Penguin, DarkHorse, and [...]
launched a series of non-[...]
history comics called the [...]
tion which covered the Civ[...]
World War II.

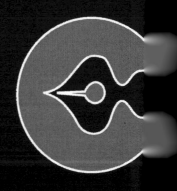

Made in the USA
Middletown, DE
09 August 2015